Lived Mission in Twenty-first-century Britain

Bishop John

Welcome to Liverpool.

— Harvey.

Lived Mission in Twenty-first-century Britain

Ecumenical and Postcolonial Perspectives

Benjamin Aldous, Harvey Kwiyani,
Peniel Rajkumar, Victoria Turner

scm press

© The editors and contributors 2024

Published in 2024 by SCM Press
Editorial office
3rd Floor, Invicta House,
110 Golden Lane,
London EC1Y 0TG, UK
www.scmpress.co.uk

SCM Press is an imprint of Hymns Ancient & Modern Ltd
(a registered charity)

Hymns Ancient & Modern® is a registered trademark of
Hymns Ancient & Modern Ltd
13A Hellesdon Park Road, Norwich,
Norfolk NR6 5DR, UK

British Library Cataloguing in Publication data
A catalogue record for this book is available
from the British Library

ISBN: 978-0-334-06553-1

Typeset by Regent Typesetting
Printed and bound by
CPI Group (UK) Ltd

Contents

Contexts

Consequences

List of Contributors

Revd Dr Benjamin Aldous is the Principal Officer for mission and evangelism at Churches Together in England, the national ecumenical instrument. Ben is particularly interested in mission, ecumenism and intercultural theology. He spent 16 years in Cambodia and South Africa, first as a church planter and latterly as a parish priest. He is the author of *The God Who Walks Slowly* (SCM Press, 2022) and is a research fellow at the Queen's Foundation in Birmingham. He lives in Devon with his wife and four children.

Dr Harvey Kwiyani is a leading mission theologian in the United Kingdom. He teaches at the Church Mission Society in Oxford. He is the Founder and Executive Director of Missio Africanus and the General Editor of *Missio Africanus: The Journal of African Missiology*. He is author of *Multicultural Kingdom: Ethnic Diversity, Mission and the Church* (SCM Press, 2020) and *Sent Forth: African Missionary Work in the West* (Orbis Books, 2014), among others.

Revd Dr Canon Peniel Rajkumar is Director for Global Mission at USPG and also teaches at Ripon College, Cuddesdon. Previously he served as Programme Executive for Interreligious Dialogue and Cooperation with the World Council of Churches in Geneva. He is author of *Asian Theology on the Way: Christianity, Culture and Context* (SPCK, 2014; Fortress Press, 2016) and *Faith(s) Seeking Justice: Dialogue and Liberation* (WCC, 2021) and co-edited *Foundations for Mission* (Regnum, 2014), *Mission At and From the Margins* (Regnum, 2013). Peniel is married to Rebecca who is an artist and theologian. They live in Croydon with their two sons Ebenezer and Cleon.

Dr Victoria Turner's research interests include World Christianity, ecumenism, youth studies, decolonial and liberation theology, interfaith, mission history and theology, and political and practical theology. Victoria is an active member of the United Reformed Church, most recently serving on the Church Life Review Group, which undertook a scoping exercise that will lead towards change in the denomination. She is the editor of *Young, Woke and Christian: Words from a Mission* (SCM Press, 2022) and *Emerging, Awake and Connected: New Theologies of Justice from a Missing Generation* (SCM Press, 2024).

Revd Dr Graham Adams is Tutor in Mission Studies, World Christianity and Religious Diversity and programme leader for the postgraduate degrees in Theology, Ministry and Mission, and Chaplaincy Studies, at Luther King Centre for Theology and Ministry in Manchester. He also teaches for the Congregational Institute of Practical Theology. His particular interest is mission in the context of empire. His publications include *Holy Anarchy* (SCM Press, 2022) and *God the Child: Small, Weak and Curious Subversions* (SCM Press, 2024).

Dr Bisi Adenekan-Koevoets received her PhD in Humanities at the University of Roehampton. She has published several works on topics including Nigerian Pentecostal diasporic missions and inter-generational conflicts (2021) and targeted evangelism and knife crime in London, exploring the relevance of mission and spirituality in the lives of second-generation children of ethnic minorities. She currently holds a postdoctoral position at the department of Sociology at the University of Essex. Her research focuses on issues of lived religion, second-generation Nigerians and socioeconomic mobility.

Dr Lisa Adjei holds a PhD in Biochemistry and Physiology from the University of Surrey. She is also the founder of Sankofa Collective, an ecumenical racial justice and reconciliation community for Christians. Lisa works for Christian Aid as a British Church Relations Manager and also sits on Churches Together in England's Racial Justice Working Group and their board of trustees. Lisa is the chair of a global ecumenical climate movement called Climate YES and attends Trinity Baptist Church in Croydon, where she serves in their young adult's ministry, Impact.

Revd Dr Boniface Carroll is a priest of the Antiochian Orthodox Archdiocese of the British Isles and Ireland, serving in the cathedral parish of St George in London. He holds a PhD in Anthropology and studies the worship, tradition and ethics of Orthodox Christianity.

Niall Cooper has been Director of Church Action on Poverty since 1997 and has been responsible for piloting a range of innovative approaches to tackling poverty in the UK, drawing on international development experience. He is passionate about enabling people struggling against poverty and exclusion to reclaim dignity, agency and power together. He has acted as policy advisor and trustee of Churches Together in Britain and

Ireland, helped shape the Methodist Church's Church on the Margins programme, and is currently helping the United Reformed Church to develop a long-term, mission-focused anti-poverty strategy.

Minister Shermara Fletcher is the Principal Officer for Pentecostal and Charismatic relations at Churches Together in England, which includes CTE's Racial Justice portfolio. She is also a minister of the gospel, international speaker, and is passionate about people living holistic and flourishing lives. Shermara is a dynamic millennial leader, which notably saw her read before 4.1 billion people at the late Queen Elizabeth II's funeral on 19 September 2022. Shermara has featured on many broadcasts including BBC radio 2, BBC radio 4, BBC world news, Talk TV, The God Channel, TBN and UBC radio.

Tom Hackett works as Children's and Youth Development Officer for the United Reformed Church Southern Synod. He is a Trustee for Gatwick Detainees Welfare Group and has been a volunteer visitor for the charity since 2017, visiting individuals detained at Brook and Tinsley House immigration removal centres. He is a member of the Refugee Tales community, which shares the stories of people with lived experience of detention, and campaigns for an end to indefinite detention in the UK. Tom is a qualified secondary school teacher and has worked in a range of social projects during time living as a community member at the Council for World Mission Europe's 'Mission House' project in Amsterdam.

Dr Elizabeth Joy is currently a Trustee at Churches Together in England and a member of the Council of Reference at British SCM. She is from the Malankara (Indian) Orthodox Syrian Church. She is the Chief Editor for the Diocesan Publications in the Diocese of UK–Europe and Africa. She is also a member of the Theology Advisory Group for Christian Aid.

Dr Heather J. Major has a PhD in Practical Theology, Rural Church and Mission from the University of Glasgow. She is convenor of the Mission Research Network for Churches Together in England and chair of the International Rural Churches Association. She can be found on Twitter at @HeatherJMajor1.

Revd Shemil Mathew is the Vice Dean of Emmanuel Theological College in the north-west of England. He is also a founding member of Anglican Minority Ethnic Network and is an elected participant observer in the Church of England's House of Bishops. His PhD research is on diaspora Anglicanism. He is proud to say that he is dyslexic.

Revd Dr Jan Nowotnik is a priest of the Archdiocese of Birmingham and Director of Mission and National Ecumenical Officer for the Catholic Bishops' Conference of England and Wales. He studied for the priesthood at the English College in Valladolid, Spain and was ordained in November 1998. Following his ordination, he worked in various parishes and pastoral settings within the Archdiocese of Birmingham before moving to Rome in September 2015 to begin further studies in theology. He specialized in ecumenical and interreligious dialogue and received his theology licence in 2017. He completed his PhD in theology at the Pontifical University of St Thomas Aquinas (Angelicum) in Rome in 2022.

Revd Dr Raj Bharat Patta celebrates his identities in multiple belongings, which include Dalit, Christian, Asian, (Im)migrant, theologian, minister, Lutheran, Methodist, Indian, British, church, academy, postcolonial, public sphere, husband, father and friend. Though a Lutheran minister from India, he currently serves as a recognized and regarded minister of the Methodist Church in Britain in the United Stockport Circuit. He completed his PhD from the University of Manchester. He is an author of *Subaltern Public Theology: Dalits and the Indian Public Sphere* (Palgrave Macmillan, 2023).

Anupama Ranawana is a Thematic Research Specialist for Christian Aid. Current research areas include: faith actors, localization, decolonizing development, race and racialization in the international development sector, civic spaces and the impact of Covid-19. She also provides advisory support across the organization on research design and ethics, particularly with regards to diversifying knowledge production, 'shifting' power in research and applied research methods. She is author of *Liberation for the Earth: Climate, Race and Cross* (SCM Press, 2022).

Emeritus Professor Dr Paul Weller is a non-Stipendiary Research Fellow in Religion and Society and Associate Director of the Oxford Centre for Religion and Culture, Regent's Park College, University of Oxford, and Associate Member of its Faculty of Theology and Religion; Visiting Fellow, Centre Trust, Peace and Social Relations, Coventry University; and Emeritus Professor, University of Derby. He is a member of the Baptist Union's Inter-Faith Working Group. His single-authored publications include: *Time for a Change: Reconfiguring Religion, State and Society* (2005); *God, Jesus and Dialogue: The Beach Lectures for 2005* (2006); *Religious Diversity in the UK: Contours and Issues* (2008); *A Mirror for our Times: 'The Rushdie Affair' and the Future of Multiculturalism* (2009).

Revd Canon Professor James Woodward is Principal of Sarum College and a Visiting Professor of Theology at the University of Winchester. He is a teacher and writer of pastoral and practical theology. He has had a particular interest in age and the place of older people in our society over the last 30 years. Presently he is engaged in some reflective writing on theological reflection and is interested in narratology and its potential to nurture flourishing. For further information about his work and publications, see: www.jameswoodward.online.

Foreword

MIKE ROYAL AND NICOLA BRADY

It is one of the great privileges of working for ecumenical instruments that as General Secretaries we are invited to contribute to major assemblies, events and dialogues taking place across our different member churches. It is always an encouragement to see how similar themes are being discussed and prayed for across the different denominations: mission and outreach to those on the margins, healing societal divisions, pastoral care of those who have been wounded by violence, injustice and abuse, and the underlying unifying theme of embracing the challenge of sharing our Christian faith in today's rapidly changing world.

The theme of mission is central to the conversations about how we might best achieve that. In this volume the editors and contributors have provided a rich tapestry of resources that help frame and inform those conversations. As a whole, the collection powerfully conveys the message that the work of mission is intrinsically relational. On the one hand this points to the need for this work to be contextualized in people's lived realities, while at the same time making a compelling case for the need to challenge ourselves to look beyond the limitations of our own personal circumstances and consider other perspectives and experiences. We are provided with a wealth of case studies examining opportunities and challenges for the work of mission in different contexts, with groups diverse in culture, identity, age and background. These experiences are analysed through a range of different academic disciplines and enriched by deep, personal storytelling that makes the examples easy to relate to and engage with. The volume seeks to formulate courageous and compassionate questions that will guide our approach to mission which must be characterized by an honest engagement with our past, a renewed energy for the present challenges and opportunities and a hopeful vision for the future.

At the time of writing this forward, our hearts are full of despair. We write on the back of a summer of protest, riots and disorder, where the flames of anti-immigrant fuelled racism has been on full display on the streets of Britain, with devastating consequences. Misinformation stirred up online and, on the streets, has led to mosques being attacked, accommodation housing people seeking asylum set on fire and individuals assaulted in public simply because of the colour of their skin. Some of the violence has been stirred up by Christian Nationalists, apparently on a mission to reclaim Britain as a 'Christian country'.

It is into this context that this book speaks. 'Lived' mission is the antidote to this kind of misinformation. It speaks honestly about the nature of mission in Britain in the twenty-first century. The contributors represent the rich tapestry of missiological praxis that informs the honest ecumenical conversation we need to have as the church in Britain now more than ever.

It's time for deeper conversations about decolonizing mission. This volume helps us listen to dynamic millennial voices and challenges us to engage with academics thinking about, and practitioners working in mission from Orthodox, African Pentecostal and inclusive church perspectives. This book is truth telling at its best and will make for an uncomfortable read for many. We can no longer afford to listen to our echo chambers, settle for the status quo and refuse by default to venture beyond our comfort zones.

Dr Nicola Brady
(General Secretary for Churches Together in Britain and Ireland)

Rt Revd Mike Royal
(General Secretary of Churches Together in England)

Acknowledgements

EDITORS AND CONTRIBUTORS

Sixteen years ago, Cathy Ross and Andrew Walls published *Mission in the Twenty-First Century: Exploring the Five Marks of Global Mission*. In some senses this present volume you hold today is the successor to that volume. Ross and Walls, using the five marks of mission as a framework, intentionally examined ideas of mission from a global perspective. Ecumenism and mission are deeply woven together. This present work is rooted in the context of Britain, but reflects a similar global diversity as, even more in the last sixteen years, the world has made its home in our midst. This volume wonders what mission, taking into account our globally diverse contexts, relationships and need for partnership, looks like, or should or could look like in Britain today.

Each of us as editors has been shaped by the gift of the global church in different ways through our studies and work. As a result of our own 'lived' experience we want to encourage an emerging generation of missional ecumenists. The royalties from the book will all be directed to the Bill Snelson Young Ecumenists Fund. The Fund has been set up to give young ecumenists – between the ages of 18 and 35 – the opportunity to experience ecumenism abroad through study, pilgrimage, volunteering or any activity that promotes church unity and mission.

We are grateful for the support of Churches Together in England for their release of resources, including time and networking. We are enormously thankful to all our authors who enthusiastically agreed to write chapters from a range of settings. The cacophony of voices in the volume is tremendously exciting. We are also grateful to David Shervington and Rachel Geddes at SCM Press for their encouragement and attention to detail in the process of publishing. Finally, we are grateful to Sharon for another beautiful linocut which adorns the cover.

Ben, Victoria, Peniel and Harvey
September 2024

Introduction: Lived Mission in Twenty-first-century Britain: Ecumenical and Postcolonial Perspectives

BENJAMIN ALDOUS AND VICTORIA TURNER

Introduction

On a recent visit to the Tate Modern on the Southbank, I (Ben) stumbled across an exhibition about the story of Black Theatre in the Redfern district of Sydney, the first Aboriginal theatre wholly led, and run, by indigenous Australians. Part of the exhibition was a film outlining the history of the theatre and how it was established and developed from 1972 to 1977. The National Black Theatre 'grew out of street theatre staged during protests over land rights and mining on Aboriginal sacred sites'. The film told the story of the 'first full-length play by an Indigenous Australian to be professionally produced premiered in Redfern in 1975, [as] its writer Robert Merritt sat chained in the audience to two police escorts for the entire performance'.[1] For the first time, Aboriginal actors, dancers, artists, musicians, directors and producers told their own story not mediated by white Australians. The stories they shared were raw, full of pain, yet coupled with pride as they reflected back to white Australian audiences what they had experienced in mass extermination, stealing of their children, almost total annihilation of their language, their cultural artefacts and their ways of being deeply rooted in their relationship with the land. The film included many interviews with the original cast and their experience of liberation in finding their voices through the Black Theatre. It was a profoundly moving account. It struck me how suppressed their voices and experiences had been and yet they found space to be themselves and write a new part of their history revealing genuine Aboriginal experience to a wider, mostly white Australia.

In an ecclesial landscape where the monolithic power of the Church of England and other historic denominations can, at times, squeeze out the stories of others, this collection of essays brings a cacophony of voices into the arena. We hear from ancient churches like the Antiochian Orthodox.

We hear from young black millennial women. We hear from those at the sharp end of climate justice activism, those working with asylum seekers. We hear from priests, academics and activists. In short, we hear from those at the institutional centres, acknowledging the dramatic contextual shifts that Britain has undergone and how the historic churches have been displaced from the day-to-day lives of people. We explore how members of those churches are working to heal these rifts, and from those at the peripheries we hear untold stories involving society's forgotten people who we know are central to God's mission.

Over 30 years ago, South African missiologist David Bosch explored what he called elements of an emerging ecumenical missionary paradigm. Bosch argued that 'missiology acts as a gadfly in the house of theology, creating unrest and resisting complacency, opposing every ecclesiastical impulse to self-preservation, every desire to stay as we are, every inclination towards provincialism and parochialism, every fragmentation of humanity into regional or ideological blocs.'[2] In this book we propose that there is still work to be done ecumenically for missiology to inhabit rightfully its role as critical friend, crosser of boundaries, advocate for justice and intellectual ankle biter.

British ecumenical history is undeniably interwoven with mission. Ecumenism did not derive from the churches but instead arose as a challenge to the churches. The World Missionary Conference of Edinburgh 1910 is often (mistakenly) pinpointed as the beginning of the ecumenical movement due to the direct line between the conference and the International Missionary Council and its inspiration for the forming of Life and Work (1925), which concentrated on the role of churches for social justice, and Faith and Order (1927), which worked for ecclesial structural unity.[3] Edinburgh 1910 was a conference of missionary societies, not churches, which also deliberately limited its conversation to co-operation in the 'mission field' to avoid discussion about unity between churches at home.[4] The energy towards co-operation between missionary societies came from the student movements. Their start can be traced to the 1890s and they famously worked for 'the evangelization of the world in this generation'. The student movements enabled young people from different denominations to pray, explore their faith and discuss the Bible together while maintaining their independent denominational ties. The two leaders of Edinburgh 1910 were both involved with student Christian movements (worldwide, in the US and in Britain) and current students were employed to work as stewards at Edinburgh 1910. It was the model devised and practised by students and young people that was replicated at Edinburgh.

The Conference of British Missionary Societies (CBMS) in Great Britain and Ireland followed in 1912, with a membership of more than 40 Protestant missionary societies. The CBMS was then closely related with the predecessor organization to Churches Together in England (CTE), the British Council of Churches (BCC, 1942). The archive, held at the School of Oriental and African Studies (SOAS), details conversations including a youth committee, correspondence with National Christian Councils in Central, East, Southern and Western Africa 'touching on educational work, political events and decolonization, African customs, Islam, social problems, and interethnic relations, including papers of the Advisory Committee on Education in the Colonies',[5] missionary work in Egypt and the Middle East with a focus on refugees, missionary work in the Caribbean – thinking about social and economic development, and work in Asia comprising medical missions, political events, wars and communism. The CBMS merged with the BCC in 1977, and today – although a study group for mission continues in CTBI – our ways of talking about and thinking about mission have drastically changed.

The call for the decolonizing of mission, present from the ecumenical missionary movement at its outset, was catalysed in 1972/1973 at the World Council of Churches' CWME Assembly in Bangkok, where South African (and other Majority World) Christians called for a temporary 'moratorium' on overseas mission. Although National Church Councils from the 1920s, and churches from the non-western world from 1948, were included in the World Council of Churches, the continued saturation of (often) well-meaning (in their terms) missionaries from the western world was stifling the ability of the churches from the non-western world to govern and theologize indigenously. One of the happy consequences of these discussions was the gradual re-theologizing of mission from many western missionary societies – and even the cessation of the former model by the prominent body that was the 1795 London Missionary Society, which became a global partnership of churches in the wake of these conversations.[6] Jione Havea, however, rightly laments that

> [t]here are more Christian bodies and communities in the global south, but the decision-making powers and the control over resources (including resources situated in the global south) have not shifted from the global north. There are more white bodies at the boards and councils of WCC and CWME even though there are more black and coloured bodies among their memberships.[7]

One of the most pressing concerns in our context is that missiological discourse is still profoundly shaped by historical churches and, by extension, whiteness, heteronormativity and the lingering vestiges of empire power. Our fellow editor missiologist Harvey Kwiyani summed up the frustration well in an interview in the summer of 2021.

We might complain that theology is a white man's discipline, but missiology is even worse. There are so few alternative voices. It feels impossible – the field is still too colonial. So, when I say I'm a recovering missiologist I'm critiquing the colonial history. I don't want to identify with that so I'm stepping back. I've been involved in mission studies for close to 20 years now. I've read and digested the literature but it's not a discipline I want to be identified with unless we own the history of colonialism which will lead us to a new missiology. That is difficult for many people to hear.[8]

Harvey conveys a common misapprehension about the future of missiological endeavours in the British context that probably resonates with many. This book hopes to be part of what we think is a new missiology – rooted in mutuality, open-handedness and genuine desire for encounter across ecclesiastical, theological and racial boundaries. A working together for the common missiological good because, as Koyama says, 'missiology only has relevance for humanity if it is fully aware of the "relatedness" of all beings'.[9] Part of that creating of a new missiology for humanity will involve the undoing of false assumptions regarding what valid theological knowledge is and where it is found.

The aim of this book is not to outline a single, agreed-upon conception of what mission in twenty-first-century Britain should look like. In fact, the aim is to do much the opposite. The organization for which Ben works, and for which Victoria is a Trustee – Churches Together in England (CTE) – has the tagline: 'One in Christ Jesus, engaged in God's mission, empowered by the Spirit.'[10] Part of the beauty of *missio Dei* is the freedom of interpretation for each of God's partners to discern for themselves where God's mission is in the world, through their own particular denominational, cultural, generational, economic, linguistic and theological lens. However, this can also easily lend itself to a lazy kind of ecumenism, where member churches avoid difficult conversations around the theology of mission, the definition of justice and the hierarchy of concern, and simply assume that mission means mission to each ecumenical partner. In one sense, each church trusting the others to follow the missionary Spirit on their own terms shows respect and upholds the diversity of *missio Dei*. If, on the other hand, we really believe that we are 'One in Christ Jesus', perhaps spiritually for the time being rather than structurally, there is surely work to be done towards us collaborating in being One in God's mission. Among the first steps, we hope, might be this present resource, which shows the theological divergence in missional practices. From remembering our rich resources in the form of saints – missional guides who have been starved (by some) of our worship – to protesting and transforming our society to Christ's vision of anti-racist peace, to really learning lessons from our newer churches that stem from the non-western world and bless our Christian landscape here, to hearing the pain that our elderly feel in being left behind as their identity is portrayed negatively by some of our traditional churches.

It's also important to remember that divergent passions can cause pain. My (Victoria's) own passion lies in societal transformation where I hope God's just vision of the equality of all people will eventually be displayed. Though my own tradition is declining numerically, I would struggle to think of mission as primarily evangelism. I hope that Jesus is present to others through me in my actions, words and compassion. We also know that some churches engage in explicit inclusive outreach to LGTBQ+ Christians, or non-believing LGBTQ+ members of society, who feel outcast by theologies that are held by another of our partner churches. So there is some kind of disingenuity, or willed ignorance, when we sit as a diverse group and simply presume that the mission we are each engaged on is one and is not in need of theological interrogation or collective wisdom and insight. I wonder if our anxiety in avoiding conflict is preventing us from really committing to each other and following God's mission collectively.[11]

Despite the different approaches to mission in our UK context, or the particular problems we each seek to solve, we do agree at least that Britain is in dire need of being reminded of the power of God's uniting, just and all-consuming mission. Near the end of 'The Kairos Document', created by an ecumenical team of South African Christians struggling under apartheid, they cry that, 'the Church of Jesus Christ is not called to be a bastion of caution and moderation. The Church should challenge, inspire and motivate people.'[12] The 'consequences' section in this book explores disturbing narratives in British society – rising anti-migration nationalism, increasing poverty, the climate emergency, continuing racism stemming from our not-far-gone colonial era – and we could add an epidemic of poor mental health and low self-esteem (especially felt by young people), class injustice, the stripping of the arts and creative pursuits, a concerning rise in hyper-patriarchy culminating in the death of 17-year-old Elianne Andam on 29 September 2023.[13] Our trans siblings feel unsafe and scapegoated by the media, and populist politics advance personal agendas rather than listen to constituents. God's mission, which embraces each of us as God's children, inherently challenges these divisive, hateful, blinded and often hopeless realities.

It can be hard to see God in desperate times. As I (Victoria) finish writing this introduction, I fear for the people in Gaza and mourn for the Israeli families who have lost loved ones. I feel isolated from my friends, partner, colleagues as I acknowledge my emotional distance stemming from the internal battle I am fighting against my despair and anger. I want to continue advocating for a cause I have been involved in for years but somehow feel paralysed from doing so. I am annoyed that our lives carry on – that some of my friends still post their Instagram stories of cosy, autumnal Starbucks drinks while others post about how Gazans have no clean water left. I struggle to know what to say to my friends living in Bethlehem and Jerusalem and feel completely useless, aware that so much of the narrative is concerned with diplomacy rather than action and tip-toed distance rather than fully embracing the human need. I wish to have such solid relationships with my Christian siblings (and ideally Muslim and Jewish siblings), no matter the denomination, that we can trust each other to talk, organize, pray, protest, cry, embrace and mourn together.

Keith Clements, the expert on Bonhoeffer's ecumenical theology, explains that for Bonhoeffer 'the church is only the church when it is there for others'. Clements continues:

> A church which confined itself to the ever diminishing 'religious' areas of life, outside the realm of everyday care, responsibilities, and joys, would be locking itself into a false kind of transcendence, the transcendence of God's assumed distance from humanity rather than the more truly biblical transcendence of otherness.[14]

Philosopher and cultural critic Byung-Chul Han, in his book *The Palliative Society*, exposes the individualism and disconnectedness of our modern-day societies that focus on a false ideology of happiness. He writes:

> The dispostif of happiness isolates us. It leads to the depolitization of society and the disappearance of solidarity. Each person has to look after his or her own happiness. Happiness becomes a private matter. Suffering is understood to be the present of personal failure. *Instead of revolution we thus get depression.*[15]

Han details how the workers' movement prevalent from the Great Depression of the 1920s has been replaced by a vicious neo-capitalist lie that expounds that our conditions are not 'social' but 'psychological'.[16] Our problems are internal rather than external. The tropes suggest that if we worked harder, meditated more, meal-prepped, grasped opportunities, took a gap-year to climb the Himalayas – we'd all be successful. Those who do not 'get lucky' under capitalism (or have generational resources and contacts behind them) are left to sift through the shame of their struggle alone – battling stigma and self-hate, isolated from others who are too comfortable to see the fallacy of the lie. We avoid their pain. As Luke Larner explains in his edited volume about the Church and class,

Confounding the Mighty, churches can also fall into this rhetoric of pure positivism in the context of class. Cuts are not touched and nursed but applauded and walked upon before they are healed. Larner names it a 'feckless faith', where solutions are posed and celebrated before the communities in working-class areas are really known. He asks provocatively what 'people from working-class backgrounds need saving from'.[17] Mission as *missio Dei* is without boundaries, it is an all-encompassing embrace of our messy, God-given-and-shared, worldly reality. I find Graham Adams' theology useful in thinking of God's work in the world, where Adams thinks of God's work as 'smallness: the chaos event of butterflies, like seeds, like yeast, like childlikeness effecting unexpected transformations'.[18] This theology would cause us to hold on to our missional aims lightly – not searching for instant results, but observing chaos lingering and connecting events, where perhaps pieces of God's mystery might become clear under our efforts.

We might also find some guidance from the Barman Declaration, drafted by Karl Barth and Hans Asmussen and adopted by the Confessing Synod of the German Evangelical Lutheran Church in 1934, directed against the rise of the Reich church that was aligning itself with Nazi Germany's ideology. The declaration stated that it rejected 'the false doctrine that with human vainglory the Church could place the Word and work of the Lord in the service of self-chosen desires, purposes and plans'.[19] An avoidance model of conflict does not lend itself to challenging each other in friendship and bolstering accountability to our shared mission of God. As we learn to get to know the contexts in which we and the mission of God are placed and constantly undertaken, let us also draw closer in fellowship – not a comfortable, kind fellowship, but a real friendship that enriches, inspires and challenges.

Norman Goodall, a congregational minister and ecumenical/missionary theological pioneer, wrote in 1964:

> The Christian mission is the transmission of this word, in thought, speech and action, and in a power of perpetual renewal ... There is only one mission field: it is the world. ... Just as the business of these historic missions ought always to have been seen as the business of the whole Church, so this Christian mission to man[sic]-in-Society, this redeeming word, attitude, and action in relation to the turbulent society of this one world – is the calling and task of the entire Church today.[20]

This care for the whole world is most aptly discerned and held by the Body of Christ in its worship. George MacLeod, Church of Scotland minister and founder of the Iona Community, wrote in 1936, 'As Christ came to earth, to preach, to heal, to feed, and by His death to save, so the congregation as the Divine Fellowship is the extension of the incarnation.'[21] Goodall similarly explained how worship embraced life through its liturgy, but was concerned 'whether in the kind of language to which we are accustoming ourselves in order to express what most properly disturbs us, we are displaying a loss of sensitiveness to the real nature of wrong and are running into a mixture of pride'.[22] Both MacLeod and Goodall were concerned with a lack of sensitivity, or thicker walls being erected, between the congregation and the context. Our missional challenges that haunt society also haunt our own ecclesial structures. We know that our churches can struggle with racism, with greed, with sexism, with abuse of power, with the disregard of the young or elderly. Our work to draw nearer to each other in worship, and our gift of learning from each other when we interpret the Word through scripture, or feel the spirit moving in our work, blesses the whole Body of Christ when it is shared, praised, prayed upon, enlarged, stretched or even questioned.

James Woodward convincingly argues in his chapter that 'it may not be an exaggeration to suggest that much of our language of mission remains obtuse, intangible and for some simply irrelevant for modernity'.[23] This book hopes that by interweaving stories of 'lived mission' in all its diversity, we can start to break the academic gatekeeping that is found in missiological discourse. The kind of gatekeeping that Jione Havea rightly posits keeps the voice of the marginalized outside and avoids the costly work of 'apology, confession, repentance, reparation and reconciliation'.[24] It is also hoped that we can bring to light the frank tensions present between the slow, present work of the kingdom and the disconnected, blinded race of neo-capitalist postmodernity.

Epistemic disobedience and mission

In order to do this work together we suggest employing what Walter Mignolo has called an *epistemology of disobedience*.[25] This is an important way of unlearning and undoing the predilection towards hegemony and the fallacy or 'hubris of zero point knowledge'.[26] Mignolo, tongue in cheek, says, 'As we know: the first world has knowledge, the third world has culture; Native Americans have wisdom, Anglo Americans have science.' These kinds of epistemic value-laden assumptions have no place in missiological recourse and writing. The South African theologian Vuyani Vellem, in a similar fashion, plays with the phrase *un-thinking* the West. There is a necessary unlearning and taking off of former assumptions about how we know. Vellem says, 'In un-thinking the West, our position is that Western civilisation can be overcome; it is crumbling as we speak. The poor and the marginalised, not Western civilisation, constitute our future for the development of life-affirming alternatives of civilisation and knowledge.'[27] In some instances in the UK context there is a degree of ignorance around the relationship between mission and colonialism and imperial thinking. But our job is not just about exploring this ignorance but about saying 'farewell to innocence', as Allan Boesak would say.[28] Not allowing ourselves to declare 'innocence' by virtue of distance from the past but to confront the mission colonial legacy squarely.

Epistemic disobedience is also a reflection of how the academic study of mission is often removed from its lived practice. In this sense, we often judge contributions on their academic prowess or formality but don't honour 'lived' forms of knowledge. Boaventura de Sousa Santos[29] notes in his *Epistemologies of the South* that the notion of western knowledge as 'normative' has corrupted knowledge production because knowledge is judged upon its ability to fit into certain descriptors. Part of deconstructing whiteness and empire is also deconstructing how mission and faith function in the world – upholding non-academic styles of writing and knowing such as feelings, relationality, spirituality and connection.

We suggest that if the Church is to truly participate in *missio Dei* in the British context with any real integrity it must begin to be a co-conspirator in epistemic disobedience. We suggest that one such act of 'disobedience' is to listen to, amplify, and be rooted and re-routed, by the voices of the Global South who have 'moved into the neighbourhood' and planted themselves in the soil of the United Kingdom. Since the end of the Second World War there has been a proliferation of churches which were carried by the waves of migration from across the world in the postcolonial era. These have shaped the ecclesial landscape in profound ways. Especially from the perspective of the national ecumenical instruments in England, this is of vital significance. When the British Council of Churches was disbanded and new instruments established in September 1990, the original group of churches that made up the members numbered just 16. By 2024 the membership had grown to 54 with others in process. The majority of these have come from Pentecostal, Charismatic and Orthodox traditions. Many of these churches bring with them fresh perspectives on the 'problem' of mission. Others bring with them an understanding of mission from their own national and denominational vantage point, planted in new soil – Serbian Orthodox or Nigerian Pentecostal for example. Another way of acting in epistemological disobedience is to give a platform to a younger generation of theological thinkers who are tired of much of the inflexibility and institutional ossification coming from the centre. In this work we hope to bring a rich, messy and polyvalent range of voices that paint a true picture of ecumenical mission in twenty-first-century Britain.

'Lived' mission and the turn to reflecting on practice and self

In the light of the above this book brings together a 'cacophony of voices', setting alongside each other both those who are well established as theologians and reflective practitioners and those who are working on the ground and have written little on their daily 'lived experience'. A number of the contributors are practitioners – those who have a more academic or institutional role have reflected on the intersection between mission and their own 'lived' experience or perhaps their own pilgrimage in mission. The volume presents an important shift away from the tendency towards the abstract to the 'lived'. The idea is to bring this about through the lenses of autoethnography or ethnographic reflection on a particular concrete situation. It is not envisioned that each of us should embark on a new, strictly academic, ethnographical study for this edited book. We are seeking more reflective-based accounts, understanding that our audience is the Church.

The contributors have been asked to consider mission as 'lived' experience, helping them to narrate their particular practices against the backdrop of their own understanding of mission in the light of the postcolonial and ecumenical. We use the five marks of mission as a broad underpinning to reflect a wide variety of practices and contexts in today's twenty-first-century Britain but acknowledge that these five marks themselves are in a sense inadequate to capture the fullness of following God in God's mission to the world. The denominational diversity has also led some authors to approach mission in ways that stretch, challenge or argue against the framework of the five marks of mission. Paul Weller's acknowledgement of our multi-faith context questions any heavy-handed approach to evangelism; Niall Cooper's chapter outlines how Christian service can only make sense when coupled with justice. If we are really to love the poor we have to work to end poverty and squash the economic gap, and Tom Hackett's discipleship does not aim to teach, transform structures (at lease explicitly), or baptize others, but his quiet determination to be with people that society would rather forget is undoubtedly a Christ-like, missional, prophetic act. Contributors in some cases also write from a particular confessional perspective.

The turn to epistemic disobedience – some reflections

It is clear that the desire to interrogate epistemic assumptions and wrestle with the gifts of theological reflection from outside the western world is bubbling up. In a recent editorial for the *Practical Theology* journal on Majority World epistemologies, Brundson and Chu say that they invited contributors to articulate epistemologies while relating practical theological thinking to contextually unique foci. Our invitation was embedded in the conviction that the sharing of epistemologies creates an opportunity not only to learn about others and the context in which they live, but from them, enhancing practical theological meaning making in the present time.[30]

Similarly, an editorial from Jay Mātenga[31] in the *Anvil* journal called for the emancipation of indigenous theological perspectives. These approaches of understanding and learning from theological knowledge created and curated from outside the hegemonic tyranny of western rationalism are important. In a recent tweet from Rebecca Chapman at a Religion Media Centre event, she posted a quote from Chine McDonald, the director of Theos: 'Most people who are Christian in the world are black & brown people. This narrative about Christianity being white & European creeps out into lots of religious coverage. There is vibrancy when you look at the global picture.'[32] Since the Second World War the landscape of Britain has changed dramatically. Waves of migration have transformed the ecclesial horizon. Today, while almost all historic churches are in decline to some degree or another, Pentecostal, Charismatic and Orthodox churches are growing – some at startling rates. Yet the centre of gravity theologically and epistemologically is still located in the cathedrals, bishops' offices, administrative centres, theological colleges and university departments. The production of theological knowledge over the past thousand years or so has, by and large, been the preserve of white men in the monastery or academy. It begs the questions, what type of knowledge do we value? Where has that knowledge been birthed, grown up and found its life? Choan-Seng Song, the Taiwanese theologian, writes about a theology being birthed from the womb of Asia.[33] Where are the theologies that will shape mission thinking in Britain for the next 20, 30 or 50 years being birthed? Not at Lambeth. Which communities, which experiences, which generations, which struggles, which peoples, or confessions? Will we take seriously a theological epistemology that is birthed out of black and brown people's experience, that is birthed among Millennials and Gen Zs, second- and third-generation men and women from South Asia, the Caribbean, the continent of Africa, from the Orthodox churches?

One of the reasons that Christianity has struggled to be open to other ways of knowledge formation and curation is because, as Kosuke Koyama says, it has 'Quite tragically produced a great number of despisers of others'. Koyama invites us to say goodbye to all 'someone else theology'. He says, 'Didn't Christianity over many centuries despise "infidels"? Don't we despise men of other religions? Don't we despise people who don't come to church? Don't we despise those who do not interpret the

Bible as we do?'[34] The 'turn' towards epistemic disobedience is a move to disrupt, supplant and renew our missiological vision, to say 'no' to being despisers. It is vitally important for the Church if she wants to be ready to meet the challenges of the rest of the century.

Epistemology and indigenous knowledge

Epistemology comes from two Greek words: *episteme* 'knowledge' and *logos* 'explanation'. Epistemology attempts to understand what it is we can know and how knowledge is constructed. In classical philosophy there are various categories or types of knowledge, broadly understood as propositional knowledge (that something is so) and non-propositional knowledge (knowledge by acquaintance or direct awareness). The rise of rationalism during the Enlightenment started with Descartes' famous method. With his method Descartes cast doubt upon the senses as an authoritative source of knowledge, and while he argues that *all* human knowledge (not only knowledge of the material world through the senses) depends on metaphysical knowledge of God, his method essentially dismisses other forms of knowledge. Later, Kant devised an approach to epistemology in his *Critique of Pure Reason* (1781) which undertakes both to determine the limits of our knowledge, and at the same time to provide a foundation of scientific knowledge of nature. He attempts to do this by critically examining our human faculties of knowledge.[35] Enlightenment epistemology was firmly rooted in scientific rationalism, in empirical observation, and was the preserve of men of the academy. Discussing this Enlightenment delineation of the world and our relationship to it, Te Ahukaramū Charles Royal, a Māori philosopher, points out that in 'the conventional western worldview, it is customary to perceive phenomena as separate from the observer – the tree is "out there" and my thoughts about the tree are "in here". This perception rests on the idea that the human being is fundamentally separate from the world.'[36] Not only is it that we are separate from the world, but more that we are masters over the separate observable world which we 'lord it over'. Seeing the 'world' as out there, apart from us, causes us to quest for control over it and to value what is controllable, calculable and predictable. This form of knowledge, rooted in scientific rationalism, became the highest form of knowledge against which all others were set, weighed and judged. As Te Ahukaramū again notes, 'Scientific rationalism risks becoming dry, abstract and lifeless. It can become detached, building authority for itself within the confines of a particular group of people who participate in this way of explaining the world.'[37] During the colonial exploits of western nations from the sixteenth century onwards, but at its height in the eighteenth and nineteenth centuries, these attitudes to indigenous and local forms of knowledge and ways of being were prevalent. It was assumed that western, rationalist ways of understanding and approaching the world were always superior. As Hoppers points out, 'part of the legacy of colonialism, and the science that accompanied it, that still lingers in academic practice in general, is that non-western societies and the knowledges that sustained them are taken as obsolete.'[38] The New Zealand Linda Tuhiwai Smith says,

> It appals us that the West can desire, extract and claim ownership of our ways of knowing, our imagery, the things we create and produce, and then simultaneously reject the people who created and developed those ideas, and seek to deny them further opportunities to be creators of their own culture (and) deny them the validity of their own knowledge.[39]

The hegemony of Western European forms of knowledge continued well into the twentieth century only really beginning to be questioned, subverted and displaced after the Second World War. As part of this questioning in his radical vision for equality and justice, de Sousa Santos argues that 'The understanding of the world by far exceeds the western understanding of the world. And there is no global social justice without global cognitive justice.'[40] Part of the process of a move towards global cognitive justice is allowing space for epistemologies that are rooted in the experiences of indigenous communities, in the voices and lives of people who have been systemically ignored, trodden down, ecclesiastically ostracized, outlawed and at times beaten, tortured and murdered. It is a flowering of a multitude of epistemologies, of ways of knowing and being often rooted in ancient wisdoms and stories whispered and proclaimed through generations. It is giving value to epistemologies which were decried and at times mercilessly ridiculed. In indigenous epistemologies of the Māori, for example, Te Ahukaramū Charles Royal says, 'In traditional pre-contact indigenous cultures, the relationship between the human being and the world was indivisible. Humankind and nature were one. There was no nature "out there", external to us, or human consciousness "in here".'[41]

For Catherine Hoppers, a renaissance and retrieval of indigenous forms of knowledge in the African context is more than just an exercise in intellectual forms of cognitive justice; it is a rediscovery of true African identity and agency. She writes:

> [E]motional dislocation, moral sickness and individual helplessness remain ubiquitous features of our time. Moreover, for a great majority of the population of Africa, the loss of cultural reference points has culminated in the fundamental breakdown of African societies, with

dire consequences for the social and human development project as a whole.[42]

Hoppers suggests that the drive for promotion of Indigenous Knowledge Systems (IKS) in South Africa, for example, needs to be at all levels: in the academy with scientists and researchers, at policy level in Government departments and alongside local indigenous communities at the grassroots level. These ways of knowing are rooted in ancient wisdom and culture.

Te Ahukaramū Charles Royal suggests two reasons why indigenous people are interested in epistemology. First, he notes that this is rooted in 'A desire for cultural restoration, the desire to restore our culture to our people, the determination to rekindle, revitalise and develop indigenous cultures damaged through colonisation.'[43] Second, the interest in indigenous epistemology lies with the closely related activity called 'decolonization'[44] – part of a focus on indigenous epistemology is about unlearning the West as Vellem says. It is part of shifting our attentiveness, or reorientating ourselves, towards other ways of knowing and valuing them – this becomes a form of decolonialization. We sense that the work you are about to read in these pages is both bound up in recovering things lost and in the process acting as a decolonizing force.

A few important caveats are necessary. First, this book is not intended to be systematically comprehensive. That would probably be impossible. Rather it offers a snapshot from a spectrum of denominations in Britain in the first two decades of the twenty-first century. As mentioned, the book draws both established and emerging voices into a matrix of mission, arguing that Britain's problem with empire and lingering residues of colonialism have not been sufficiently dealt with to birth new forms of mission and evangelism robust enough to navigate the multiple challenges present today. Second, since it is not systematic there are gaps. We have a voice from Scotland but none from Wales or Northern Ireland. We acknowledge this fact. We have a range of voices from particular denominations, but others are missing. Nevertheless, we hope it gives voice to a whole range of people, theological confessions and traditions that you may not think belong together but are part of an ever-growing ecumenical diversity found in Britain in the third decade of the twenty-first century.

Confessions, Contexts and Consequences

The book is divided into three sections entitled 'Confessions', 'Contexts' and 'Consequences'. In Part One, **Confessions**, we invited our authors to write from their particular confessional location. This includes

Catholic, Orthodox, Free Church and Pentecostal lived experiences. The book begins with a reflection on mission and synodality from **Jan Nowotnik,** the director of mission and the national ecumenical officer for the Catholic Bishops' Conference of England and Wales. Decidedly occupying the institutional centre, Nowotnik outlines something of the synodal process that Pope Francis has set into action and which has been called the greatest listening exercise ever undertaken. Nowotnik argues, drawing on the papal exhortation *Evangelii Gaudium*, that mission and synodality are rooted in a renewed understanding of the joy of the gospel. **Shemil Mathew,** Anglican theologian and vice principal of Emmanuel Theological College, outlines some work on Anglican diaspora, mission and postcolonialism from his PhD work researching two Anglican diaspora communities of which he is part and their views on mission in the UK. Antiochian priest **Father Boniface Carroll** sets out the often 'mis-remembered' history of Orthodoxy in the British Isles, arguing that only when the Church of these fair isles begins to venerate her own saints will the Church grow again.

In Parts Two and Three, **Contexts** and **Consequences,** we showcase several authors reflecting on concrete situations and the consequences of their actions. These include work alongside children, refugees and diaspora Christians, action around the climate emergency, and the challenges of rural settings. **Harvey Kwiyani** draws upon the tools of World Christianity, where the secularity of the West is being met with the dynamic faith of the non-western world, especially from the myriad contexts of Africa. The chapter with **Tom Hackett** is in the form of an interview with Victoria Turner, where they discuss Tom's work of visiting a detention centre for asylum seekers and the struggles of powerlessness but with the gift of grace seeping through the unjust system. **James Woodward** reflects upon the elderly, often used to demonstrate the 'problem' of many of our churches. James pulls us away from anxious styles of mission and draws upon a slower, counter-cultural, care-ful style of missional engagement. **Heather Major** shares some of her recent PhD work on the fragility of churches in rural Scottish contexts. **Elizabeth Joy** argues that *missio Dei* is best understood as marginality and outlines a decolonizing of mission from her perspective as an Orthodox woman who has served with the Council for World Mission (CWM). **Bisi Adenekan** perceptively gives voice to the experiences of second- and third-generation Nigerian Pentecostal Christians and their understandings of mission and evangelism and the challenges that these bring for the future.

Lisa Adjei and **Shermara Fletcher** share their experiences of growing up as black millennials in Britain and their pursuit of racial justice in their dynamic ministries. **Raj Patta** helps us to think about love, and how a pedagogy of love enlivens our biblical readings for mission. **Paul Weller**

uses quantitative census data to explore how we should relate to our plural society – not as a threat, but as a gift we could embrace as relational, embracing followers of Christianity. **Niall Cooper** shares some of his profound experience in anti-poverty campaigning to question how we mission alongside people who are hurting, forgotten and overlooked in society. He asks how we can develop relationships of mutuality and solidarity, where people with experience of brokenness can lead the way to fixing our cracks. **Anupama Ranawana** draws on cultural theorist Ambavalaner Sivanandan's idea of 'communities of resistance' as a framework for the hostile environment that migrants encounter in the UK and its relationship to climate justice.

We hope this collection can inspire, unsettle and advance our conception of *missio Dei* in the world. We hope it will be a catalyst for conversation – from our ecumenical instruments to our local churches – across denominations, communities, perhaps even in interfaith work. We aspire that it will be a helpful tool for practitioners and a book of lessons for academics. As editors we are full of gratitude to the authors for responding and writing so richly, and grateful to our team for the process of getting to know each other better, enabling creativity, poking for deadlines, laughing through disagreements and crafting a beautiful contribution to the eternal discussion of how we see and worship, work and love God, who is ever present and ever walking with us in our broken, enlightening, painful and awe-inspiring world.

Notes

1 S. Dow, 2022, '"It had no filters": The legacy of Australia's provocative National Black Theatre', *The Guardian*, 9 November, https://www.theguardian.com/stage/2022/nov/09/it-had-no-filters-the-legacy-of-australias-provocative-national-black-theatre, accessed 04.06.2024.

2 D. Bosch, 1991, *Transforming Mission: Paradigm shifts in theology of mission*, Maryknoll, NY: Orbis Books, p. 496.

3 Life and Work and Faith and Order united in 1948 to form the World Council of Churches. The International Missionary Council joined in 1961.

4 See Brian Stanley, 'The World Missionary Conference, Edinburgh 1910: Sifting history from myth', *The Expository Times* 121 (7) (2010): 325–31.

5 British Missionary Societies, 'Conference of British Missionary Societies Archive', *Jisc Archives Hub*, https://archiveshub.jisc.ac.uk/search/archives/8d977ba7-fbb6-390d-8b41-29f702f5355e, accessed 04.06.2024.

6 See Victoria Turner, 2023, 'A Happy Ecumenical Legacy for the London Missionary Society? Exposing the coloniality between churches engaged in mission' in Anthony Reddie and Carol Troupe (eds), *Deconstructing Whiteness, Empire and Mission*, London: SCM Press, pp. 120–36.

7 Jione Havea, 2020, 'Repatriation of Native Minds' in Jione Havea (ed.), *Mission and Context*, Lanham, MD: Fortress Academic, p. 6.

8 B. Aldous, 2022, *The God Who Walks Slowly: Reflections on mission with Kosuke Koyama*, London: SCM Press, p. 86.

9 K. Koyama, 2009, 'Commission One after a century of violence: The search for a larger Christ' in D. Kerr and K. Ross (eds), *Edinburgh 2010: Mission now and then*, Oxford: Regnum, p. 50.

10 Churches Together in England, 'Welcome', *Churches Together in England*, https://cte.org.uk/, accessed 04.06.2024.

11 I owe this insight to Bishop Humphrey Southern, who explored the Thomas-Kilmann five models of conflict for a class at Ripon College Cuddesdon in our module Leadership and Theology for Ministry and Mission (17.10.2023).

12 The Kairos Document, 'Challenge to the Church: A theological comment on the political crisis in South Africa', British Council of Churches, 1985, p. 27.

13 Elianne Andam, 2023, 'Boy, 17, appears in court over murder of schoolgirl in Croydon', *BBC News*, https://www.bbc.co.uk/news/uk-england-london-66942594, accessed 18.07.2024.

14 K. Clements, 2017, *Dietrich Bonhoeffer's Ecumenical Quest*, Geneva: World Council of Churches, p. 264.

15 Byung-Chul Han, 2021, *The Palliative Society: Pain today*, trans. Daniel Steuer, Cambridge: Polity Press, p. 12. *Dispostif*, in the translation from the German, implies 'the all-consuming goal of'.

16 Han, *The Palliative Society*, p. 11.

17 Luke Larner, 2023, 'Feckless Faith' in Luke Larner (ed.), *Confounding the Mighty: Stories of church, social class and solidarity*, London: SCM Press, p. 15.

18 Graham Adams, 2022, *Holy Anarchy: Dismantling domination, embodying community, loving strangeness*, London: SCM Press, p. 112.

19 United Church of Christ, 'Barmen Declaration', *United Church of Christ*, https://www.ucc.org/beliefs_barmen-declaration/, accessed 15.12.2021.

20 Norman Goodall, 1964, *Christian Missions and Social Ferment*, London: The Epworth Press, pp. 87–8.

21 George MacLeod, 1936, *Speaking the Truth in Love: The Modern Preacher's Task*, London: SCM Press, p. 96.

22 Norman Goodall, 1954, *Gathered for What? An Address from the Chair of the Congregational Union of England and Wales delivered in Westminster Chapel, London on 10th May 1954*, London: Independent Press, p. 10.

23 James Woodward chapter in this collection.

24 Havea, 'Repatriation of native minds', p. 3.

25 W. Mignolo, 'Epistemic disobedience, independent thought and decolonial freedom', *Theory, Culture and Society* 26 (7–9) (2009): 1–23.

26 Mignolo, 'Epistemic disobedience', p. 2.

27 V. Vellem, 'Un-thinking the West: The spirit of doing Black Theology of Liberation in decolonial times', *HTS Teologiese Studies* 73 (3) (2017): 2.

28 A. Boesak, 1977, *Farewell to Innocence: A socio-ethical study on Black Theology and power*, Maryknoll, NY: Orbis Books.

29 B. de Sousa Santos, 2016, *Epistemologies of the South: Justice against epistemicide*, Abingdon: Routledge.

30 A. Brundson and C. Chu, 'Special themed issue: Majority world epistemologies', *Practical Theology* 16 (2) (2023): 134. It should also be noted that the November 2023 edition of *International Review of Mission* 112 (2) dedicated its theme to 'Mission and Decolonisation: Again'.

31 J. Mātenga, 'Editorial: The emancipation of Indigenous theologies in light of the rise of World Christianity', *Anvil* 39 (1) (2023): 2.

32 Rebecca (Bex Chapman), 2023, *Twitter*, 12 June, https://twitter.com/bex chapman3boys/status/1668214939280973825, accessed 04.06.2024.

33 C. S. Song, 1988, *Theology from the Womb of Asia*, London: SCM Press.

34 K. Koyama, 1975, *Theology in Contact*, Madras: The Christian Literature Society, p. 34.

35 W. Bristow, 2017, 'Enlightenment', *The Stanford Encyclopedia of Philosophy*, Edward N. Zalta (ed.), https://plato.stanford.edu/archives/fall2017/entries/enlightenment/, accessed 04.06.2024.

36 Te Ahukaramū Charles Royal, 2009, *Let the World Speak: Towards an indigenous epistemology*, Wellington, New Zealand: MKTA, p. 7.

37 Royal, *Let the World Speak*, p. 17.

38 C. A. O. Hoppers, 2002, 'Indigenous knowledge and the integration of knowledge systems' in C. A. O. Hoppers (ed.), *Indigenous Knowledge and the Integration of Knowledge Systems: Towards a philosophy of articulation*, Claremont: New Africa Books, p. 4.

39 L. T. Smith, 1999, *Decolonizing Methodologies: Research and indigenous peoples*, London: Zed Books, p. 1.

40 De Sousa Santos, *Epistemologies of the South*, Preface.

41 Royal, *Let the World Speak*, p. 5.

42 Hoppers, *Indigenous Knowledge*, p. 3.

43 Royal, *Let the World Speak*, p. 30.

44 Royal, *Let the World Speak*, p. 30.

Confessions

I

The Synodal Pathway in the Catholic Church

JAN NOWOTNIK

Introduction

Synodality is not a word that many Catholics had come across until recently. It is fair to say that most had never really heard the word until Pope Francis started to use the term in October 2015 and more precisely when he spoke on the 50th anniversary of the institution of the Synod of Bishops at the end of the Second Vatican Council. On that occasion Francis said:

> We must continue along this path [the synodal pathway]. The world in which we live, and in which we are called to love and serve, even with its contradictions, demands that the Church strengthen cooperation in all areas of her mission. It is precisely this path of synodality which God expects for his Church in the third millennium.[1]

In this chapter I will address how I see that the world in which we live helps us to a deeper appreciation of what Pope Francis wants from the synodal pathway not only for the Catholic Church, but also set in an ecumenical framework. Therefore, I would like to suggest that the synodal pathway is not just important for Catholics and for the mission of the Catholic Church, but what it implies will be important for how she engages with other Christians so that together we can discover what the Lord's plan is for us. In this way Christians from our various traditions will together love and serve the world more faithfully, which I believe is something the world needs; a deeper cooperation between us all.

Pope Francis and the synodal pathway

In the same address of October 2015, Pope Francis said, 'From the beginning of my ministry as Bishop of Rome, I sought to enhance the synod, which is one of the precious legacies of the Second Vatican Council',[2] so that we would be members of a Church

> which listens, which realises that listening is more than simply hearing. It is a mutual listening in which everyone has something to learn. The faithful people, the college of bishops, the Bishop of Rome: all listening to the Holy Spirit, the Spirit of Truth in order to know what he says to the Churches.[3]

Pope Francis here is speaking of the Synod of Bishops set up by Pope Paul VI at the end of the Second Vatican Council to be a mechanism whereby principally the bishops of the Catholic world could engage more fruitfully together to discuss how best the Church may serve the needs of the world and its people. Before delving into the principles of synodality suggested by Pope Francis and what he exactly meant when he said that he wanted to enhance the synod that had been instituted by Pope Paul VI in 1965, let us first go back to the beginning of his ministry as the Bishop of Rome to see how this notion of synodality was part of his pontificate from the very start. Pope Francis was elected pope, the Bishop of Rome, on 13 March 2013 and made his first appearance to the city and the world on the balcony of St Peter's on that March evening. It was a moment charged with huge emotion at the end of the second day of a conclave. Unusually, this took place not after the death of a pope but instead after the shock resignation of Pope Benedict just a month earlier, who had suggested that he could no longer lead the Church through the challenges that she was facing. Pope Benedict had believed that the Church needed a fresh pair of eyes to guide her.

The fresh pair of eyes was incarnated in the person of the man who up until then had been Cardinal Archbishop of Buenos Aires, Jorge Bergoglio, and who now introduced himself to the world as Pope Francis. Everyone was waiting to hear what he would say and what he would be like, and when he began with the simple Italian greeting of '*Buonasera*' we knew that we might be in for something different. Here was the simple greeting of a man who has made it his priority to connect with those around him, especially the most vulnerable and those on the margins.

I believe what Francis is trying to teach the Church is that it is often in the small gestures that we witness most clearly to those around us, those whom we are called to love and to serve. This is certainly true for me as I reflect on my own priestly ministry and on my role as national ecumenical officer. It is very easy to become weighed down by all that divides us and separates our different traditions and not see a way out, but this barrier is broken when we make the starting point what we have in common; our humanity, our desire to connect with another and our hopes to bring our relationship with Christ to others. This, surely, is at the heart of a synodal experience of the Church in which we all learn to accompany each other on life's journey.

This is the sense that I get with Pope Francis, that it is the small gestures that sometimes have huge implications which bring about a true change of heart, something which is not always experienced when we try to change structures or years of history. Therefore, I would like to suggest that the real 'Franciscan reform', or synodal understanding, is more about how we as human beings allow space for God in our lives and let that encounter spill over into our human relationships. Quite simply, what Pope Francis offers is a vision of a church which attempts to discern faithfully what the Holy Spirit is saying to her through all her members, so that she can be a more effective sign of God's love in the world.

The synodal pathway as a journey that we embark on together

To speak of the synodal pathway only in terms of change is unnecessary and could be alarming for some within the Catholic Church. It is true that the synodal pathway demands change, but this is primarily a personal change of heart, and in my own desire to know the Lord through my prayer and in my service to the other. To be involved in the Lord's mission begins by hearing Jesus call me by name and sensing that I am deeply loved by him; when I know that I am loved and am forgiven of my sins, my guilt and shame when I turn to him, then I am impelled to share this with others. In this way, the Church's mission is predicated on how we share together the common space which is the world in which we live and how we come to share in each other's joys and sorrows.

Set in this context, what Pope Francis offers is not the path of radical change of doctrine or Church teaching; rather, he is asking us to consider the ways in which we are called to be disciples, which he claims are rooted in the journey we take together, as he said on his first appearance: 'And now, we take up this journey – bishop and people – the journey of the Church of Rome, which presides in charity over all the churches.'[4]

For me, this sense of journey finds its echo in the Acts of the Apostles, where we see how the early Church began to arrange herself, first by attempting to share all in common, united in prayer and fraternity. This is also seen in the road to Emmaus story in Luke's Gospel, which presents the Christian life as a journey lived through the experience of the two disciples and their encounter with Jesus.

The context is clear: the Christian life is a journey or pilgrimage where we listen to the Lord amid our daily tasks and where we learn to accompany each other or, as the word synod suggests, we walk with each other.

This is so much more than seeking structural development and so much more about sharing in the joys and sorrows of each other's lives. To go back to my experience of walking with my friends in other Christian traditions, as we get to know each other and know what makes us tick we sense what is important to each other and this is what gives rise to our unity, which in turn gives us the confidence to speak of what, at times, divides us.

For me, this is the broader context of the teaching of the Second Vatican Council which reminded the Catholic Church of the need for her members to enter into a dialogue with the world; this, as we know, is also at the heart of what Pope Francis is currently attempting to achieve. This means that the synodal pathway is very firmly linked to what we received in Vatican II, with its focus on a return to the significance of the scriptures as the fountain from which to drink deeply to appreciate the Lord's teaching as experienced in the Tradition of the Church. Cardinal Walter Kasper frames this beautifully: 'What will be the path of the new pope, together with the people of God?' The answer is clear, 'Of course, it will be the path or way of discipleship of Jesus Christ. There is no other path for the Church.'[5] Kasper is clear that the way forward is a radical discipleship which flows from the inheritance of our common baptism revealed in the life of the Christian community that accompanies each other on life's pilgrimage.

The challenge that Pope Francis offers

In Pope Francis's first Apostolic Exhortation, *Evangelii Gaudium*, or in English, 'The Joy of the Gospel', he says that this Gospel joy 'fills the hearts and lives of all who encounter Jesus'[6] and that he hopes to 'encourage the Christian faithful to embark upon a new chapter of evangelisation marked by this joy, while pointing out new paths for the Church's journey in years to come'.[7] The task of the Christian life is to find the joy and peace which only the gospel can bring, with its potential to transform our lives for the better and help us to pass on to others what we have received.

The joy of the gospel

Pope Francis embodies this in his life, where he teaches us how to be immersed in the joy of the gospel, where we are drawn from self-preoccupation to appreciate the needs of those around us. Therefore, when he writes about the 'joy of the gospel' Pope Francis believes that in the outreach to others we must speak to the challenges presented by contemporary societal structures. So today the Christian is called to speak to the challenges of life brought on by economic problems, the crisis in family life, and the devastating consequences wrought by war. He suggests that we give answer to these challenges through the balm of the gospel, which is the antidote to the sorrow and offers the Christian person fresh ways to proclaim the joy of the gospel which attempts to relieve burdens and not create more.

Pope Francis speaks of the social consequences brought about by the Church's missionary zeal predicated on the Christian's focus on Christ, who shows himself most of all in the poor and weak. The Christian is invited to go to the margins or the peripheries where not only the poor and the weak can be found, but also those who feel excluded from the Church's life and mission. This journey to the periphery is not just for us to bring the healing that is needed but also affords us the opportunity to get a distinct perspective that is good for the Christian soul. At the margins we mix with those who are misunderstood and badly characterized and who so often feel let down by societal structures. What then are we called to do? Not just to stay at the margins for a short while and then walk away, but surely to be the bearers of a Gospel joy which offers the balm that Francis speaks of.

The synodal journey

Moving on from the 'joy of the gospel' I want to introduce the theme of the synodal pathway in a more focused way. For me, the synodal pathway flows from a renewed vision of the Church offered by Vatican II's constitution on the Church, *Lumen Gentium* or 'The Light of the Nations'. In this document we read of the Church as the People of God, highlighting that all of us are part of the People of God, pastors and people together, and together are called to the pathway of holiness. It is the teaching of the Second Vatican Council which paves the way for a deeper appreciation of synodality.

For a moment I want to describe what Pope Francis means when he says that he wants to enhance the structure of the Synod of Bishops. He is speaking about the result of Pope Paul VI setting up the Synod of Bishops in 1965, at the end of the Second Vatican Council, as a place where the bishops of the world could share ideas about how to be faithful to the gospel in a contemporary situation. What Francis does in 2015 is to attempt to broaden this structure so that it is not just for the bishops, but that all the baptized should have an opportunity to both speak and discern. Pope Francis clearly links this with the 'joy of the gospel', saying that 'the world in which we live, and which we are called to love and serve, even with its contradictions, demands that the Church strengthen cooperation in all areas of her mission. It is precisely this path of synodality which God expects of his Church in the third millennium.'[8]

What we see here is how Francis makes a link in a chain which takes us back to the fresh approach of Vatican II but at the same time broadens it for the needs of twenty-first-century Christianity. By developing the structure of the synod, Francis is responding to the needs of the time, where laywomen and -men want to step up to be involved more fully in the Church's mission. The synodal pathway speaks to the needs set out in *Evangelii Gaudium* and steps out tentatively to put them into practice. The ongoing question is how to make this more real each day.

The pathway of dialogue beginning in prayer

The key to a renewed sense of mission must be to develop the relationship we have with the Lord in the Church's liturgy and in our personal prayer which forms our hearts and minds. When we come to know the Lord in prayer and through formation, we are more capable of speaking about him and witnessing to him. This is a dialogue of the heart, our hearts entwined with the Lord's, akin to the motto of Cardinal John Henry Newman, 'Heart speaks unto heart', '*Cor ad cor loquitor*'.

This perspective is illustrated beautifully in Luke's Emmaus story, which I would like to return to for a few moments. St Luke offers us this story of the two disciples as they walk away from Jerusalem on their way to Emmaus after the events of the Lord's passion and death. It is an emotional journey that starts off with two downcast disciples, not able to come to terms with the events of the past days and all that had happened to their friend Jesus. They are so upset that they are prevented from recognizing Jesus when he walks alongside them and so it is Jesus who begins the conversation with them, with the simple, yet effective question, 'What matters are you discussing as you walk along?' That is enough; they start to tell their story, sharing the events of the last few days, pouring out their hearts and taken aback that this stranger is not familiar with these events, which they felt sure everyone must know about.

Jesus can converse with them and engage with them as he takes them through the history of salvation. He tells them who he is, that he is not a stranger, he is their friend Jesus, and he explains his relationship with the Father. No wonder that they are captivated by the stranger, no wonder that as they approach the village, and when he makes as if to go on, they beg him to stay with them. They want to remain with the man who could stir their hearts and explain their deepest emotions; it is no wonder that they hearts burn within them as he speaks to them on the journey.

This is one of my favourite moments in scripture, it is so full of human emotion and fragility and ordinariness. It reminds me not just of my need for Jesus but also how he shows himself to me, not just in the Breaking of the Bread but also in my daily encounters where others share their story with me and vice versa.

The Emmaus story helps me to understand how Pope Francis sees the synodal journey. It is about letting go to experience the Lord's love, amid our own human emotions and disappointments. We too need the release of feeling our burdens lifted by the Lord of love, which allows us to move forward with a new sense of purpose and our hearts uplifted. This story speaks to us of what happens to us when we abandon ourselves to the Lord in prayer and how we are moved to dialogue with one another in the work that we are called to do in the Church.

The pathway of dialogue extends from prayer

I want to set the pathway of dialogue, or what we may now be able to call the synodal pathway, in the teaching of Paul VI during the time of the Council. I speak here of what remains for me one of the most significant papal documents of the last 60 years or so, the *Ecclesiam Suam* of Pope Paul VI. This teaching letter of Paul VI of 6 August 1964 is about who the Church is and what she is called to be and do in the world.

Paul VI begins this, his first encyclical – or teaching letter to the whole Church – in the following way: 'The Church was founded by Jesus Christ to be the loving mother of the whole human family and minister to its salvation.'[9] From the outset Paul outlines what will be the important markers of his pontificate; the very *raison d'être* of the Church's existence is to minister to people's salvation. The Church exists to heal the wounds of the broken-hearted and to offer them a new way of being, just as Jesus did with the disciples on the road to Emmaus. We could liken this to how Pope Francis has spoken of the Church as a field hospital that helps the wounded to get back on the journey. The idea of the field hospital is that it is ready to minister to the wounded where they are, not from the luxury of the centre but at the peripheries. The implication is clear: the members of the Body of Christ, the Church, are called to accompany each other on the journey, and integral to this is the healing of our mutual wounds.

This idea resonates with what Pope Paul VI had spoken of nearly 60 years earlier when he stated that 'The aim of this encyclical will be to demonstrate with increasing clarity how vital it is for the world, and how greatly desired by the Catholic Church, that the two should meet together, and get to know and love one another.'[10] Paul had reinforced Pope John XXIII's hopes that the Second Vatican Council would remind the Church of the need to enter into a dialogue with the world, and especially with those who share Jesus' teachings. Francis suggests that the best way to do this is to heal each other's wounds as we walk along the way. This is what will draw us into the path of salvation.

In *Ecclesiam Suam* Paul VI had given us a charter for the type of dialogue that we can enter. When we review it in the light of the present call for a synodal Church, it seems to me that in Paul VI we can see the direct precursor for what we are experiencing in the Church today. The true image of the dialogical or synodal Church is the Holy Trinity, where we see the communion of the three persons of the Trinity in one God. In our prayer we are drawn into a communion of love in the Trinity, and our dialogue with each other is an echo of that communion as we are drawn together with our companions on the journey into the life-giving mystery of the Triune God.

Paul VI articulates for us the main attributes of a truthful and truth-leading dialogue. When we speak, we must do so clearly, but with a sense of humility and meekness. We must be confident in what we say, but, like the prudent teacher who both listens to and engages with our interlocutor, able to adapt to new situations while at the same time remaining faithful to the Truth.[11] In this way Paul VI provides a simple framework for the synodal pathway, which must be first centred in the dialogue that we have with the Lord in prayer.

The first steps into a synodal Church

In many ways it could be said that Pope Francis has inherited that same sense of the importance of dialogue with the world that his predecessor Pope Paul VI had and spoke about in *Ecclesiam Suam*. To that end, Francis has begun to reform the institution that is the Synod of Bishops to encompass the entire People of God. He began in 2021 by postponing the next Synod of Bishops' meeting by one year so that it could be a true consultation of the People of God under the theme of 'For a Synodal Church, Communion, Participation and Mission'. He invited parish and diocesan groups to participate in synodal gatherings to listen to the Lord in prayer and to each other, to inform one another what it is like to be a Catholic today.

Pope Francis has also changed the way that the bishops will gather in synod in Rome by providing the opportunity for laywomen and -men, and religious men and women to participate alongside the bishops; thus in the 2023 synod there were at least 70 participants who were not bishops. This was so that the synod would become truly representative of the People of God, and so that the bishops could hear directly from the lay faithful and they in turn could speak directly with the bishops, who have the charism of leadership, or governance in the Church. This invites the whole gathering to share honestly the joys and sorrows of being a follower of Christ and so seek ever fresh ways to proclaim the joy of the gospel. Some have argued that by extending the remit of the synod, Francis has cast aside the discernment of the bishops. I hope, rather, that what he is doing is allowing the bishops, priests, religious and lay faithful the time to be together and so discern together what the Lord wants of his Church today, the Church which includes all the People of God.

Consultation or discernment?

Before the meeting in Rome a widespread consultation took place among the People of God. This was not always easy, because many Catholics would admit that this was the first time that they had been asked their opinions by and of the Church. It has been challenging, I think, to differentiate between criticism of the Church and her teaching and what the Spirit is saying to the Churches. So, wisely, the consultations moved slowly, too slowly in some people's minds, so that at every level of the Church's life there was a reflection on what had been heard, at the local parish level, at diocesan level and moving into the continental before arriving at the synod in Rome.

There is the inevitable tension between the Church's teaching and the lived experience of faith, and it seems as if we are back at Vatican II, or at least developing its teaching to see what is required of us at the present time. I cannot speak for every place, but having been involved in the process in England and Wales I can assert that we have felt that tension too, but underpinning it is the desire to serve the Lord in a church that people love, even knowing its human flaws.

The consultation has brought similar patterns of thought to the surface across the Church and not just in England and Wales. One of the biggest questions is how we include all people in the life of the Church, and certainly the role of women has been mentioned at the top of this list. There is also the inclusion of those in the LGTBQ+ community, alongside those who are divorced and remarried. The role of young people in the Church remains an important question as we seek to help those setting off in life to know the joy of the gospel. The main tenet of the discussion is how we as the Church become more welcoming and more open to accompanying each other.

From these discussions flow a new sense of purpose and a sense of where the People of God may be heading in these days and certainly a renewed desire to accompany each other on the journey. This is consolidated by the possibility of a deeper appreciation of our need for a formation that helps us to speak the Truth tempered with a healthy dose of mercy. A mercy that comes from our own experiences and most certainly the knowledge of our own need for God and his mercy in our own lives. The synodal Church demands a healthier sense of formation and a better formation for both clergy and laity as we learn to appreciate one another's gifts and how to listen to one another's wisdom.

What is the next step in the synodal Church?

The simplest way to answer what next for the synodal Church is to reflect on the outcomes of the first synod in October 2023. There these themes were discussed in the presence of Pope Francis and the representatives of the world's bishops and for the first time the group of non-bishops, laywomen and -men, priests and religious who make up this renewed synodal assembly. This is an important staging point for a synodal Church, not the end but part of the ongoing journey. It is already clear that the synodal process is open to reforming some of the Church structures so that they better reflect the sense of the Church's mission today.

I feel sure that there will be a call for ongoing formation for the People of God, that there will be a cry for inclusivity, and that those who have leadership roles will listen carefully to all the voices. In this there will be the sharing of the story, just like on the road to Emmaus; there will be much emotion and some apprehension and perhaps even some blind spots, but in the midst of it all will be the Lord who walks with his people. This is what makes sense of the synodal journey, the Lord is among his people.

Conclusion

One way or another, the last few years of my life have been taken up with the study of synodality. I have read about it, given talks about it and been both excited by it and sometimes challenged by what it brings up. That said, I end where I started – with Pope Francis and his desire for a synodal Church – and I remain convinced that the journey we have started must continue.

Synodality, or the way that it is currently being imagined, is a recent theological concept. However, it is rooted in the very essence of the

Church, which from the outset has met together to resolve issues and defend doctrine. From the Council of Jerusalem, the Church has met in a council or synod in one form or another. Current thinking suggests that what synodality now calls for is a mechanism by which we can gather more imaginatively to resolve issues and defend doctrine. The needs of the present time may be expressed differently, but at heart the mission is always going to be the same – to proclaim the gospel and bring people to the Lord.

I feel sure that when Pope Francis speaks of synodality he does so inviting us to enlarge the space of our tents (this the title given to the document for the continental synodal phase). Making a tent bigger is a risky business; we must move the tent poles a little wider, which may cause tension in the tent material, it may even cause it to tear! Moving the tent poles and making space means that there will be more room for others, meaning that those who have not been in before will get a chance to shelter in the tent, and those inside the tent may have to move to another area in the tent and mix with new people. That is where I think we are.

We might express the four poles of the tent as the expressions that we so often hear of the synodal pathway; encounter, journeying, formation and accompaniment. These are the four ways in which we may be called to enlarge the space now and open the tent to see what happens. There will be risks, and it will necessitate courage and trust in the Lord – this is what Pope Francis has been calling the Church to since March 2013. The signals were there in the gestures that he used; we have the examples, now we must try to make them our own.

I would like to end on a personal note. Since September 2020 one of my tasks has been to be the National Ecumenical Officer for the Catholic Bishops of England and Wales. It is a role that I never imagined myself in, but I give thanks to God each day for the opportunity it gives me to enlarge the space of my own tent. I have learned much from my Christian brothers and sisters, and I hope that I am able to offer them something in return. What I have learned is like an Emmaus relationship, in that we walk together, we discuss the challenges that arise because of our disunity and in our midst is the Lord who walks alongside us all. For me this is the image of the synodal Church that I love best, all-encompassing and all-inclusive, and surely this is what God wants for his Church.

So, my final words are a hope and a prayer. A hope that what I have written may inspire you to read more about the synodal pathway and learn what it may mean for you in your life. A prayer that we as Christians would continue to walk together and in doing so let it be the way in which we resolve challenges and disappointments and give witness to the world. My hope and my prayer are that one fruit of the synodal journey is that it will bring us closer to the unity for which Christ prayed, unity among all those who profess the name of Jesus. I pray that our words and gestures, however small we may think that they are, will help to enlarge the space of the tent and bring us the fruits of a synodal and unified Church.

Notes

1 Pope Francis, Ceremony commemorating the 50th anniversary of the Synod of Bishops, 17 October 2015.

2 Pope Francis, Ceremony, 17 October 2015.

3 Pope Francis, Ceremony, 17 October 2015.

4 W. Kasper, William Madges (trans.), 2015, *Pope Francis's Revolution of Tenderness and Love*, New York: Paulist Press, p. 2.

5 Kasper, *Pope Francis's Revolution*, p. 2.

6 Pope Francis, 2013, *Evangelii Gaudium, The Joy of the Gospel*, London: Catholic Truth Society, p. 1.

7 Pope Francis, *Evangelii Gaudium*, p. 1.

8 Pope Francis, Ceremony, 17 October 2015.

9 K. McDonald (ed.), 2014, *The Gift of Dialogue, The Encyclical Ecclesiam Suam and the key documents of Vatican II on Interreligious dialogue and Ecumenism*, London: Catholic Truth Society, p. 43.

10 McDonald, *The Gift of Dialogue*, p. 43, quoting Pope Paul VI's encyclical *Ecclesiam Suam*, 6 August 1964, p.3.

11 McDonald, *The Gift of Dialogue*, p. 84.

2

Mission in the Colonial Matrix of Adult Power: Child-centredness as Way, Truth and Life!

GRAHAM ADAMS

Introduction

While writing this chapter, I was also working on a book called *God the Child*.[1] Among the connections, I recognize a desire to value my own childlikeness, allowing curiosity, imagination and playfulness to colour how 'the adult me' writes about children. This isn't an attempt to mimic someone outside of me, but is a desire to listen to and recover a part of my whole. As Christians we also affirm Jesus' call to 'receive the kingdom of God as a little child' (Mark 10.15), so the intentional recovery of child-like ways of seeing and being is a discipline worth practising.

In Walter Omar Kohan's philosophical biography of Paulo Freire, the liberative educationalist, he notes Freire's focus on his childhood – it honed his curiosity and yearning for change.[2] Kohan suggests that Freire's childlike language 'appears as an expressive force that exceeds and goes beyond adult academic language ... [and] the things that we can name with childlike words are precisely not the unimportant things.'[3] This is a challenge to me, as I value 'adult' discourse, but in the spirit of this challenge, parts of this reflection are in a different tone, something a little more playful, as I try to hear my childlikeness. Of course, this could be enhanced by social research with the voices of real children, but more humbly, this chapter is a *contextual* reflection on my experience, a *personal* project in recovery of childlikeness, and a *transient* marker towards further possibilities, rather than purporting to be at all definitive.[4]

The pattern for the chapter is in four phases: stories, questions, framework and dreaming. I begin with some stories, representing the kind of experience I am trying to think through. The stories are rooted in questions about worship, but they 'interface' with missional assumptions and challenges, so when I draw out the questions concerning them, I will make the connections with mission more explicit. In the third section, I bring an 'adult' concept to bear, notably identifying 'the colonial matrix of adult power', but with a childlike twist, to reflect further on the issues and possibilities. Finally, I offer a brief dream, believing we need the dreams and visions to orientate our direction of travel.

Story time

Number One. It was a church service. There was one child. It included a 'Mini Olympics', with some challenges – first, to move some tiny seeds between your fingers between two containers as quickly as possible; second, another task, which I've forgotten; and third, to crawl through a plastic tunnel, again seeing who could be faster. I had two volunteers – an adult and a child (I had asked my daughter beforehand, and she was willing). The adult didn't hold back. He was trying to win. He did win the second task. I said something like, 'Don't try too hard!' He said, 'If she's going to win, it should be because she is better than me!' She did win. She was quicker with the seeds and much faster through the tunnel. He was just too big.

The point was: Jesus told stories about the value that God gives to small things (seeds, yeast, children). Not just value; it's how God does things. It's how God changes things. The power of the small. But obviously another point arose because of the brief exchange with the adult. From one angle, it is a question of whether children should be patronized ('don't try too hard') or taken seriously with the gifts they bring ('if she's going to win ...'). But from another angle there is a different question about whether succeeding on merit is always good or whether there are times when it is appropriate to give an advantage to little ones. While located in worship, these issues speak to the challenge of mission: how well we affirm and do not patronize small things, not least children, valuing their agency and capacity.

Number Two. It was an all-age event and worship with activities beforehand, where everyone is invited, but mostly children and parents or grandparents come. Followed by the 'usual' service, but in a child-friendly way: shorter, interactive, relaxed. The activities had included preparing an impromptu 'rap', so while I called the congregation to gather for worship, a colleague led the children and families in a procession – entering the worship space to the sound of a very vocal response, assisted by the banging and shaking of freshly made musical instruments. The gathered congregation, their eyebrows raised, could not help but notice the arrival of children making clear: we are here, this is our space too. This is also a call for children's agency in God's mission: we are here, this is our vocation too.

Number Three. While a minister was leading the congregation in prayer, a young child was crying. I noticed another woman going to the parent to say something. She looked very serious. She went back to her seat. The parent's reaction was difficult to identify. What had the woman said to her? I immediately feared she had said something unhelpful to the parent about keeping the child quiet. It was just a suspicion. My mind raced. At the end of the service, I asked the parent quietly if the woman had said something unhelpful, but the parent said 'no'. Of course, I had put the parent on the spot. It would have been difficult to acknowledge that there had been any awkwardness; it might exacerbate things; perhaps she wanted to leave the moment behind. Or perhaps the woman had been supportive, not critical. But I was left with questions: if someone had told a parent to silence their children, what should be done? What message should be given from leaders at the front? Whose space is this? Whose job is it to determine the space and its ownership – and whose job is it to police the community's behaviour? This is both about the missional nature of worship (that is, how worship has a place in forming missional community) and relates to the very nature of mission too: who controls it; who determines its parameters, content and goals; whose story is it?

What are the questions?

In telling those stories, I have begun to show the connections between worship and mission; this is not an incidental relationship – it runs deep. I recognize that some people in churches do not believe worship and mission need to be connected; in fact, they apparently see value in keeping them separate. In particular, work with children may be more effective if child-friendly activities and worship are seen as distinct. After all, what we traditionally offer as worship is not immediately engaging of or attractive to many children. Even when we create something intentionally 'all-age', it is often not as 'all'-inclusive as we imagine. This is an issue identified in relation to cultural diversity in church too: a dominant group may *aim* to be multi-cultural, but what happens may be relatively small movements on the part of the dominant group, merely 'allowing' minority cultures to participate. Of course, some go much further, and the ideal is something far more mutual, with different groups interchanging with each other, sharing space and power. Truly 'intercultural church' is, then, demanding.[5] This is why truly 'inter-generational church', rather than merely 'all-age worship', is a more demanding direction of travel: it requires people to give and receive, to share power, to co-create space and experience. I will come back to this, because the same applies to mission.

In the face of such overwhelming demands, some people frame the question like this: 'Aren't children happier engaged in activities designed for children, and aren't adults happier engaged in experiences designed for adults?' This applies to mission and it applies to worship. It is, though, an assertion with its own assumptions: that children and adults are rarely happy engaged in the same things, and that all groups should be targeted with activities that make them happiest. Both assumptions are flawed, even if understandable. Not that the converse is wise: because the answer isn't that everything should be uniform; nor is it to make people unhappy! Nevertheless, we ought not to assume that certain activities are exclusively for particular generations; many people do not comply with our assumptions.

> I like quiet. I like doing things. I like prayer. I like listening. I like films. I like making films. I like running. I like drawing. I like being on my own. I like being with people. I like stories. I like Jesus. I like Grandma. I like friends. I don't like mean people. I don't like war. I don't like puppets.

Of course, Messy Church (incorporating creativity, hospitality and worship)[6] and the more recent innovation Muddy Church (involving wonder and exploration in the natural world)[7] are models that seek to bring the two together: the activities are woven together with worship. Such is the integration, that Messy and Muddy Church constitute people's encounter with church, without any expectation that people who attend them should eventually 'move on' to more inherited models of worship. After all, they engage people in wonder and mystery, in story and tradition, in creativity and community, often making stronger connections between those who attend than a 'traditional' service can.

As I articulated in a forum recently, when we were asked how worship builds community (a missional goal), I do not often feel that a traditional act of worship enables me to be more deeply embedded in community. This is because traditional worship asks us to be relatively passive, to receive what is offered but not particularly to give to it, except through joining in corporate prayer and song. Conversely, Messy and Muddy Church have become key models in engaging new generations of families in Christian story and community, because Sunday worship is increasingly not a space in which many families easily find a home.[8] There are exceptions – not least because different kinds of church have very different cultures. So sacramental traditions, for instance, give space for children to participate in the multisensory 'drama' of worship; and Black-majority and Pentecostal churches often worship with all ages together. All traditions have challenges, of course, but for many churches the issues are particularly clear: how to sustain the interest of those who already belong, how to connect with those who don't, and how to give place to children among the church's ministry overall.

In the church where I belong, with a team of worship leaders and with several different engagements with children, I detect some explicit differences in approach to the question of mission among children, and there are presumably many implicit differences too. It is an active church, with a Toddlers group, Messy Church, Muddy Church, as well as a Sunday programme for inter-generational worship (focused on one Sunday per month). On the one hand, people are relaxed about whether children are present with the largely adult congregation or not – relaxed in the sense that it is good that children are engaged in the various midweek activities, so it does not matter that few attend on Sundays. After all, adults should not treat children merely as instrumental means of making us feel that the church is what it should be (or worse, what it was); they are more intrinsically valuable than that. Generally, though with the occasional exception, people are also relaxed about what children do during a service; that is, they can move between the main space and a room at the back. This may be because there has been a collective effort to create an environment in which movement is not a distraction but a part of the whole, normalized at least to some extent.

On the other hand, it would be wrong were adults *indifferent* to the presence or absence, vitality or silence, of children. Yet sometimes there is indifference, at least implicitly, since the majority seem satisfied for it to be an issue which a minority seeks to address. But some are also explicit that we should not see Sundays as the time for children, because it is a dying model of engagement with children. What, then, when children do come? Have we already resigned ourselves to the impossibility of engaging well with them? (A rota barely meets the twofold challenge: having enough people who are happy to engage with children and having enough children to justify the rota.) But no, we have not resigned ourselves to its impossibility; we continue to wrestle with the challenge – because it is important. If we were indifferent to the question, we would not only be neglecting children in our midst but also overlooking the potential for our own childlikeness. For we are called to receive the kingdom as children (Mark 10.15) and to become like little children (Matthew 18.13). Jesus even urged us to welcome children on the basis that, when we do so, we welcome him and even the one who sent him (Mark 9.37); in other words, God comes to us in a child, not exclusively, but nevertheless, in the welcoming of a child, we welcome God. The centrality of 'welcome' is elaborated on many levels by Joyce Ann Mercer, including the importance of children as gift and fully human.[9]

But do you believe it? That Jesus puts this huge focus on welcoming children?

If you do, perhaps you hope he only meant the nice ones, the obedient ones, the quiet ones.

But why wouldn't he also mean the noisy ones, those not easily contained, who keep asking 'why?'

What if, in the welcoming of the most disruptive child imaginable, you welcome God ...?

The inclusion of children – or even the desire to create inter-generational church (in both worship and mission) – should certainly not be a way for adults to congratulate themselves that they are performing well. Rather, it ought to confront us again and again with the challenge that goes to the heart of our faith: to demonstrate ever deeper neighbour-love, our neighbours being as diverse in culture, age and story as they can be. The gospel, after all, is a social project – in the sense that it is not merely a relationship between God and each individual but is a vision of a renewed world, the kingdom of childlikeness on earth as in heaven. That social vision suggests to Paul Joshua Bhakiaraj that 'it takes a whole church (which cannot be conceived without children and young people) to raise a Christian'.[10] In other words, it is not only adults who nurture children, but children play their part in nurturing adults – and indeed, in discerning and leading mission. Such centring of children, in the biblical story, church and society, is developed in R. L. Stollar's *The Kingdom of Children*.[11] For me, this alternative (anti)kingdom – or Bhakiaraj's 'upside-down Kingdom'[12] – is a world in which the Spirit-infused dreams of the young are recognized and pursued (Joel 2.28). A world in which children are free to play, even in adult-dominated streets (Zechariah 8.5). A world in which we are challenged to see ourselves through the eyes of children's experience, those who play tunes, anticipating others will join in solidarity (Matthew 11.16–17). A world in which a child leads restored creation (Isaiah 11.6).

As we begin to reflect on these debates and aspirations, there are many questions emerging, but I identify four in particular to explore:

1. What exactly is worship for? In the context of the church's missional challenge of engaging with children, what is the place of worship?
2. Whose space is it? When we speak of creating worship in which children may feel at home, who is presuming control of the space – and why? This is a missional issue.
3. What are the expectations? When we envisage an experience in which adults and children contribute mutually, what sorts of expectation are appropriate – low ones or high ones, and who expects what of whom? This, too, is related to mission.

4. What is the relationship between what we do now and the future we hope for? This is certainly a missional matter.

So, first, what is worship for?

I continue to be drawn to the insights of James K. A. Smith, for whom the primary purpose of worship is to redirect our desires so that they align with God's desires.[13] At first hearing, it may sound strange. There may be many reasons why people worship – to give God honour, to set aside time for reflection and prayer, to have our 'batteries' recharged. None of these is wrong, but Smith's insight helps to integrate and re-purpose the story: to honour God, to show God that we give worth to God's nature and involvement with us, we must learn to desire what God desires, God being a force of desire, yearning that particular purposes – or the divine will – shall be done on earth as in heaven. That is to say, we cannot simply have our batteries recharged if we are not also being reoriented, our yearnings and aspirations re-centred in God's yearnings and aspirations.

This speaks to the church's engagement with children: for at the heart of God's desire is an alternative realm, the kingdom, which Jesus suggests we may enter if we (re)learn childlikeness. If worship is the space in which we are reoriented towards a new world, which is coming among us, central to worship is the vitality of the call to be like children. This shapes worship *but also mission*.

The implications are huge. On the one hand, if we are to rediscover the call to childlikeness, it is the presence of children which can most aptly prompt and feed this rediscovery, as they become our teachers. Of course, adults have things to teach children too; but at the very least, as the engine of this alternative social project, worship fuels our mission to be reoriented towards child-shaped dreaming and discipleship. So adults ought to let children disrupt adult-ness.[14] Adults ought not to be indifferent to children's presence. Adults ought to be intensely attentive to who children are and what they bring, no matter how much children distract adults from what they thought they were doing.

On the other hand, children are not merely adults' teachers or trailblazers, because they matter in themselves, as humans and disciples in their own right; as bearers of the ministry of Christ, witnesses to the alternative horizon, even if they are infants. It can seem like nonsense to us as adults, assuming that our knowledge, experience or capabilities are the necessary means by which the Christian story is kept alive. But Jesus tells us that God revealed these things to infants (Matthew 11.25), humbling us if ever we suppose our wisdom and articulacy are the answer.[15]

This resonates with Ben Aldous's insights into the appropriate inefficiency which frames Christian faith and discipleship. Drawing from the wisdom of Kosuke Koyama,[16] he argues that churches are too often focused on efficient approaches to the challenges we face – in part, no doubt, due to our limited resources which need to be deployed wisely – but that what is important to remember is that the way of Christ, being deeply relational, takes time and patience, which can feel painfully inefficient. The child engaged in a task, in such a way that an adult desperately wants to accelerate the process, inadvertently teaches us what it means both to be attentive and simultaneously immersed in the flow of the act.[17]

Children matter, because worship reorientates us towards the kingdom of childlikeness.

> I like communion. It tells us what we are remembering – a meal with friends. Sadness and joy. Things break and God puts things together again. It's about the power of love. It's also about the future – what kind of world we hope for. Where everyone has enough. Even a little amount shows us God loves everyone. Little things matter. Everyone matters. In the thing we do right now, in this bit of time, it's like those things are connected – what we remember and what we hope for. And like I say, it's about the power of love. And food. I like eating.

Second, then, whose space is this?

In order to make children feel at home, it is understandable that we give them a space which is more immediately child-friendly, perhaps slightly separate from 'the main space'. In our church, they can go to a room with windowed doors, so they can see and hear what is happening but can be occupied on their own terms. The advantage of this is that, in their space, they can be children more freely; but the disadvantage is that, even if only implicitly rather than explicitly, the message they receive is that 'the main space' is not their space, and that adults prefer not to be distracted or disrupted within it – even though, actually, many do not mind.

Imagine if we could have the confidence, as many churches do, not least sacramental traditions, to 'allow' the space to be children's space too. But even that aspiration is limited. Imagine instead if the space could be co-hosted, co-created, by children and adults together. Imagine if children can be not merely the tenants temporarily entering adult property, or like students learning how to be on adult terms, but co-owners, co-learners, co-teachers – in fact, in some respects, *more* the teachers, *more* the trailblazers, showing adults how to be, how to dream, how to dance, how to play, how to worship. After all, it is the gospel of the alternative kingdom in which children lead the way.

Yet more colouring? But can I colour outside the lines and can I colour through these doors?

Can I colour what's happening over there? It looks like it needs a bit of colour.

If we're going to be people who colour, I think Jesus would want colour all over the place.

Black and white is OK, and the shades in between, but what about some colour everywhere?

Scribbling across the spaces, making lines that connect and patterns that join us together.

What might this mean for how we engage in discussions about worship *and mission*? Our task is not merely to create space in which children may feel at home, but to co-create space with children and adults together, in which we experience a mix of 'home-ness' and 'strangeness', because neither worship nor mission is simply a matter of being at home. It is about engaging on frontiers: venturing like a risk-taking child into unknown territory, towards alternative horizons. Both worship and mission lead us across thresholds, between the world as it is and the world as it may become – and it is children who represent this movement between spaces. But care must be taken in enabling one another to live in this threshold-environment, whether in worship or in mission – with its fusion of comfort and disruption, both a restorative space and an empowering space. For who determines which has the upper hand? Who presumes to make decisions about what will happen and who should be in which space? It is not for adults to control either worship or mission; rather, we should be attentive to the voice of 'little ones', not presuming to speak for everyone, but seeking to co-create worship that fuels mission, and the very nature of mission itself, in which childlike curiosity and imagination are vital.

In the next section, as we reflect further on the question of the colonial matrix of power, the adult-ness of our assumptions must be addressed and challenged. At the heart of the colonial matrix, there are surely notions about whose space this is, who controls it and who relinquishes control? Mark Scanlan's 'interweaving' approach speaks to this: how, in the church's engagement in youth work, the various boundaries and claims to control are dynamic not static; it is a matter of ambiguity, potential and creativity.[18] This resonates, too, with my notion of 'the awkward body of Christ',[19] a site in which we struggle to fulfil the goals we pursue, but we rightly struggle with them – and the ambiguities involved in that quest are worthy of being taken seriously. After all, in order to dismantle the 'matrix of power', whereby certain groups – such as dominant adults – must have their status destabilized, there will necessarily be some 'chaos', some pushing against patterns of False Order.[20] Catherine Keller argues, 'chaos is the border along which creativity takes place',[21] which is to say that this dynamic reworking of the space – such that co-creation and co-ownership can emerge – will be messy but generative,[22] because new life has this capacity to emerge from mess. Why else have 'messy' or 'muddy' church, if not to affirm that creativity is best rooted in places of muddle, ambiguity, awkwardness? This is surely true not only of worship but of mission, which is inherently a messy and generative process, laden with unpredictability and possibility. This is why, for instance, Al Barrett and Ruth Harley affirm 'edge-places',[23] those sites between one kind of land-use and another, where mingling and cross-fertilization make new things possible. Exactly the sorts of space that children explore – so in the case of the church engaged in mission and recognizing these ambiguous interfaces, it allows itself to be open to interruption, disruption, unexpectedness. I will return to necessary ambiguity below.

Third, what of the expectations?

This is an important and difficult issue. In relation to each of the questions, there are understandable tensions, with good intentions on many sides, and this question is no exception. What strikes me, though, is that our expectations of different groups can differ hugely. For some people, it is too much to expect the older members of the congregation to be capable of adapting enough to create meaningful space for children. The challenge is obvious enough; the congregation is steeped in its traditions, it values the style that it values, and in some regards people's limitations are simply determined by their health, mobility or energy. It is better, the argument goes, to leave a traditional congregation as it is, and for children's ministry (worship and mission) to be designed for children. Why struggle to make co-created space in which no one may be satisfied? Why put people through the experience of dislocation for the sake of a well-meaning vision, a high-minded ideal of everyone being together (but usually together on the terms of a dominant group)? These questions have strong arguments behind them. But what I notice in respect of expectations is that they are relatively low – or perhaps we should say 'realistically low'.

At the same time, this approach has realistic expectations of children: that they will like what they like and not what adults like; that they should not be expected to 'fit in' with something alien and unfriendly; that any attempts to force something different is going to be unfulfilled.

Whereas I am drawn to a contrasting approach: one of high expectations, where we dare to believe people are capable of something more, encouraging but not demanding it. This will also be developed in relation to the fourth question – the connection between what we do in the present and the future we hope for – but here I simply note that we *can* expect things of adults, including older adults who have needs to be met as well. We can expect that, as a community of fellow travellers, worship is not owned by any one group but is space in which we continually remind ourselves to be reoriented towards God's desires – and what God desires is the kingdom of childlikeness on earth as in heaven. We can expect that worship is a journey, not a stable state; an adventure towards a different horizon, and a horizon which is closer at hand than we imagine, even under our noses. We can expect, too, that the way in which we worship will be directly related to our aspirations for mission.

I am drawn to the (high) expectation that children can be faithfully who they are among a community of people who are striving to be truly themselves and are travelling together. Sometimes in quietness, sometimes lively; sometimes sad, sometimes joyful; sometimes reflective, sometimes creative. After all, I am increasingly convinced that worship feeds and facilitates mission when it is a balanced diet of different food types, not designed to meet the needs of different age groups but grown and shared as varied ways of nourishing our diverse personalities and the various dimensions of community. That is to say, if we co-create worship that embraces art, movement, conversation, silence, symbol, as well as listening – a variety of things, suitable for a mix of ages – this will similarly facilitate a breadth of approaches to mission. The expectation is not that everyone should do all of it, but that everyone should be encouraged to understand the need for variety; a range of ways for people to engage enabling a range of people to engage differently in mission.

Of course, there are risks in imagining that seemingly high expectations of everyone are appropriate – and as I say, they shouldn't be imposed but co-created, a culture being nurtured in which we seek to journey together, believing it is worth putting in the effort, while also ensuring there is room for struggle and awkwardness. In other words, we try to understand why not everyone finds such space or such aspiration easy; we foster empathy with one another; and we see that both worship and mission are works in progress.

So, in short, expectations should be mixed – realistic and idealistic, rooted and rising – as we reckon with the realities of who we are while encouraging each other towards what could be.

Fourth, what of the present and the future?

Essentially, the tension is this: on the one hand, should we focus on doing what is appropriate for this very moment, working with what we have got, the desires and needs currently known and expressed? Even if we aim for such efforts to build us up into becoming something different, the focus is on the present (not the past or the future). On the other hand, might the different future only come into being if we practise it presently, if we demonstrate inter-generational church and its capacity to witness to the kingdom of childlikeness *right now*?

How we expect things of each other will clearly inform our approach to the future, so again there is wisdom in holding the two options in creative tension together: being attentive to the church and the world as they are, while also daring to practise the future we desire. As Kelly Brown Douglas says, 'we hope by showing up. Showing up for the future we claim we believe in.'[24] Kohan shows us that such tension between one state and another was integral to Freire's affirmation of childhood: in particular, his notion of 'childhood as schooling' represents 'a type of possibility for passage between two worlds';[25] that is to say, childlikeness is a necessarily dynamic state in which the truth of the current moment (our present practice) is not denied but is held in creative tension with what could be (our future hopes). In other words, a focus on children not only reminds us to aspire to a way of being church that better reflects the kingdom of childlikeness towards which God orientates us; it also represents the dynamic relation between 'now' and 'not yet', the energy beckoning us to the horizon,[26] which is where the fruits of God's mission are fully realized.

The matrix

It is all very well dreaming dreams and chasing horizons, but we live in a matrix of power. In decolonial thought, Walter Mignolo works helpfully with the ideas of Anibal Quijano to capture the reality as 'the colonial matrix of power',[27] a network of vested interests, norms and habits which condition how we think, how we perceive, how we act. It is obviously a matrix, or web of connections, that goes far beyond the life of the Church, framing politics, economics, knowledge and education, and even our sense of self – but we should acknowledge that it also colonizes religious thinking and practice.

The matrix may be further qualified in a number of ways, with reference to wealth and class, 'race', gender and sexuality, dis/ability, and so on. But adult-centredness is also integral to it. That is, it is a colonial matrix of *adult* power, controlled by adults, essentially serving the vested interests of adults, some rather more than others. Of course, children do not have consistent experiences around the world, so the adult/child axis will intersect with the other axes (wealth, race, gender, disability, etc.). But even so, children are objects of the matrix, not its subjects determining its direction of travel. I have argued elsewhere that, even where children seem to have many rights and dignities, they are nevertheless subjected to conflicting impulses that deny them life in its fullness.[28] On the one hand, adults like to conceive of children as innocent – something to be preserved even when we fail to see their alertness to the realities of life; so they become objects bearing our own longing for naivety. On the other hand, our economic system – an adult game – encourages children to be economic agents, adults-before-their-time.[29] Freire also speaks of this 'double existence', such that children are 'simultaneously childlike and adult'.[30] (Adults are as well.) In *God's Heart for Children*, these tensions and challenges are addressed by global contributors, exploring how issues such as climate change, trafficking, displacement and gender discrimination impact children[31] – in a sense, these are all the consequence of adults playing their games of domination.

All of the questions I identified are framed within this overbearing matrix. The nature of worship, the control of space, the level of expectations, and our relationship to the future are all informed by the matrix of power, how it conditions us as adults to see things a certain way and to maintain a status quo. If worship orientates us towards an alternative kingdom which is at hand, a kingdom marked more by childlikeness than adult power, then the mission to which we are called is one of dismantling this matrix and living a different future now. For Corneliu Constantineanu, it is such radical transformation of society that 'welcoming a child' calls forth; the hospitable embrace of God, in Christ, epitomized by inclusion of children, signalling the total reversal of power and status.[32]

Elsewhere I suggested a new version of 'the five marks of mission', one which places emphasis on the imperial nature of the system we live within and so calls us to be anti-imperial – or decolonial. It strikes me that a shift from adult power to childlikeness offers an important re-reading of them, such as this:

1. Dream of a healthy Earth – and work for it, because this planet is God's, not ours. So listen to the voices of children who help us to notice the creepy crawlies and the humongous webs of life in which humans are only one part.
2. Hear the cries of people who are at the bottom of the pile or forgotten. Listen to them and change the world so that everyone can have a good life.

3. Love people: care for them, whoever they are – because they are all our neighbours.
4. Make better churches: places where we love each other, listen to each other, play nicely together, eat together, and dream better dreams.
5. Tell good stories: ones that don't avoid pain or weakness, but help us see the potential for transformation, even if it's messy.

This is how to dismantle the colonial matrix of adult power, so that our worship and mission are better oriented towards the kingdom of child-likeness, and our churches keep working at the challenge of co-creating the space we share. This will enable the broader and deeper participation of diverse people in pursuit of the new horizon, and hold realistic and aspirational expectations in tension, such that we take the present reality seriously while venturing boldly towards what could be.

Dreaming

The thing is, what if Jesus called us to be like children because he under-stood how childlike God is?[33] It seems he may have understood it, because he also appeared to embody it: a childlike quality – not 'mild, obedient, good', but disruptive, defiant, destabilizing, with a lively curiosity about the world as it is and a subversive energy committed to making it what it could be. What if ...?

> If Jesus the Child is the way, the way of mission is playful adventure.
> If Jesus the Child is the truth, the truth of mission is inquisitive disruption.
> If Jesus the Child is the life, the life of mission is a feast with room for everyone.

These themes do not give us answers to the questions I have named, but they may help us struggle better with them: daring to be adventurous in our worship, our conversations about inter-generational possibilities, our aspirations for what could be: seeking to be inquisitive, not avoiding the awkward questions but asking them defiantly; and determining to be communities of feasting, where everyone's gifts, questions and potentials are held and loved.

Notes

1 G. Adams, 2024, *God the Child: Small, Weak and Curious Subversions*, London: SCM Press.

2 W. O. Kohan, 2021, *Paulo Freire: A Philosophical Biography*, London: Bloomsbury, pp. 118–19.

3 Kohan, *Paulo Freire*, p. 123.

4 See also M. J. Bunge (ed.), 2021, *Child Theology: Diverse Methods and Global Perspectives*, Maryknoll, NY: Orbis Books.

5 See, for instance, H. Kwiyani, 2022, *Multicultural Kingdom: Ethnic Diversity, Mission and the Church*, London: SCM Press; and B. Aldous, 2022, *The God Who Walks Slowly: Reflections on Mission with Kosuke Koyama*, London: SCM Press, pp. 87–90.

6 See https://www.messychurch.org.uk/.

7 See https://www.muddychurch.co.uk/.

8 According to Youthscape (https://www.youthscape.co.uk/services/youth-work-news/youth-decline), as of 2020 in the UK, 38% of churches have no 0–16-year-olds and 68% have fewer than five young people; the attendance of under 16s is declining faster than any other age group in the CofE (it has fallen by 20% in the last five years); and the concentration of young people is narrow: '44% of all of 0–16's are to be found in 6.4% of churches and parishes'. In a report from New Wine (https://www.new-wine.org/stories/the-future-of-church/), we see that, in 2017, the average British Anglican church had three children attending. And according to Madeleine Davies in the *Church Times*, following the pandemic, children's attendance at church has not recovered as fast as it has for adults, reaching 71% of 2019 levels, compared with 79% for adults; and during the course of the pandemic, the most likely Fresh Expressions (new, creative ways of exploring how to be church) to have ceased were 'child-friendly', such as Messy Church. See Madeleine Davies, 'Cutting services is a key cause of decline in attendance, report suggests', *Church Times*, 3 April, https://www.churchtimes.co.uk/articles/2023/6-april/news/uk/cutting-services-is-a-key-cause-of-decline-in-attendance-report-suggests, accessed 04.06.2024.

9 J. A. Mercer, 2005, *Welcoming Children: A Practical Theology of Childhood*, St Louis, MO: Chalice Press.

10 P. J. Bhakiaraj, 2014, 'The Whole Household of God: How Children Can Deepen Our Theology and Practice of Missional Ecclesiology' in Bill Prevette, Keith White, C. Rosalee Velloso Ewell and D. J. Konz (eds), *Theology, Mission and Child: Global Perspectives*, Oxford: Regnum, p. 129.

11 R. L. Stollar, 2023, *The Kingdom of Children: A Liberation Theology*, Grand Rapids, MI: Eerdmans.

12 Bhakiaraj, 'The Whole Household', p. 130.

13 J. K. A. Smith, 2009, *Desiring the Kingdom: Worship, Worldview and Cultural Formation*, Grand Rapids, MI: Baker Academic.

14 See also Bhakiaraj, 'The Whole Household', p. 130.

15 G. Adams, 2022, *Holy Anarchy: Dismantling Domination, Embodying Community, Loving Strangeness*, London: SCM Press, p. 136: 'The sheer prospect of God's revelation coming to those who cannot communicate it is revelatory in itself – *because* it confounds us.'

16 Aldous, *The God Who Walks Slowly*: 'walking and plodding' (p. 34) as opposed to 'efficiency, calculability, predictability and control' (p. 37). Kosuke

Koyama himself reflects on welcoming children in 'A Holy Mystery: Welcoming a Little Child', in *The Living Pulpit* (October–December 2003), p. 4.

17 D. Hay and R. Nye, 2006 (rev. edn), *The Spirit of the Child*, London and Philadelphia, PA: Jessica Kingsley Publishers, pp. 65, 68.

18 M. Scanlan, 2021, *An Interweaving Ecclesiology: The Church, Mission and Young People*, London: SCM Press: he speaks of 'not ... delineating solid boundaries' (p. 157), 'porous or ambiguous boundaries' (p. 158), 'an openhanded vision for church' and 'practices of interruption' (p. 159) and 'releasing creativity' (p. 229). See also footnote 23 below – Al Barrett and Ruth Harley's 'edge-places' in which possibilities intermingle.

19 Adams, *Holy Anarchy*, pp. 155–7.

20 Adams, *Holy Anarchy*, p. 67.

21 Catherine Keller, 2002, 'Process and chaosmos: the Whiteheadian fold in the discourse of difference' in Catherine Keller and Anne Daniell (eds), *Process and Difference: Between cosmological and poststructuralist postmodernisms*, Albany, NY: State University of New York, p. 66.

22 Scanlan, *Interweaving*, p. 213: there are indeed 'relational dynamics' to be worked with.

23 A. Barrett and R. Harley, 2020, *Being Interrupted: Reimagining the church's mission from the outside*, London: SCM Press, p. 119.

24 K. B. Douglas, speaking at the Society for the Study of Theology annual conference, 4–6 April 2023.

25 Kohan, *Paulo Freire*, pp. 128–9, referring to Paulo Freire and Sergio Guimarães, 1982, *Sobre educação: diálogos*, Rio de Janeiro: Paz e Terra.

26 I pursue the notion of this horizon, and God as horizon-seeker, in *God the Child*. Similarly, for Bhakiaraj, children are 'co-members in the household' who 'deepen' our theology and practice of ecclesiology and mission oriented towards the kingdom ('The Whole Household', p. 132).

27 W. Mignolo, 2012, 'Decolonizing Western epistemologies/building decolonial epistemologies' in Ada María Isasi-Díaz and Eduardo Mendieta (eds), *Decolonizing Epistemologies: Latina/o theology and philosophy*, New York: Fordham Press, pp. 27–8.

28 G. Adams, 2016, 'Doubting empire: growing as faithful children' in Vuyani Vellem, Patricia Sheerattan-Bisnauth and Philip Peacock (eds), *Bible and Theology from the Underside of Empire*, SUN MeDIA MeTRO. See also Olive M. Fleming Drane, Anne Richards et al., 2018, *Through the Eyes of a Child: New Insights in Theology from a Child's Perspective*, London: Church House Publishing.

29 Adams, 'Doubting Empire', p. 84. See also Mercer, *Welcoming Children*, pp. 73–6.

30 Kohan, *Paulo Freire*, p. 127.

31 Rosalind Tan, Nativity A. Petallar and Lucy A. Hefford (eds), 2022, *God's Heart for Children: Practical Theology from Global Perspectives*, Langham Global Library.

32 Corneliu Constantineanu, 2014, 'Welcome: Biblical and theological perspectives on mission and hospitality with a child in the midst' in Bill Prevette, Keith White, C. Rosalee Velloso Ewell and D. J. Konz (eds), *Theology, Mission and Child: Global perspectives*, Oxford: Regnum, pp. 139–40, 146–7.

33 Adams, *God the Child*.

3

Contexts and Consequences: Enduring Pain versus the Intentional Erasure of Colonial Legacy

SHEMIL MATHEW

This chapter explores enduring pain and intentional erasure, tracing the intricate threads of colonial legacy and their contemporary implications. It begins with a personal account of my experience at the Union of Black Episcopalians Conference 2023, then transitions to an exploration of my current context: I am an Anglican theological educator and advocate for racial justice, and in this role – as someone with Indian heritage – I frequently witness the intentional erasure of colonial history. I then turn to an examination of the far-reaching consequences that this intentional erasure has on the present-day *missio Dei* in Britain, with a particular emphasis on the Church of England and its members from the UK Minority Ethnic (UK ME) and UK Global Majority Heritage (UK GMH) communities.

Enduring pain: UBE 2023 experience

I was privileged to attend the Union of Black Episcopalians Conference 2023, held in Montgomery, Alabama. This enriching experience was made possible by the support of the Church of England's Racial Justice Directorate. The primary goal of the conference delegation from the Church of England was to foster connections and learn from the remarkable racial justice efforts within the Episcopal Church in the US.

During our time at the conference venue we could not fail to notice that we were situated just 200 metres away from the bus stop where Rosa Parks, a courageous African American woman, made her historic stand by refusing to give up her seat to a white man on 1 December 1955. Her brave act of defiance led to her arrest, sparking a year-long bus boycott that eventually culminated in the landmark Supreme Court ruling deeming bus segregation unconstitutional. Also, while in Montgomery, we had the opportunity to visit significant historical sites associated with the 1965 marches from Selma. We listened to powerful testimonies from survivors of the infamous 'Bloody Sunday' on 7 March 1965, when nearly 600 protesters were viciously attacked with batons and tear gas while peacefully marching for civil rights.

Furthermore, conference delegates went to see Montgomery's Legacy Museum, which bears the tagline 'From Enslavement to Mass Incarceration'. Confronting the historical reality of the slave trade is inescapable in this location, as it is situated on the very site of the infamous Montgomery slave market – an institution that, prior to the American Civil War, leveraged the new railroad and the steamboats that navigated the Alabama River to emerge as a national hub for the slave trade. The museum's brochure unequivocally states: 'In the final two decades of American slavery, none stood as more prominent and significant than Montgomery, Alabama's slave market.'[1] Historical records suggest that from 1848 to 1860, no fewer than 164 licensed slave traders were actively involved in the formal buying and selling of men, women and children within Montgomery's slave markets.

I was particularly struck by the way in which the museum recognized that the enslavement of approximately 12 million Africans during the period spanning from 1619 to 1865 (acknowledging that not all were liberated in 1865) resulted in profound cultural and religious colonialism: given this central feature of American history, I wasn't surprised by the palpable eagerness to delve deeper into the 'African' facet of African American heritage shown by conference participants. The museum itself, as its name declares, frames the history of slavery alongside its enduring legacy in the US: central to this perspective is the disproportionate representation of Black Americans within the modern-day prison system. Despite comprising only 13 per cent of the overall population, Black Americans account for a substantial 38 per cent of the prison population: 'Black Americans, in particular, are disproportionately likely to be incarcerated and to receive the harshest sentences, including death sentences.'[2]

The persistent reminders of the grim history of slave ownership trade, the vivid memory of racial segregation, and the current stark reality of mass incarceration remained a central theme in our discussions throughout the conference. Revd Dr Gale Stewart, who served as a police officer with the NYPD for several decades and now holds the position of NYPD chaplain, shared a thought-provoking insight into the contemporary police system: its inherent design, as she articulated it, primarily safeguards and favours White individuals while upholding the existing order.[3] This observation prompted a collective realization among us that while the tragic death of George Floyd acted as a catalyst for acknowledging global racism, it merely scratched the surface of the deeply entrenched institutional violence and organized brutality experienced by Black communities in the United States.

Across the pond: attempts of intentional erasure of colonial legacy from memory

I was invited to join the Montgomery delegation due to my role as a founding member of AMEN (Anglican Minority Ethnic Network) and my role as a theological educator. All of the other delegates were also Church of England clergy or laity, and all of us are actively engaged in its ongoing pursuit of racial justice. The conference provided us with profound experiences and insights, leaving no doubt that racism, racial discrimination and race-based brutality persist openly in the USA. However, this also underscored the significant disparities in the historical experience of racism within England and the Church of England. Even though Britain could be considered as a nation that benefited greatly from the transatlantic slave trade (some estimates suggest that British ships transported approximately 3.4 million individuals across the Atlantic from Africa), the country managed to maintain its mainland free from the presence of enslaved people and slave markets. This separation allowed the British consciousness, both at institutional levels within the Church and state and in the collective public mindset, to keep the realities of colonial exploitation and the slave trade at arm's length. This convenient distance often enabled a facade of blissful ignorance, providing a sense of innocence and comfort. Instances of prominent racial violence and pervasive everyday micro aggressions against Global Majority/Minority Ethnic communities have been experienced in Britain, but unlike the USA, there was never a period akin to the Jim Crow era. Memories of signs reading 'No Irish, No Blacks, No Dogs' may linger, but there has never been a phase of overt state-enforced segregation in England or any other part of Britain.

Different manifestations, same legacy

Despite the differences, it is also necessary to examine the parallels between the UK's Minority Ethnic (UK ME) or Global Majority Heritage (UK GMH) individuals and Black Episcopalians in the US. One undeniable shared element is that contemporary individuals of UK ME and GMH in Britain can also trace their ancestral lines to those who were transported to various plantations worldwide, particularly in the Caribbean and West Indies, or to those whose forebears experienced colonization during the colonial era. This connection is more evident than ever. The 2021 census data for England reveals that 87.9 per cent of the population identifies as white, white British, or white other, leaving the remaining 12.1 per cent identifying as non-white. Within this non-white demographic, the most prominent groups include people of Indian descent or heritage at 3.1 per cent, individuals with Pakistani heritage at 2.7 per cent, those tracing their heritage to Black African roots at 2.5 per cent, individuals with Bangladeshi heritage at 1.1 per cent, and those with Black Caribbean heritage at 1.0 per cent.[4]

While historical trajectories may have slightly diverged for the UK ME and UK GMH communities compared to their US counterparts, the undeniable common thread among them is the legacy of colonial exploitation, predominantly orchestrated by European nations, with a particular emphasis on Britain. This legacy is intertwined with the distressing history of subjugation and the forced transport of human lives.

It can be said that the racial landscape in Britain is far from a simplistic White–Black demarcation, and the term 'White' cannot and should not be confined to skin colour alone. For example, there have been many instances of Irish immigrants in this country being labelled as non-white, such as the aforementioned 'No Irish, No Blacks, No Dogs' signs: racial distinctions are intricate and multi-layered, transcending mere skin colour and complicatedly tied to one group of people's privilege over another. Additionally, according to the UK Government's Race and Ethnic Disparities Report, published on 31 March 2021, the challenges faced by ME communities in the UK 'often do not have their origins in racism': it even suggests that white supremacy and racism are waning in the UK.[5]

I would claim, however, based on my personal and collective experience as part of the ME and GMH communities in the UK and on recent academic research, that the government's report is quite misguided. For instance, just a few months before writing this chapter, in April 2023 Policy Press released *Racism and Ethnic Inequality in a Time of Crisis: Findings from the Evidence for Equality National Survey*. One of the report's foremost discoveries was that 'experiences of racist assault and racial discrimination are widespread'. Furthermore, it stated:

> Over a third of ethnic minority participants reported having experienced one or more racist assaults (verbal, physical, or property damage) throughout their lifetimes, with one in six reporting instances of physical assault. The responses from ethnic minority participants also indicated pervasive encounters with discrimination within institutional settings – nearly a third reported experiencing racial discrimination in education, a similar proportion in employment, and approximately a fifth while seeking housing. In social settings, almost a third reported racial dis-

crimination experiences in public, and nearly one in six experienced racial discrimination from neighbours. Furthermore, over one in five reported facing discrimination from the police.[6]

Despite the absence of a history of slave markets or immediate memories of struggles for civil rights in Britain, this contemporary violence and discrimination indicates the core connection between UK ME and GMH individuals and Black Episcopalians: the enduring legacy of nearly five centuries of colonialism and racial oppression.

The parallel between racism's presence in the broader state context of Britain and within the Church of England is evident. Creating the Anglican Minority Ethnic Network (AMEN) in 2014 stemmed from direct experiences of racism and racial discrimination during the selection and training process for Anglican ordination. More recently, A. D. A. France-Williams' 2020 book *Ghost Ship* has forcefully addressed the same issues. In 2021 the BBC's *Panorama* programme aired a documentary entitled 'Is the Church Racist?', investigating allegations of racism within the institution. Above all, perhaps the most compelling evidence of racism within the Church of England is the candid acknowledgement by the Archbishop of Canterbury, the Most Revd Justin Welby, that the 'Church of England is still deeply institutionally racist'.[7]

Erasing uncomfortable memories!

Disputing the conclusions presented in the Race and Ethnic Disparities Report, I would argue that racism has not simply vanished; instead, it has evolved into a phase of collective forgetfulness. This phenomenon is thoughtfully illuminated by Sathnam Sanghera, a British-born journalist of Indian heritage, in his 2021 book *Empireland*. This societal amnesia tends to erase the less favourable aspects of Britain's imperial and colonial history, while highlighting the benevolence of the empire as a force that established a 'Pax Britannica', advanced mass education, introduced modernity, and played a role in leading the world from obscurity to enlightenment.[8]

The carefully chosen and favourable recollections of the empire that Britain once held, along with its established connections to the Commonwealth, proved advantageous during both World Wars. This was evident in the form of soldiers from the colonies fighting for the mother country, even after some of those colonies had achieved liberation. Furthermore, members of the Commonwealth rallied to assist in rebuilding Britain after the Second World War. However, this is not a memory that resonates universally. While the process of postcolonial deconstruction of history may be confined to academic realms within the UK, for the descendants of the populations that were once subjected to colonization and enslavement, they continue to exist within the framework of a postcolonial reality. This reality is likewise evident in their political discourse and their interpretations of history. For instance, consider Shashi Tharoor, an Indian diplomat who later became a prominent national politician and author. His book, *An Era of Darkness: The British Empire in India*,[9] meticulously deconstructs the prevailing British myths of a benevolent imperialism, systematically addressing and debunking each notion.

With its lasting impact, the curated and positive memory of the British Empire continues to play a role in political discussions and attempts to shape public opinion in England, too. An example of this can be observed in the proponents of Brexit, who frequently invoked what is known as the 'Commonwealth factor'. This argument posited that Brexit would facilitate stronger trade relationships with nations within the Commonwealth. There were two major flaws in this plan: first, even though Britain may have forgotten the past through an act of selective amnesia, the Commonwealth nations do remember that the last time they entered into a trade relationship it did not end well for them; second, as *The Financial Times* pointed out, Commonwealth countries will be more worried about maintaining and developing free trade agreements with the EU than building new ones with Britain.[10]

Many proponents of the notion of benevolent colonialism might argue that Britain's rise to economic prosperity is not tied to its colonial endeavours but is largely attributable to the success of industrialization and its adept management of a global open market. There is no doubt that modern Britain and her wealth was created by the Industrial Revolution, but it also needs to be accepted that this would not have been possible without the colonial exploitation of the rest of the world. The tally of 3.4 million transported individuals, accompanied by an estimated excess of one million lives lost during the harrowing transatlantic passage, represents but the visible fraction of the expenses underpinning Britain's ascent as an industrial juggernaut. The markets often characterized as open by proponents of the benevolent view of colonialism were anything but open. Instead, they were structured in a manner that consistently favoured the British establishment and were frequently maintained through coercive means, even enforced through military intervention.

An illustrative instance is the exploitation India endured throughout the dominion of the East India Company and later under the British Raj. Manchester's mills, now embodying the echoes of William Blake's 'satanic mills', were sustained by cotton and indigo sourced from farmers coerced into cultivating these crops instead of the sustenance they needed to shield their families from famine. Furthermore, the industrialization of

Britain was propelled by the concurrent deindustrialization of India. This was facilitated by restricting Indians from engaging in the production and export of handloom goods while also coercing them into buying woven cotton that was produced from raw materials exported from India.[11] Imran Khan, a correspondent for Al Jazeera, aptly captures this reality, proclaiming that 'The labour and spirits of enslaved individuals laid the foundation for Britain's growth – the toil of those who worked in cotton fields and plantations within British colonies, as well as the spirits of those who succumbed en route.'[12]

It can be said that Christianity and colonialism did not always go hand in hand in the history of British imperialism: though influential, the Church of England was not involved in a calculated, premeditated endeavour orchestrated by the British government or trading companies to disseminate the Christian gospel. Contrary to narratives depicting a mission of enlightenment and global Christianization by the western powers, the fact is that the British East India Company consistently maintained that the presence of Christian missionaries could potentially harm their trade interests. For example, again looking at India (as it is the context I am most familiar with), the earliest British missionaries and mission organizations were dispatched primarily as chaplains to cater to the spiritual needs of the company's officials and soldiers stationed there. Only after the establishment of the British Raj in 1847 did India become more receptive to Christian missionaries.

However, setting this aspect aside, it is evident that the Church of England, being the Established Church, held significant sway over and reaped benefits from Britain's colonial expansion. As an example of the former, the modern missionary movement, drawing inspiration from Britain's colonial expansion and benefiting from the protection of colonial military forces, played a pivotal role in laying the foundation for what we now recognize as the Anglican Communion. With regard to the latter, the Church's buildings and foundations and institutions owe much to the success and growth of Britain as an imperial power. One tangible reminder of these is the plaques and monuments in our historic churches and cathedrals. More poignantly, the Church also benefited in the past and sometimes still benefits from investments and capital donations bequeathed to the Church that were made with profits from colonial exploitation and the slave trade. There was a recent reminder of this history in 2021, when the Church Commissioners of the Church of England opened an investigation into the possibility that the £9.2bn investment fund known as Queen Anne's Bounty, which supports parishes across the country, had its origins in the slave trade: the report published at the end of the investigation concluded that this fund does indeed have links with transatlantic slavery.[13]

Intentional erasure

The shared, selective amnesia about the empire in Britain is far from co-incidental. Narrating the national story involves celebrating the people of a small island nation who came to rule an empire over which the sun never set; for this myth to function, it is important also to forget the darker aspects of colonialism and slavery.

The country's education system reinforces this narrative by failing to adequately address Britain's colonial past and its role in the slave trade. In 2021, when a petition that garnered 268,772 signatures demanded the inclusion of lessons about colonialism and Britain's involvement in the slave trade, the Minister for School Standards Nick Gibb dismissed the idea, asserting that such teaching could potentially stifle teachers' creativity and compromise the quality of education.

This situation is mirrored in the educational landscape within the Church of England and its theological colleges. The theology disseminated to individuals undergoing ministerial training often remains confined to a one-dimensional viewpoint, neglecting the richness of diversity that authentically reflects the intricate composition of a multicultural and multi-ethnic Britain. This exact insufficiency was underscored in *From Lament to Action: Key recommendations*, published in 2021:[14] this report provided directives to address this concern, although at the time of writing there is no available data to oversee and assess the execution of these guidelines.

Making disciples, reflecting and celebrating the memory, breaking the kingdom in

The mission of the Church revolves around nurturing followers by spreading the transformative message of hope. Jesus' public ministry began with the imperative call to 'repent' (Matthew 3.2), signifying the imminent arrival of the kingdom of God. This initial proclamation sought a change of heart. Present-day portrayals of Jesus often diverge from the bold preacher depicted in the Gospels. Popular culture often depicts a gentle and passive Jesus as an innocent infant in a manger or a vulnerable figure crucified on the cross. However, it's essential to recognize that Jesus did not initiate his ministry by declaring universal love (though undoubtedly, he embodies it), but by emphasizing the urgency of repentance due to the nearness of the kingdom of God. The Christian understanding of repentance (*metanoia*, μετάνοια) signifies a profound shift, encompassing not only a transformation in thought but also a behaviour change. It marks the pivotal juncture where a genuine reversal occurs, initiating our journey as disciples. This change is only possible through a sincere recognition of our collective shortcomings as a church community in instances where we have fallen short of God's love and acted unjustly towards our siblings. It entails recognizing not only personal guilt but also the collective inadequacies of the human race, acknowledging our failure to keep the commandment to love one another as we love ourselves.

Just as the Industrial Revolution has bestowed wealth upon Britain in the present day, the enduring legacies of colonialism and the slave trade continue to cast their influence over countless lives across the globe. The simple fact that it took 180 years to settle the compensation extended to former slaveholders by the British government raises the question of what reparations should be provided to those who were stripped of their ancestral heritage and subjected to racial injustices. The ongoing injustice stemming from past wrongs persists, and we must acknowledge that the state and many people in this country still reap the advantages of colonialism and slavery. These benefits manifest indirectly through the existence of various educational and financial institutions that have roots in these historical injustices. Additionally, more direct associations, such as the Church of England and other comparable establishments, derive income from investments originating in the colonial era. While achieving financial reparations that directly address the historical harm inflicted by colonialism and slavery might prove extraordinarily challenging or unfeasible, the imperative to initiate acts of reparation remains crucial. These actions are vital for redressing the persistent, systemic racial inequalities entrenched within our society.

Reflecting (and lamenting) and honouring memories is central to the Judeo-Christian faith tradition. The Hebrew Bible has a recurring motif of the Lord's providence, highlighted most prominently by the narrative of Israel's liberation from Egypt. Similarly, the foundation of the New Testament church rests upon the memory of Jesus breaking bread with his disciples. So when we grapple with historical accounts of colonial exploitation and slavery, Christians must engage in the same practice of reflection and lament, of mourning and rejoicing. There exists a responsibility to faithfully document the events that unfolded and subsequently endeavour to interpret them within the context of present-day moral perspectives.

A genuine disciple of Christ living in Britain in our century, who is shaped by the path of repentance, must liberate themselves from the nation's collective ignorance of colonial history. Their dedication should revolve around transforming their own lives, accompanied by a resolute commitment to rectify the persisting consequences of past injustices. By doing this they/we will be demonstrating the values of the kingdom of God, which is 'righteousness and peace and joy in the Holy Spirit' (Romans 14.17, NRSV).

The Church, composed of repentant disciples, is obliged to ensure that its leaders in training possess not only an understanding of the history of colonial exploitation and the slave trade but also an awareness of this history's ongoing legacies in the present era. Instilling these teachings in our emerging leaders might appear daunting; nevertheless, adopting a global perspective and humbly seeking assistance from our fellow brothers and sisters worldwide can prove invaluable.

The Global Theology module we offer at Emmanuel Theological College aims to exemplify this approach by demonstrating how seeking collaboration beyond our borders can contribute to fostering a more comprehensive understanding of these crucial matters. The module commences with a concise overview of the evolution of the global Church and the Anglican Communion. It subsequently delves into the development of contextual theologies from around the world, consistently probing how these insights can enrich the learning experiences of our students. Notably, a significant proportion of these students are undergoing training for diverse forms of licensed Anglican ministry in the north-west of England. Emmanuel Theological College capitalizes on its extensive network within the Anglican Communion and beyond to provide students with a window into the expansive scope of the worldwide Church. Within this module, scholars from various regions – including India, Kenya, Singapore, Malaysia, Palestine, the EU, Malawi, Pakistan and Burundi – participate in interactive learning sessions facilitated by platforms such as Zoom. This innovative approach links the classroom in Liverpool with voices spanning the globe, fostering a more holistic understanding of theological perspectives.

As a nation experiencing ever-growing cultural and ethnic diversity, there should be no evasion in providing younger generations with an education that covers the profound realities of colonial exploitation and the transatlantic slave trade. This educational effort must extend to the descendants of both the colonized and the colonizers, encompassing those who were once enslavers and those who were enslaved, ensuring a comprehensive understanding of this harsh yet undeniable history. In essence, this education demands an unwavering exploration of the stark truths surrounding colonial exploitation and the slave trade, juxtaposed with accounts of industrial progress. It is of utmost importance to recognize the manner in which history is interpreted and communicated. We are tasked with consistently re-evaluating our approach to historical interpretation and instituting a practice of periodic review concerning the narratives presented on monuments and plaques. This practice can help ensure that our understanding of history remains accurate and comprehensive.

Conclusion: What would our ancestors say to UK ME and GMH people of our generation?

At the beginning of this chapter, I outlined my narrative and analysis of my participation in the UBE Conference 2023 in Montgomery, Alabama. I want to conclude the chapter by returning to this event. Given my roles as both a theological educator and advocate for racial justice, a significant highlight of the event was the keynote address presented by Dr Catherine Meeks. With a fitting self-description as a mentor tending to the spirits of her students and workshop participants, her influential talk carried the following title: 'The Ancestors are Observing with Reverence!' At the end of her keynote speech, she delivered this powerful statement:

> The Ancestors are looking back at us, and they want to know. What are we doing about the legacy that they gave us? How are we working to overcome the illnesses of colourism and other racialized trauma?[15]

With the persistent reminders of the grim history of slave ownership and trade, and the vivid memory of racial segregation, along with the current stark reality of mass incarceration, this question struck a chord with the participants.

Meeks' questions hold significant relevance for people of UK ME and GMH. Our predecessors endured the hardships of enslavement and colonization, losing their cultural heritage, language and religious practices. They held limited rights and there were few opportunities to challenge the injustices inflicted upon them or oppose their oppressors. However, we, the current generation, are fortunate to have avoided the yoke of colonial dominion or enslavement. Further questions then arise: how are we using the freedom, or the perception of freedom, that we possess? Are we courageous enough to challenge the intentional erasure of the colonial and slave-trading past of our nation and our Church?

Notes

1 Equal Justice Initiative, 2018, Slavery in America: The Montgomery Slave Trade, Montgomery, AL: Equal Justice Initiative, https://eji.org/files/slavery-in-america-summary.pdf, accessed 10.10.2023.

2 Prison Policy Initiative, 'Race and ethnicity', *Prison Policy Initiative*, https://www.prisonpolicy.org/research/race_and_ethnicity/, accessed 10.08.2023.

3 Gale Stewart, 'Plenary', 26 July 2023, UBE 2023.

4 Gov.uk, 2022, 'Ethnicity facts and figures', *Office for National Statistics*, 22 December, https://www.ethnicity-facts-figures.service.gov.uk/uk-population-by-ethnicity/national-and-regional-populations/population-of-england-and-wales/latest, accessed 04.06.2024.

5 Commission on Race and Ethnic Disparities, 2021, *The Report of the Commission on Race and Ethnic Disparities (March 2021)*, London: HM Government https://assets.publishing.service.gov.uk/government/uploads/system/uploads/attachment_data/file/974507/20210331_-_CRED_Report_-_FINAL_-_Web_Accessible.pdf, accessed 04.06.2024.

6 Nissa Finney et al. (eds), 2023, *Racism and Ethnic Inequality in a Time of Crisis: Findings from the Evidence for Equality National Survey*, Bristol: Policy Press.

7 BBC News, 2020, 'Church of England is "deeply institutionally racist" – Welby', *BBC News*, 12 February, https://www.bbc.co.uk/news/uk-51469566, accessed 04.06.2024.

8 S. Sanghera, 2021, *Empireland: How imperialism has shaped modern Britain*, London: Viking, pp. 185–206.

9 Shashi Tharoor, 2016, *An Era of Darkness: The British Empire in India*, New Delhi: Aleph Book Company.

10 J. Blitz, 2018, 'Brexiters focus on the Commonwealth factor', *Financial Times*, 14 February, https://www.ft.com/content/bb199160-1175-11e8-8cb6-b9ccc4c4dbbb, accessed 04.06.2024.

11 Tharoor, *An Era of Darkness*, p. 7.

12 Imran Khan, 2020, 'Britain was built on the backs, and souls, of slaves', *Al Jazeera*, 11 June, https://www.aljazeera.com/features/2020/6/11/britain-was-built-on-the-backs-and-souls-of-slaves, accessed 04.06.2024.

13 H. Williams, 2022, 'Church Commissioners Acknowledge that Slave Trade boosted Early Funds', https://www.churchtimes.co.uk/articles/2022/17-june/news/uk/church-commissioners-acknowledge-that-slave-trade-boosted-early-funds, accessed 18.07.2024.

14 *From Lament to Action*, https://www.churchofengland.org/sites/default/files/2021-04/FromLamentToAction-report.pdf, accessed 18.07.2024.

15 Catherine Meeks, 'The Ancestors are looking back in wonder!' Keynote Speech, 26 July 2023, UBE 2023.

4

'When the Church of the British Isles Begins to Venerate Her Own Saints, Then the Church will Grow'

TIMOTHY BONIFACE CARROLL

This chapter frames the question of twenty-first-century mission in Britain against the background of the early centuries of Christian mission in these islands. Looking at what we know of St Aristobulus of the Seventy, whom one could name as the first British Cypriot, and those other early apostles, from St Joseph of Arimathea to St Theodore of Tarsus, this chapter considers how the Christian history of Great Britain and the wider British Isles is a product, first and foremost, of missionization from the Eastern Mediterranean region. As these are the first martyrs (even before St Alban), this is the blood that first watered these God-blessed islands. With this background, the chapter then moves to address the work of St John of San Francisco, who, while bishop of Paris and Brussels, began to push for the recognition of the pre-schism saints. This, along with the prophecy of St Arsenios of Paros about the importance of the Church in Britain venerating 'her own' saints, frame the contemporary period of mission in the UK and Ireland.

Introduction

While some early histories of Christianity in Britain, most notably that of the Venerable Bede,[1] start with St Lucius, king of the Britons, in the second century AD, our history is older than this.[2] Within the anthologies of hagiographies, known as synaxaria (single synaxarion), of the Orthodox Christian Churches, several first-century saints are remembered. Popular accounts, for example, connecting St Joseph of Arimathea to Glastonbury, hint at the scattering of the apostles and the other disciples within the first generation of Christ. In the Orthodox synaxarion, as well as the Menaion, a 12-volume set of saints' feast days arranged according to the calendar, we also find St Aristobulus of the Seventy. Depending on the calendar in question, he is remembered either on 15 or 16 March; and there is also some disagreement in the record if he died in peace or was martyred in Wales – but more on this later. Nonetheless, this brother of the Apostle Barnabas, who along with his brother followed Christ as one of the Seventy (see Luke 10) and joined in at least some of the missionary journeys of St Paul, is remembered as having been sent by St Paul to Roman Britain.

Three points emerge from this example. The first is that Orthodoxy in these God-blessed islands is ancient. Second, within Orthodoxy and its lived tradition today there is disagreement, not only about calendars and details of hagiography, but wider issues, too. Third, how memory, death and peace are of core importance in Orthodox Christian tradition. And a fourth thing, like the first, is that Christianity came to these God-blessed islands from Asia and the eastern Mediterranean.

As discussed briefly below, the history of Orthodox Christianity in Britain is, by some accounts, very recent. However, this is an error, one born of the loss of memory. Saints like St Aristobulus serve as a point of continuity with an ancient and enduring tradition of Orthodox Christianity. The fact that he is remembered in the Menaion, even if only briefly, speaks to the continual practice, over the centuries, of his commemoration. Elsewhere in the Church, even while there was no Orthodox Church in Britain, at least some of the saints of Britain were commemorated. There is, then, a link between the contemporary Orthodox community in Britain with their religious forebears. There is, likewise, a link between the Church here and the Church elsewhere. This is not only true of the Church universal, or the Church triumphant – though this is also important – but the Church in other places, each in their own 'here'. Just as British and Celtic saints were remembered by the Church in Greece and Russia, for example, during the period when Orthodoxy was absent from these shores, so too should the Church here support the Churches suffering periods that risk 'memory loss', such as that experienced by the Russian Church under the Soviet yoke.

St Aristobulus is by no means alone or unique. Notable saints of the Eastern Church also include many recognized in the West. For example, St Augustine of Canterbury, St Theodore of Tarsus and St Cuthbert. Missionary saints from Britain such as St Boniface, apostle to the Germans, and his cousin St Lioba, for example, also speak to the history of the Church in Britain as a source of further apostolic mission. During the first millennia, thousands of Christian saints lived in Britain – and the Orthodox Church recognizes them as her own. Thus the continuity of Christianity from the time of St Aristobulus, even with its complications and tensions both interior and exterior, is understood by the Orthodox Church to be Orthodox. There is breakage, however, after the millennium. Some name St Edward the Confessor as the last Orthodox saint-king from antiquity in the British Isles. Others extend this honour to his successor Harold, seeing him as the king and also a martyr at the hand of William of Normandy.

For many Orthodox, the Norman Conquest is seen as a point of severance. In the years following the conquest, the last of the Orthodox bishops were driven out and their sees given to Roman Catholics. Coming in the wake of the Great Schism and the excommunications of 1054, the Conquest is understood to have been done under the blessing of an excommunicated bishop and to the detriment of the Orthodox Church in Britain. This process is understood to fulfil the deathbed prophecy of St Edward when, in a vision, he learned that because

> those who have climbed to the highest offices in the kingdom of Eng-
> land, the earls, bishops and abbots, and all those in holy orders, are not
> what they seem to be, but, on the contrary, are servants of the devil, on
> a year and one day after the day of your death God has delivered all this
> kingdom, cursed by Him, into the hands of the enemy, and devils shall
> come through all this land with fire and sword and the havoc of war.[3]

In fulfilment of this prophecy, William's coronation was a year and a day after the repose of St Edward.

The ecclesiastical rift between Orthodox Christians and other Christians in Britain was then made worse by the destruction of Orthodox heritage and sacred artefacts. The Dissolution of the Monasteries undertaken by Henry VIII, between 1536 and 1541, destroyed much of the material remains of Orthodox Christianity. There is, within Orthodox circles, some variation in how non-Orthodox Christians are viewed. But suffice it to say that, by this point in history, only the ecumenically minded Orthodox Christians would consider the monastics in Britain to have been spiritual brothers. Nonetheless, there is a great loss felt, not only because of the loss of lives, but because the destruction included many ancient relics, icons and monasteries that were extant from the period before the Schism and Conquest. This moment in the history of Christianity in Britain marks a worsening by degrees of an already dire situation. As an Orthodox historian once told me: 'While the Roman Catholics were bad, the Protestants proved much more hostile and destructive.'

One might ask, in a book about lived mission in the twenty-first century, why there is this attention to the past. This is an excellent question, because it belies a fundamental difference in approach to what has happened. Within Orthodoxy, and within the Temple Judaism that preceded it, memory is fundamental to the faith. The role of memory is not one of remembering the past, but – not unlike the phenomenology of time as set out by the philosopher Edmund Husserl – is one of participation. Or, to take a different philosophical analogy, in the opening lines of the dialogue *Phaedrus*, Socrates asks 'Whither and whence': where are you coming from and where are you going? If we are to discuss mission, today, in these God-blessed islands, we must remember the witnesses sent from Mount Olivet and receive the tradition handed down by them.

This memory and participation is rooted, ultimately, in the Eucharist. 'Do this', the Lord says, 'in remembrance of me.' The symbol of the rite – the liturgy and the movements therein – draw the person towards God, to participate in him. This idea, set down by St Dionysius the Areopagite, is too deep to delve into fully here. However, this form of participation via apophatic symbols – summarized in the beguilingly simple invitation to 'come and see' – forms the basis of Orthodox missional work. It is against the background of this practice of participation – in Christ, in the Eucharist, in the memory of God – that the history of the Church is understood. Coming into this understanding, and with it recognizing the apostolic faith and its theology and practice, is often spoken of as gaining 'the mind of the Church'. Almost as a sense of shared familial history, a form of memory and mutual understanding that holds together a wide inter-generational and multi-ethnic family, the remembered history is held as common lived memory. In fulfilling the commandment to 'honour thy father and mother', this remembering of our forebears and rejoicing in their triumph through Christ in the act of veneration, helps ground the Church today. Knowing from whence we have come helps us know where hence we must go. Thus periods of violence and suffering – periods of Roman persecution, Ottoman and Soviet yokes, the Iconoclastic Era, the Crusades, and the Dissolution of the Monasteries, among others – are all events that shape the Church here in Britain and its relationship to the land and people herein. This is a land, a God-blessed island, which is often hostile to the Church, but is also rich with – all too oft forgotten – ancient testimony to God.

A brief modern history

Since the late seventeenth century there has been a slow re-introduction of Orthodoxy into Britain. First with labourers, sailors and merchants, as well as scholars being sent to study at Oxford University, a trickle of Greek and Russian communities became established in Britain.[4] In 1677, a Greek parish dedicated to the Dormition of the Mother of God was opened in Soho, London, under the auspices of the Duke of York, later James VII and II. However, this parish met protest from the Anglican Bishop of London who forbade the use of icons and required them to forfeit 'Romish' doctrines. Under such rather absurd constraints it was closed shortly thereafter. Then, in conjunction with the four-month stay of Tsar Peter the Great in England in 1698, a small parish was established under the auspices of the Russian Embassy. This parish, though soon to outgrow its space, appears to be the first permanent Orthodox parish in Britain in modern history.

Over the next century a handful of parishes sprang up around Britain, but it was only in the 1920s that the population of Orthodox immigrants was large enough to warrant local episcopal oversight. This was introduced first by the Patriarchate of Constantinople in 1922, with the formation of the diocese of Western and Central Europe under the Metropolitan Germanos (Strenopoulos[5]). Then, in 1929, seeking to meet the needs of the large numbers of Russians fleeing the Revolution, the Russian Orthodox Church Abroad (later ROCOR[6] consecrated their first bishop of London, Nicholas (Karpoff). Bishop Nicholas helped establish the community in London, but his work was cut short when he died three years later. His Eminence Germanos, however, was quite influential, but there are two contrasting narratives concerning his influence. The first – though I have not been able to find concrete evidence of this – is the suggestion that there was an 'infamous agreement' between His Eminence Germanos and the Church of England. The details of this agreement are vague, but there is a general sense that Germanos agreed not to proselytize nor receive converts from the Church of England. This would be scandalous if true. The second narrative suggests that he was an astute ecumenist. As the first metropolitan bishop of the Orthodox Churches in Great Britain, H. E. Germanos participated with particular zeal in dialogues with the Church of England as well as with Old Catholics on the Continent. The Church in Constantinople joined the ecumenical movement in earnest in 1920 and, as a western-trained scholar, the then bishop of Seleucia, Germanos, was involved from the start. At the time, there was much, though probably naive, optimism that unity could be found between the various Christian Churches worldwide. Despite ongoing dialogue between the Church of England and the Orthodox Churches, currently such optimism is hard to find.

The succeeding years saw Orthodoxy in Britain undergo four more periods of growth worth mentioning. The first was the influx of Cypriot immigrants because of the Turkish invasion in 1974. The second was composed of various Eastern European communities emigrating following the fall of the Soviet Union. The third is seen in the migration, most notably of Romanians, who made use of free movement during the UK's participation in the European Union to enrich the Church and wider society in Britain. The fourth is a 'native' movement, largely of former Anglicans who came to Orthodoxy following years of increasing discontent with the liberalizing and modernizing forces within the Church of England.

This last group was received into the Antiochian Greek Orthodox Church in 1995 by Patriarch Ignatios IV (Hazim), by the hand of the then vicar, later Metropolitan, Gabriel (Saliby) of Paris. While notable for the number of people who joined the Orthodox Church in one movement, echoing similar groups in North America,[7] there has been a continual stream of converts joining the ranks of the Orthodox Church. Some, like these, come from other Christian backgrounds; but the Church also has a regular growth of people from non-religious and other religious backgrounds alike. In some ways, by God's providence, the Covid-19 pandemic gave people time, stuck on the internet at home, to explore beyond what they knew. In the last few years, more people have sought out the Orthodox Church. In some cases, literally knocking at the doors asking to be let in.

Coming to see

The Eastern Orthodox Christian communities in the UK, as is common across the regions of the world that did not fall within the boundaries of the Eastern Roman Empire, are characterized by a certain ecumenical ambivalence. This is to say that, while all the Chalcedonian Orthodox Churches are One, singular, Holy Catholic and Apostolic Church, they are also each independent, autocephalous (self-headed) Churches. In the lands of the eastern Mediterranean it is easier to see how the Churches relate: for example, the Patriarch of Serbia, Porfirije, called on his people in February 2023 to help the people of the Church of Antioch, having been informed by the Patriarch of Antioch, John X, of the situation in Syria and Turkey after the earthquakes in the region. Like the contributions of the Churches in Macedonia and Achaia to the Church in Jerusalem (Romans 15), the Church in Serbia, like many others, gathered contributions to help the local Church in the affected lands. One land, or region, and one Church of that land. This is the ideal. The Patriarchs, or their representatives, make irenic visits to each other and send letters of support and encouragement. They concelebrate liturgies together and send seminarians to train in their sister's institutions.

However, the historical migration of people, and the ways in which pastoral care and episcopal oversight often followed the congregations by several years, means that the Church(es) outside the Eastern Roman Empire grew in a somewhat haphazard, overlapping manner. Thus, as mentioned above, the Russian, the Greek and the Antiochian Churches all have, in the brief history of the regrowth of Orthodoxy in the UK, had episcopal representation in the islands. The situation today is even more complex in terms of administration. And yet the fundamental principle of being the same One Holy Catholic and Apostolic Church is still true. Thus, when a new member is welcomed into the Church, they are not bound to one jurisdiction but to the Orthodox Church. Particularly for weddings and baptisms, it is not uncommon for concelebrations to happen across the jurisdictional boundaries of administration. On one hand, this may be understood as ecumenical relations; however, this is not the best way to understand this, as it is fundamentally within one Church.

With this ecumenical ambivalence in mind, it is easier to understand how the various Eastern Orthodox traditions – for example, Russian, Greek, Serbian or Romanian – speak into each other's traditions. One saint, though glorified by a local Church over 'there', is universally recognized 'here', too. While the administrative differences are important in terms of the governance of the local body, the spiritual unity of the Church, in all her local variation, allows for an easy translation of teaching from one place to another.

In this context, I now turn to two recent Orthodox saints in order to frame the role of memory and participation within the context of British Orthodoxy. The first is St Arsenios of Paros. St Arsenios lived from 1800 to 1877, first in mainland Greece then on the island of Paros where he became a beloved spiritual father. He never came to Great Britain, but did prophesy concerning it. It is often retold as: 'The Church in the British Isles will only begin to grow when she begins to venerate her own Saints.' This need to venerate 'her own' was also taught by St John Maximovich. St John was a Russian bishop, for a time located in Shanghai, then in Paris and Brussels for 12 years before being moved to San Francisco. During his tenure in Europe (1950–1962), he also oversaw the ROCOR Church in Britain. From one visit to England, the following memory was recorded by Archimandrite Ambrose (Pogodin):

Vladyka[8] John routinely visited churches of other faiths, where the grace of Orthodoxy might still manifest itself, especially in the form of the holy relics of saints who had been glorified before the Schism. Following this practice, Vladyka John expressed the intention of visiting Westminster Abbey. At one time it may have been a holy place. In spite of the devastation wreaked by Henry VIII, the Abbey had miraculously been preserved as a working church. Now, however, it no longer possesses the holiness it once had as an ancient church. Now people simply go to see it as one of London's tourist attractions. Vladyka also went to see it, but after spending only a short time there, he left, saying: 'There is no grace here.' It is true, there could be found the remains of famous English figures, of the country's political founders, writers and scholars, but not of saints.[9]

This pattern of going into non-Orthodox places of worship in order to venerate the relics is not unique to St John, but it is extraordinary. The remarkableness of the practice comes in its juxtaposition with canon law. Among the most ancient, and thus most important, canons is Apostolic Canon LXIV. It reads, 'If any clergyman or layman shall enter into a synagogue of Jews or heretics to pray, let the former be deposed and let the latter be excommunicated.'[10] By canonical standards of Orthodox ecclesiology, Westminster Abbey, and indeed any edifice of the Church of England, is a 'synagogue of the heretics' – though more friendly terms, such as 'heterodox' are now more often used. Vladyka's decision to enter Westminster Abbey could have been cause to strip him of his clerical rank if it were not for Orthodox *oikonomia* – economy – and our theology of relics. *Oikonomia*, literally 'keeping of the house', is the practice of interpreting the canons according to the local need at the time as it concerns the salvation of those persons involved. Paired with *akriveia*, which denotes a strict reading of canon law, it guides how a canon may be applied. Within Orthodox practice of *oikonomia* it is deemed permissible to enter into the 'synagogue of the heretic' in order to venerate the relics of Orthodox saints.[11] Thus, should sacred things have fallen into the hands of those outside the Church, Orthodox Christians are allowed to break the literal meaning of the canon and go to pray there. There are two conclusions that come out of this account of Vladyka John. In the first instance, it demonstrates the real power of the historic witness of the Church over what is otherwise perceived to be a harmful and spiritually toxic environment. Following from this, it reiterates the degree to which Orthodoxy perceives the Anglican witness as a hostile force. As St John Maximovich said, 'There is no grace here.'

St John's practice of visiting 'churches of other faiths' was part and parcel of a wider instruction for the Orthodox Christians from the East now residing in the West to learn about and venerate the ancient saints of the pre-Schism Church. There is harmony between St John's teaching and St Arsenios's prophecy, and through the work of St John Maximovich much was done towards cataloguing and venerating the local saints.[12] The continuity of the Church, both living and dead, is central to Orthodox ecclesiology. Therefore the saints of a region are fundamental to the well-being of that local Church. For this reason, in the Orthodox liturgical calendars globally, the first Sunday after Pentecost is dedicated to All Saints, and the second Sunday to All Saints of that region.

Recognizing the importance of celebrating – and remembering – the local witness of the Church, the intra-Orthodox ecumenical endeavours under the Episcopal Assemblies,[13] which were organized in 2010, sought to complete this process.[14] Although many lists of saints exist, they do not all agree; and, as seen with St Aristobulus, when they do all attest to a certain saint, the biographical accounts may differ. Despite the variance, what is important to note is a strongly felt need at all levels and across ethnic boundaries to establish an Orthodox Christian practice in the British Isles that is a continuation of what was before and is still retained in part. Britons and Irish find themselves living in a group of islands rich with a religious history with which they both identify very closely and from which they are markedly separated. The practice of Christianity in the British Isles has become something with which many Orthodox can only partially identify. The labour to regain, or create anew, an iconographic tradition of known saints, and to write hymnography for their veneration, is work that has been done by various Orthodox artists across Western Europe.

Work to compile extant witness of pre-schism saints, done by local parishes and lay fellowships, also often provides information on how to make pilgrimage to various local saints and holy wells. In celebrating the lives of ancient saints, it is not simply a practice of national heritage and pilgrimages are not simply an excuse to ramble in remote parts of the islands – though there certainly may be some aspect of this at times. More importantly, though, is the sense that this is 'our' faith; it is the 'holiness of our own region', as one announcement reads, in inviting people to visit the site of an ancient monastery destroyed by Henry VIII.

In the case of the British saints, there is often only limited evidence for what they would have looked like, due in large part to sixteenth- and seventeenth-century iconoclasm. Thus iconographers working in the traditional Orthodox aesthetic styles must work to recreate a sense of the situated character of the British and Celtic saints that is true to the land from which they came, the land in which they lived their lives, and the region which is 'ours'.

This 'holiness of our region' is best understood in both senses of 'our'. The holiness found in the ancient pilgrimage sites, and sought in the burgeoning iconographic tradition of the British saints, is 'ours', that is, belonging to the Orthodox Church in Britain. It is understood to be the spiritual heritage of all Orthodox Christians residing in these lands, regardless of ethnic bloodlines. St Aristobulus, after all, was Cypriot; and St Theodore of Canterbury – known for establishing the administrative order of the English Church, still extant in parts of the Church of England – was from Tarsus, in the Church of Antioch, sent to England by the Patriarch of Rome. This 'our' is not limited to 'native' blood, it is not nationalism,[15] nor ethnophyletism. While this heresy has had influence in some contexts in recent centuries, and the nationalism discourse, as seen for example in the establishment of the modern Greek nation state, is difficult to parse from Orthodox notions of belonging, the emphasis on locally inscribed belonging is about the communal pursuit of holiness – fulfilling the incarnational ministry of Christ – not ethnic division. This sense of 'our' holiness is, ultimately, a eucharistic 'our'; being bound in the blood of Christ, made present – here, now and in eternity – in his saints. Thus, this 'our' is also best understood as our means to holiness, both personal and communal. The bond between the well-being of the local Orthodox Church in Britain and her treatment of her saints can be seen on each level.

This bond, however, like forgiveness as it is discussed in the Lord's prayer, is conditional. St Arsenios says *when* the saints are venerated, *then* the Church will be healthy and grow. So the work to grow the Church must include the work of venerating the saints of these God-blessed islands. The Orthodox mission is, fundamentally, one of memory and prayer. It is a mission of memory and sacrifice. It is a mission of martyrdom; and, if martyrdom is not literal – as it is in many parts of the Church today – then it must be one of participation: participation in the suffering of Christ and his body. Either way, though, our land, these God-blessed lands, must be watered, either by blood or the tears of repentance.

Even in cases where the individual is not ethnically 'British', there is a felt connection between the region in which they live and the religious devotion which has deep roots in British soil. The long history of the Church in the British Isles, spoken of briefly at the beginning of this chapter, is held to be not just something of national heritage but something that actively shapes the spiritual flavour of the region; these are events within the lived memory of British Orthodoxy. Thus the growth of Orthodox Christian veneration of Orthodox saints of the British Isles must not be an innovation of Byzantine or Slavonic Orthodoxy in Britain, but a growth of something local, specifically the holiness of our region.

Of martyrdom and repentance

There are, however, difficulties at times, and impediments to unity in mission. There are various excuses and rationale for these impediments – all above my pay grade; but let us gesture to this simply as a way to remind Orthodox Christians, both in the British Isles and abroad, to pray – as the anaphora of St Basil says – that God might 'stop schisms among the Churches'. St Cyril of Jerusalem, in the earliest extant catechism we have, warns his flock against gossip and instructs them to ignore news of what the emperor or clergy have done. Instead, he tells them to 'lift up your eyes' because 'you need Him who is above'. The first Christian martyr, St Stephen, looked up into heaven and saw the Son of Man standing at the right hand of God (Acts 7.56); in his martyrdom he asked that the sin of those who killed him not be held against them and committed his spirit to Christ. In his martyrdom he attained peace. And so, if we think about the disagreement between the hagiographic detail of St Aristobulus – that one source says he died in peace and another says he was martyred – maybe the two are not so different. The point of Christian mission is to reconcile all humankind to God. It is to bring healing to the broken, and to make people – who may be separated by various divisions – 'one' even as Christ and the Father are one. Healing is often uncomfortable. Healing is often experienced as suffering; but to suffer in Christ is to die to the self and attain peace.

Conclusion

In closing, it is worth highlighting that there is nothing particularly British about what is happening here. Every land, watered by the blood of Orthodox martyrs, is a God-blessed land. Every land, with saints born and raised there or who have moved to live there – for remember St Theodore of Canterbury was a Greek from Tarsus – is God-blessed and has its own 'our'. Our Christianity here, in Britain, came from the Levant. It came from Jerusalem, brought by a Jewish Cypriot bishop. If we think that Christianity is a western religion, or a European religion, we have forgotten our fathers and mothers. From the outset, the centres of Christianity have predominantly been in Asia and Africa: places like Antioch, Jerusalem, Cappadocia, Alexandria, Carthage, etc. This true religion, however, has been brought to Albion by the apostles and their heirs time and time again: St Aristobulus, St Theodore, St John Maxim-ovich, and many others. It has been watered by the blood of martyrdom and the tears of repentance, so that we may receive the peace Christ promised. This requires serious labour to be faithful to the traditions handed down to us. The fidelity to the theology, custom and practice of the Orthodox Church is part of 'our holiness' – it must not cultural, nor national, but a regional – local – expression.

Notes

1 Bede, 2008, *The Ecclesiastical History of the English People*, B. Colgrave, J. McClure, R. Collins (trans.), Oxford: Oxford University Press.

2 The history presented in this chapter and parts of the wider argument draw on T. Carroll, 2015, 'An ancient modernity: Ikons and the re-emergence of Orthodox

Britain' in T. W. Jones and L. Matthews-Jones (eds), *Material Religion in Modern Britain: The Spirit of Things*, London: Palgrave MacMillan.

3 F. Barlow (ed.), 1992, *The Life of King Edward who Rests at Westminster Attributed to a Monk of Saint-Bertin*, 2nd edn, Oxford: Clarendon Press.

4 See T. Catsiyannis, 1993, *The Greek Community of London (1500–1945)*, London: privately printed. J. Harris, 2009, 'Silent minority: the Greek community of eighteenth-century London' in D. Tziovas (ed.), *Greek Diaspora and Migration Since 1700: Society, politics and culture*, London: Ashgate Publishing. C. Birchall, 2014, *Embassy, Emigrants and Englishmen: The three hundred year history of a Russian Orthodox Church in London*, Jordanville, NY: Printshop of St Job of Pochaev.

5 I follow the Orthodox convention of placing family names as a parenthetis following the given name for clergy. The family names of monks, priests and bishops are rarely ever used in speech, except to distinguish priests with exceptionally common names.

6 Russian Orthodox Church Outside of Russia.

7 For example, P. Gillquist, 1989, *Becoming Orthodox: A journey to the ancient Christian faith*, Chesterton, IN: Conciliar Press.

8 This is a Russian honorific for 'bishop' which is also connotative of affection.

9 Quoted by Fr Andrew, 'Orthodox Holiness: St John the Wonderworker in England', available online at: www.orthodoxengland.org.uk/stjohnen.htm, accessed 31.05.2023.

10 P. Schaff (ed.), 1899, 'The Canons of the Holy and Altogether August Apostles' in *Nicene and Post-Nicene Fathers Series II, Volume 14, The Seven Ecumenical Councils*.

11 This view was supported most notably by the twelfth-century canonist, Theodore IV (Balsamon) of Antioch.

12 The influence of St John Maximovich on this matter can be seen in the creation of icons of All Saints of the British Isles and a service to the same, which was commissioned by his successor.

13 These are local synods of bishops that have been called together based on geographic region across the traditionally non-Orthodox parts of the world. Every local bishop, from each of the self-ruling Orthodox Churches present in a region, is a member of these Episcopal Assemblies tasked with specific pastoral and administrative duties within their local geographic context.

14 Unfortunately, following political machinations upsetting the peace of the Church in Ukraine in 2018, and the rippling consequences felt further afield, the Episcopal Assembly in the United Kingdom has ceased to function.

15 See also the work by Dr Nicholas Lackenby on the concept of '*narod*' (the people) in Serbian Orthodoxy.

Contexts

5

This is Our Land:
Africans Evangelizing in Britain

HARVEY KWIYANI

Introduction

In this chapter I will explore, from an African perspective, some aspects of the lived missiology that I see being lived out in the UK, with a focus on the missional implications of the growing African Church scattered around the country. I wonder, as an African theologian, what missiological thought shapes a great deal of our missional practice in Britain and how this can be invigorated and enriched by the missiologies of migrant Christians, for instance those of the African Church in this country. I write in agreement with Lesslie Newbigin and others, that Britain needs a fresh missional engagement, and I suggest that such an engagement must reflect the cultural diversity that makes British Christianity today. The African part of this engagement is reflected in the ways that African churches are serving and evangelizing their host communities.

Mission field Britain

A great deal of British missiology looks outward, from Britain to the rest of the world, especially Africa, Asia and Latin America, where thousands of British missionaries have worked for more than 200 years. Indeed, when most British Christians hear the word 'mission', they think of the many ways in which people from these great islands go across the seas to share the gospel with those who do not follow Jesus in other parts of the world. There is a sense in which it has become acceptable among some Christians in Britain, especially of the Evangelical wing, to speak about evangelism right here in Britain. The Evangelical Alliance's report of 2022, 'Talking Jesus', is evidence of this.[1] However, as far as mission is concerned, the general understanding is that it happens out there, in other parts of the world, especially among the so-called unreached people groups. Of course, there is some sense in this. This is part of the legacy of the era of European Christendom when to be a European was to be a Christian and, to some extent, to be Christian was to be European. In this context of Christendom, mission and evangelism happened among the 'heathendom, papists, and Mohammedans', as William Carey put it.[2] Evangelists and missionaries were never needed in Britain when everyone was believed to be a Christian. That is why the history of world mission since the late 1700s is full of British names who left their homes in Britain to serve Christ overseas. We speak with a sense of pride about the great achievements of people like William Carey, Robert Moffat, David Livingstone, Hudson Taylor, Mary Slessor, and many others on the mission field overseas. The rise of the British colonial empire in Asia and Africa in the nineteenth century to a considerable extent overshadowed the great work that British missionaries were doing around the world. Yet, when the colonial empire collapsed, Christianity had been planted in most of the British colonies in Africa as well as in parts of India.

One of the British mission theologians of the twentieth century was Lesslie Newbigin (1909–1998). Newbigin went to India in 1936 and served there as a missionary for 38 years, being the bishop of the South India Church for an extended period. During his time in India he encountered a missionary situation that was resistant to Christianity, and this opened his eyes to the realities of missionary work. When he returned to England after nearly 40 years in India, he was shocked to find that the Christian Britain that had sent him to India was now secular.[3] He was further shocked that most British Christians did not even realize that Britain was no longer Christian. He would later say that the situation he met back in Britain was worse than that which he saw in India. In his autobiography he describes the British situation in no uncertain terms. 'It [the ministry] is much harder than anything I met in India. There is a cold contempt for the Gospel [in England], which is harder to face than opposition.'[4] He would later continue, 'England is a pagan society, and the development of a truly missionary encounter with this very tough form of paganism is the greatest and practical task facing the church.'[5] Though public institutions and popular culture in Britain, like those of Europe and North America, no longer made people culturally Christian, the British church still ran its ministries assuming that a stream of traditionally moral people who looked favourably upon Christianity would simply show up in services, eager to join and belong. Evangelization and mission were still thought of as activities with which churches engaged in far-away unevangelized lands overseas. Newbigin realized that the church in the West had not adapted to the secular reality of its context. As such, he argued that the Western Church had to become completely missionary in its own context if it were to be engaged with the non-Christian society surrounding it. It needed to develop a missiology for the western post-modern culture just as it had done for other unevangelized cultures.

The secular England that he returned to in 1974 forced Newbigin out of his retirement. He would devote the next 24 years of his life articulating a contextually relevant missionary theology for the West which would start a ripple in theological conversations around the world that, in the opinion of this writer, has yet to be fully realized.[6] His books *Foolishness to the Greeks*[7] and *The Gospel in a Pluralistic Society*[8] received a warm acceptance among many scholars worldwide and thereby opened a wider audience to his theology of mission. His exegesis of the western culture was astonishingly accurate. He did not shy away from criticizing the influence of the Enlightenment and modernity on western Christianity.[9] The themes in his theology of mission have drawn interest from many other mission scholars. In the early 1980s, Newbigin had been involved with a British Council of Churches programme, The Gospel and Our Culture, which laid the foundation for the book *The Other Side of 1984*. His influence remains, although, to some extent, his observation of Britain as a mission field is forgotten. The United Kingdom has become even more secular since Newbigin's return from India. Both the British Social Attitudes Survey and the National Census have been very clear on the declining numbers of Christians in the UK. Christianity has been losing adherents for decades and efforts to slow down or reverse the haemorrhage have mostly been unsuccessful. Census figures for 1991, 2001 and 2011 reflect rather clearly that the numbers of those who identify as Christians are not holding up – falling from 72 per cent in 2001 to 59 per cent in 2011. The British Social Attitudes survey of 2016 concluded that the number of people in England and Wales who identify themselves as having no religious affiliation has reached 49 per cent, exceeding – for the first time – those who self-identified as Christians at 44 per cent.[10]

African Christians to the rescue

Christian mission is migratory in nature.[11] It has been that way since its very early days. It remains the same today. It is in this sense that Christianity spread rather easily along the trade routes of the Roman Empire, using the Greek language that was spoken in most of its cities. It does the same today, following the migration trends precipitated by the politics of the global economy, which of course includes the selling of higher education, the need push and pull factors of labour export and import, the ease of international travel, and migration laws in many countries. For many African Christians, the English language is usually not a major problem. The British colonial empire prepared the way. It was in the early decades of the twentieth century, in the glory days of European colonialism in Africa, that Christianity was successfully planted in the continent. By the mid-twentieth century, Christianity had started to show signs of waning in Britain while it was beginning to explode in Africa. When we get to the end of the century, Africa had become predominantly Christian and was beginning to send back missionaries to the West.

Following the collapse of European colonization of Africa in the 1960s, many Africans began to come to Europe. Access to western education as well as the general European life was a major factor. Longstanding migration patterns that had seen Europeans migrate to the world for 450 years began to slow down and, within a short time, started to reverse as people from the colonies and the wider rest of the world found their ways to the West. With these, many more African churches emerged in Britain.[12] These congregations were particularly grounded in 'the social and religious traditions of the African communities from which they draw most of their members'.[13] In 1964, the first African Independent Church, the Church of the Lord, *Aladura*, emerged in the UK, led by the late Primate Adeleke Adejobi.[14] Since then, thousands of African congregations have mushroomed across the UK. Every major town and city in the UK will have more than a handful of African congregations – Nigerian, Ghanaian, Zimbabwean and many other nationalities.

By the 1980s the migration of Africans to the UK was beginning to grow steadily. As a result, African Pentecostal denominations also started to establish their congregations in the country. A good example of those is the Redeemed Christian Church of God (RCCG), a Nigerian Pentecostal church that was registered in the UK in 1989. It has 200,000 members in 1,000 congregations scattered across the UK. Three in four of these congregations are in England, and half of them are in the south east, with a special concentration in London. When they gather in the London ExCel centre for prayer vigils, which they do at least twice a year, more than 50,000 people show up. They seek to 'plant churches within five minutes walking distance in every city and town of developing countries and within five minutes driving distance in every city and town of developed countries'.[15] To fulfil this vision, they attempt to plant 50 new churches every year. Another Pentecostal denomination from Ghana, the Church of Pentecost, also registered in 1989, has grown in its presence in the UK, having around 160 congregations (largely concentrated in England as well). These two are just the largest among the numerous smaller denominations, networks and associations of African churches in Europe and North America; Christ Apostolic Church (Nigeria), Winners' Chapel (Nigeria), Living Waters (Malawi), Deeper Life (Nigeria), Light House Chapel (Ghana), the Apostolic Faith Mission (South Africa), to mention but a few. In addition, there are thousands of independent nondenominational congregations of African origin in the UK. For example, Kingsway International Christian Centre (KICC), one of the largest churches in the UK, was established in 1992 and is led by a Nigerian, Matthew Ashimolowo, and claims to have over 12,000 members.

This is our land

In 2013, I served as a mission consultant for a network of Zimbabwean congregations in England. The network had formed of a group of congregations that had just broken away from the Apostolic Faith Mission (AFM), a South African Pentecostal denomination with a strong presence in Zimbabwe. As a young network of African congregations, they were keen to harness all their energy to grow their membership. As a result, they were absolutely focused on evangelism. To show their commitment to evangelizing their cities, every time they got together they chanted in English:

This is our territory
This is our land
Devil, move over
This is our city.

Since then, they have continued to declare every Sunday that England is their territory, their land and their country. The chant continues to be an anthem for the entire network, which has now become much larger. Hundreds of African Christians declaring that England is their land is the story of evangelism in the mission field of Britain. The political nature of the chant has not of course been missed at all, and to some extent has hampered their evangelism efforts. A government official once asked them, 'Who are you to say that this is your city?' Some locals have expressed concerns over the militant tone of the song – it sounds as if these Africans have come to claim rights to the land that belongs to the British, like Cecil Rhodes did in Zimbabwe in the late 1800s. The irony is hard to miss and it touches people's raw emotions – the song exemplifies reverse colonialism.[16] For them, though, the anthem is a powerful spiritual chant – a prophetic declaration – that chases the enemy forces that keep people in darkness and allows them to claim God's promise that 'every place on which you set foot shall be yours' (Deuteronomy 11.24). The whole endeavour, from their planting of new churches to their prayer vigils, the establishing of food banks and their claiming 'this is our city', is shaped for 'evangelism'.

Unpacking the story: African lived missiology in the UK

In the early years of the twenty-first century, a saying has emerged in Britain that says, 'London Christianity is a black religion.' Others joke that, in terms of Christianity, 'As Lagos goes, so does London.'[17] There is some truth in these riddles. The spiritual revival going on in sub-Saharan Africa inevitably leads to an increase in Christianity in the UK, even when mainline white British Christians continue their exodus from the Church. African Christians make up a considerable part of British Christianity today. London Christianity as a whole, not only migrant congregations in London, depends on migration. Without the migration of Christians from the current Christian heartlands of Africa, Asia and Latin America, the decline in European Christianity would be more pronounced. This means that migrant Christians in the UK, including Africans, must bear some responsibility for the engagement in mission in our cities. The future of UK missions and, to some extent, of UK Christianity as a whole, depends on migrant Christians taking seriously their missionary calling to the UK. African missiology in the UK is characterized by its focus on evangelism and the power of the Spirit of God. In the end, of course, African missionaries in the UK have yet to contextualize their approach for the UK population, their post-Christian worldview and their religious needs in general. I will now discuss the two key hallmarks of African missiology in the UK.

Evangelism-focused missiology

Not many African Christians in the UK sing 'This Is Our Land', but they all take evangelism as seriously. They often speak about evangelizing their cities while, just like the wider British Christian population, they think of mission as something that happens elsewhere. They call themselves 'the missionaries that God has sent to the UK for such a time as this', but they limit their sense of mission activities to evangelism and food banks. Thus they primarily think of themselves as evangelists. Many of them will engage in evangelism, especially giving out gospel tracts on the high street. Of course, this kind of evangelism does not yield much fruit here but they do it anyway because it is what worked in Africa. In these days of the cost-of-living crisis, food banks have become even more popular. These reflect an awareness of the need to engage with the hurting in their communities, but of course they do not give them easy pathways to converting people.

This emphasis on evangelism among African Pentecostals is grounded in two key convictions: the fact that they believe Jesus is about to return, and that they will get rewards in heaven for saving people. Indeed, for many African Pentecostals, the delayed *parousia* is finally about to be resolved – the trumpet will soon be blown and Jesus is about to appear.[18] Their theology on the return of Christ is shaped, to a large extent, by their reading of Peter's appropriation of Joel's prophecy (Joel 2.28) in Acts 2 (verse 24), where he replaces Joel's 'And afterwards' with 'In the last days'. They believe that the last days started at Pentecost. Living in the twenty-first century, 2,000 years after Pentecost, means we are in the very last of the last days – often described as the very last few seconds of the eleventh hour, right before midnight when Christ will appear.[19]

Spirit-empowered missiology

When they declare 'This is our land', these African Christians are not making a political statement, even though the statement may carry those overtones. For them, the declaration is a prophetic utterance that establishes things in the Spirit first, before they are manifested in the material world. This missiology is grounded in the African understanding of the world. For most African peoples, the entire human life-journey, from the cradle to the grave, is one continuous religious adventure, punctuated by moments of intense spiritual activity including puberty, marriage, child-bearing and, indeed, death. It is, generally speaking, impossible to separate African culture from African religion. In most African societies, religion shapes all life and, conversely, all of life revolves around religion. This expansive African religious heritage creates a culture in which people pay attention to the unseen world of spirits – including the Supreme Being (or god) who is above all a Spirit, in addition to the many created good and evil spirits and ancestral spirits. An African traditional life is impossible without a continuous engagement with the spirit-world of the invisible. This is what informs their missiology. Whatever mission they conceive of is first understood as spiritual wrestling with the powers and principalities that dominate this land. The main thrust of the song says, 'Devil, move over.' As the devil moves over (sic) the land is liberated for Christ and the kingdom of God is made manifest. A missiology that is shaped by such an understanding of the world will be rooted in fervent prayer, for it is through the exercise of fasting and night vigils that the spirits dominating a land are chased away.

When done in Africa, this understanding of mission and evangelism is deeply connected to the performing of miracles. In line with African traditional religious thought, the god that can provide for its people and heal them of their diseases is the one that must be followed. Among African Pentecostals, the power of the Spirit of God is seen when people are miraculously healed or provided for.[20] Throughout sub-Saharan Africa, it was Reinhard Bonnke's healing crusades that accelerated the growth of the Church in the 1980s and 1990s. Of course, those crusades were famously grounded in the ministry of intercession that gathered strong praying communities to make the miracles happen. Here in the UK, however, this aspect of their ministries fails to deliver. Yes, God still heals but the people are not necessarily looking for healing, at least not from God. Even the message of provision, which emphasizes that God provides for people and, in some cases, wants them to prosper materially, is not attractive to many UK people. As such, there is often a disconnect between what the Africans offer and what their neighbours are looking for – between their missiology and the needs of the context in which they are working. Their prayers may be transforming the spiritual atmospheres of their cities, but they are not translating into conversions among their non-African neighbours and are certainly not bringing white people into their congregations. This highlights the limitations of their spirit-empowered missiology in this Enlightenment-shaped context.

Challenges facing African missiology in the UK

The life of an African missionary in the UK is not trouble-free. This explains why, even though many Africans believe themselves to be missionaries, most of them end up in the migrant churches of other Africans. These churches, usually divided along national identities, come into being as a result of the disconnection between the ecclesiologies of African communities and their missionary expectations in the UK. If they are not their first choice when it comes to finding a place of worship, it is often the last, and once they have found it they settle. There are many factors to this. Here we will look at just four of these.

Communication

It is often difficult for African migrants to integrate into local communities in their new host societies in the UK. There remain some deep-seated systemic tensions that lead to suspicion, one against the other. In most cases, racism and anti-immigration convictions among some locals make it hard for Africans to assimilate. Further, communication styles differ greatly between the two groups. While there is a great passion and fervency in the way most Africans pray and minister, a greater part of the impact from these is lost in translation. Even negotiating communication styles that are understandable to their neighbours is a challenge for many. Cultural norms like the length of the worship service and the sermon make a big difference. While it is common to spend more than two hours in a church service in African churches, a typical UK worship service generally lasts no longer than 90 minutes. This is a huge cultural barrier that must be negotiated if immigrant churches are to connect with local Christians.

Theology/missiology

Andrew Walls observes that the representative theology of this century may as well be African.[21] Of course, it may be more non-western than just African. Most of it will be charismatic and conservative, dominated by the voices of the southern hemisphere and Asia. Many such expressions of theology are suspicious of western theology, which was shaped greatly by the Enlightenment and modernity. Feminist theology rightly argues for recognition of the fact that western theology is male-dominated, and it is opening up space for women to have a voice. Liberation theology rose in the face of oppression under the hierarchical structures within the Catholic tradition in Latin America. Black Theology, from the Americas and South Africa, is a theological reflection of black people's understanding of God. African theology has emerged in the context of colonialism, neo-colonialism, poverty, exploitation, globalization, corrupt leadership, diseases, among many uniquely African social issues. African missiology follows in the footsteps of these theologies, to image a way of talking about God and mission that is shaped by African cultural sensibilities. Such a missiology will look different from that of the UK.

Essentially, there is – and must be – a difference in the way Africans read scripture from that of the West. While UK theology continues a 2,000-year heritage mediated through science and reason in Enlightenment and modernity, contemporary African theology is 70 years old. Certainly, a missiology born among colonized peoples, struggling with poverty and diseases, articulates a God that identifies with those at the margins. African Christianity as a whole has exploded among the poor. To a great extent, then, an African missiology should lead migrant Christians in the UK to a closer identification with those at the margins on the UK community. Mission, in this theology, transcends the works of charity to the poor. It seeks ways to be with and among those in need. This is, generally speaking, different from the wider UK mission endeavours that are shaped for middle-class living. When done well, this theology allows African church plants to happen in lower-income areas. For instance, in my neighbourhood in Liverpool, which is low-income, I have seen three intentional church-plant attempts between 2017 and 2022. They realize that the poor are also called to follow Jesus.

Politics of immigration

Immigration is always a highly sensitive political issue these days. In 2023 we are having an intense discussion about how to deal with the *problem* of migrants. Anti-immigration sentiments form a major part of the political agenda leading up to every election. Even those migrants who are legally living in the UK usually live with the struggle of prejudice against them. The growing cultural diversity in the UK is a source of major concern for those who worry about the growing population of migrants in the country. Migration from Africa is targeted.[22] Of course, work permits for Christian ministers of religion from Africa are almost impossible to get. The UK, like most western countries, does not recognize missionaries as 'professionals' worth a work permit. As a result of all this, African Christians must seek to always be on the right side of the law, even though this is extremely expensive. Pastors as well as members are usually deported for staying illegal. Many African denominations have got around this by sending bi-vocational professionals to lead their congregations in diaspora. The West is a creative-access mission field for them. Many West African churches, for example, make use of medical doctors with legitimate work permits in their fields to plant and lead churches.

Church versus cultural centre

Finally, there is the problem of identity. Many African migrant congregations identify themselves as churches and places where the mission of God is carried out. However, for many of the members, migrant churches are social places where they can find a home away from home. They become small cultural enclaves where news and food from home are shared. Worse than that, at times they become gossip mills where people update one another on the current affairs in their communities. It is common knowledge among some migrant communities that if one wants to hear whose marriage is having problems, they just need to go to church. It follows, then, that since they are perceived as social gathering spaces for nursing homeland nostalgia, one does not necessarily have to be a Christian to belong. Therefore it is hard to really press for Christian morality and responsibility from the congregants. This makes their missionary work difficult. They cannot reach their societies without a clear identity of what it is they are called to do.

Moving forward

In this twenty-first century, mission in the UK will include the works of many non-western peoples trying to make sense of how to re-evangelize the country. To a small extent, we are already seeing this beginning to happen. Jehu Hanciles has suggested that western Christianity in this century will depend largely on the impact of the many Christians that are migrating from the southern hemisphere and Asia to Europe and North America.[23] In this case, the currently dominant missional conversations in the UK must engage the voices of those non-westerners living and working among them. It has to be noted that the missionary congregation conversation here in the UK was started by a *stranger* in the person of Lesslie Newbigin, who came back from almost 40 years of missionary work in India. That conversation today could be greatly enhanced if this engagement with a stranger's voice could be sustained.

For African Christians, the attempt to evangelize the UK will be a difficult one. The cultural differences are rather too big to be ignored. There will be a great need for intentionality in the way that they engage their UK neighbours. Certainly, there is need to study the UK culture and language, just like the western missionaries did in Africa and other places. It is quite probable that as we move further into the century there will be missionary training available for non-western missionaries in the West. Non-western missionaries will begin to articulate the anthropology of the western peoples. The West will be forced to look at itself through the strangers' eyes. This is the reversed gaze.

As globalization and postmodernity get further entrenched in western culture, there will be more room created for intercultural dialogue. This will make possible further non-threatening spaces for majority-world Christians to learn how best to engage the West. While postmodernity encourages the West to listen to the 'other', it does so in a way that most non-western Christians would need to learn. The dynamics of communication, especially with the stranger, are critical for missionary engagement in the UK. Many Africans sound judgemental and unwilling to listen to UK Christians, whom they condemn as belonging to a dead form of Christianity.

There will also be a great need for UK Christians to make ways for their non-western counterparts to do mission work in the country. Instead of treating them as inconvenient foreigners and economic refugees, which is what most people do, they need to look at them as co-labourers in the mission field. In many cases, when western churches are overflowing with resources, the immigrant churches are struggling with poverty. UK leaders will need to learn ways to be hospitable to such needy churches. Some of that learning will happen as they share resources like worship spaces.

It is also important that non-western Christians muster their courage enough to share their voice with their western counterparts, even when doing so risks their very existence. In sharing their convictions, they offer a critique to UK Christians to listen to global theology. But this is a two-way street. Non-western theologians also need to listen to western theology. That is how they will learn how best to have a conversation with western Christians.

Conclusion

Within the past century, Christianity has moved from being a western religion to becoming a global one. Even though many UK Christians still think that the West is at the centre of Christianity and its theology, the truth is that the centre of gravity for the religion has been spread into many cities and villages in the southern hemisphere and Asia. In the same way, the centre for missionary activity and missionary-sending is also slowly catching up with the southward shift. It is in this context that Africa, which is mostly in its second Christian century, is sending missionaries to all the other continents. This will continue for the foreseeable future because, of course, it is impossible for the UK to stop migration of Africans entirely. When they come, they bring with them an African expression of Christianity that places great emphasis on evangelism and the power of the Holy Spirit. This essay points us towards a future when Africans serving as missionaries in the UK is not strange. It is my hope that the African missiology discussed here also begins to be heard in the missiological conversations of the UK missions landscape.

Notes

1 The Evangelical Alliance UK, 'Talking Jesus Report', https://talkingjesus.org/.

2 W. Carey, 1961, *An Enquiry into the Obligations of Christians to Use Means for the Conversion of the Heathens*, London: Carey Kingsgate.

3 D. L. Stults, 2009, *Grasping Truth and Reality: Lesslie Newbigin's theology of mission to the western world*, Cambridge: James Clarke, pp. 35–6.

4 L. Newbigin, 1985, *Unfinished Agenda: An autobiography*, Geneva: WCC Publications, p. 249.

5 Newbigin, *Unfinished Agenda*, p. 249.

6 Newbigin's theology of the Spirit (which was perhaps influenced by his experiences in India) has yet to find a place in western theology. The western interpreters of Newbigin have not fully engaged this aspect of his missional theology.

7 L. Newbigin, 1986, *Foolishness to the Greeks: The Gospel and western culture*, Grand Rapids, MI: Eerdmans.

8 L. Newbigin, 1989, *The Gospel in a Pluralist Society*, Grand Rapids, MI: Eerdmans.

9 See L. Newbigin, 1983, *The Other Side of 1984: Questions for the Churches*, Geneva: WCC Press.

10 See the British Social Attitudes Survey 36, 'Religion', https://natcen.ac.uk/sites/default/files/2023-08/BSA_36.pdf, accessed 06.06.2024.

11 See J. J. Hanciles, 2021, *Migration and the Making of Global Christianity*, Grand Rapids, MI: Eerdmans.

12 I. Olofinjana, 2015, *Partnership in Mission: A Black Majority Church perspective on mission and church unity*, Watford: Instant Apostle, p. 16.

13 G. ter Haar, 1998, *Halfway to Paradise: African Christians in Europe*, Cardiff: Cardiff Academic Press, pp. 94–5.

14 Olofinjana, *Partnership in Mission*, p. 26.

15 The Redeemed Christian Church of God, 'Mission and Vision', https://www.rccg.org/mission-and-vision/, accessed 06.06.2024. Also see J. J. Hanciles, 2008, *Beyond Christendom: Globalization, African migration, and the transformation of the West*, Maryknoll, NY: Orbis Books, pp. 354–7.

16 Given the colonial entanglements of European mission in Africa in the twentieth century – the history of Christianity in Zimbabwe bears great testimony to this – and the British awareness of that history – a few thousand British farmers once owned 60 per cent of all productive land in Zimbabwe – Zimbabwean Christians declaring that England is their land is unnecessarily provocative. See B. Raftopoulos and A. Mlambo, 2009, *Becoming Zimbabwe: A history from the pre-colonial period to 2008*, Johannesburg: Jacana, p. 170.

17 I have heard this said numerous times, almost always with negative connotations. However, Africans take it with pride. They celebrate the fact that their Christianity is quite visible in London.

18 A Malawian preacher friend of mine has, for the past 40 years, started all his sermons with a strong statement that, while he looks forward to the ministry at the end of his sermon, he hopes his preaching will be interrupted by Jesus' return (which he expects could happen at *any moment*). He encourages people to believe that Jesus' return is by far much better than anything he could ever wish for – it brings an end to the need for him to pray for people.

19 On this belief, Lazarus Chakwera (the current president of Malawi), being one of the key mission leaders in Africa, formed a missions academy in the late 1990s called The Eleventh-Hour Institute'; its purpose was to prepare and send missionaries from southern Africa to the rest of the world, beginning with North Africa where Christian populations are very small. See L. McCarthy Chakwera, 2000, 'The development of the Eleventh Hour Institute to be utilized as a means of mobilizing, training, and sending missions workers from Malawi and nearby countries to unreached peoples', Unpublished Doctor of Ministry Thesis, Trinity International University.

20 There are numerous African Pentecostal denominations that still believe that true faith means that they do not take medicine when sick. The Apostolic Church of Nigeria, with seven congregations in the UK, is a good example. Many of their young people, especially in Nigeria, are discouraged from studying anything to do with health.

21 C. Fyfe and A. F. Walls, 1996, *Christianity in Africa in the 1990s*, Edinburgh: Centre of African Studies University of Edinburgh, pp. 139–48.

22 Paul Seddon, 2023, 'Many foreign students to lose right to bring family to UK', *BBC News*, 24 May, https://www.bbc.co.uk/news/uk-politics-65683046,

accessed 06.06.2024. While this seems to include all foreign students, Nigerians were singled out for 'bringing to the UK their dependents during their study, hoping that they can stay in the country when done'.

23 Hanciles, *Migration and the Making of Global Christianity*, Introduction.

6

Second-generation Nigerian-British and Contextual Mission in Britain

BISI ADENEKAN

Mission must be about building relationships. If you have the same compassion of Jesus, that deep compassion and you are like, 'I want to know about you and what's going on in your life', you will be very surprised how many people actually open up. [Apostle] Paul didn't give out leaflets, they just went into the fold and like ... said, you make it personal to people. It is about how you make people feel. (SG focus group, London, 2018)

Introduction

This quotation captures the viewpoint of second-generation (SG) Nigerian-British who participated in my doctoral research about the strategies that Nigerian Pentecostal churches (NPCs) in Europe utilize in the effort to establish multi-ethnic and truly multicultural congregations. Until recently, academic studies on African migration and spirituality have focused mainly on the perspectives of the first-generation (FG). Over the past four decades, however, their children and grandchildren, who have different life experiences, have grown in population, age and social mobility. There is therefore the need for academic studies that give more attention to their narratives when discussing diaspora Pentecostal Christianity. Increasingly, a number of studies have emerged focused on different aspects of the lives of the SG.[1] In particular, Caleb Nyanni's monograph, *Second-Generation African Pentecostals in the West* focused on Ghanaian FG and SG members of the Church of Pentecost (CoP) and some of the conflicting views between them regarding spirit beliefs.[2] My doctoral research investigated more broadly the perspectives of second-generation Nigerians on mission and other beliefs and practices of their parents, the inter-generational differences that arise and the impact on the SG's spirituality and mission proclivities.

Historically, Nigerian church planting in the UK can be traced to the 1960s. These were churches established first to cater for a growing number of Nigerians who had left a postcolonial and post-civil war era in their country, as well as migrants from other African and Caribbean communities. The initial wave of Nigerian church planting was the *Aladura*-type African Independent Churches (AICs), the foremost being the Cherubim and Seraphim (C&S) and the Christ Apostolic Church, which generally grew across the European religious scene in the 1960s and have continued to grow.[3] This was followed in the 1980s by neo-Pentecostal churches like the Redeemed Christian Church of God (RCCG), Winners Chapel, House on the Rock (HOTR) and so on – which were branches of denominations with Nigerian headquarters. The next wave was initiated from the 1990s by individuals who had migrated either for secular employment, to further their education, or as missionaries from Nigerian-origin denominations. These Nigerians then founded 'independent' churches that had no connection with any sending denomination at home or elsewhere. The foremost in the UK is Kingsway International Christian Centre[4] and most Nigerian churches are still largely populated and led by this founding generation. Although their children have been religiously socialized, both at home and through regular church participation over the years, they do not yet constitute an effective majority in leadership. In these congregations, 'home' belief systems and leadership styles predominated (and still prevail) among the mostly Nigerian members, which implied little or no need for contextualization.

With the growth and expansion of NPCs over the years, the second group of people they aspired (and still aspire) to evangelize were White Europeans. This is the concept of reverse mission, and it implies a historic shift in the direction of mission both geographically and in terms of power dynamics. That is, a reversal in the geographical direction of mission and in the direction of colonization such that the formerly colonized and missionized now return to evangelize generations of the former colonizers and missionaries.[5] In the case of Nigerian and other African Pentecostals, the limited level of success of reverse mission, in terms of membership by White westerners, remains a matter of academic debate.[6] Several reasons have been given for this limited achievement. For example, Nigerian Pentecostals in my study blame the 'devil' for stopping White people from being 'converted' to Pentecostalism. In that way, it is interpreted as a spiritual battle that needs continuous prayer for peoples' deliverance so that the 'weapons' being used to hinder the salvation of souls will be destroyed. Other participants point to the Enlightenment[7] and postmodernism, with the intellectual and cultural worldviews woven around these ideas, as possible culprits. Nevertheless, participants say they will remain committed to reverse mission even if their efforts have not yet yielded the desired results. They argue that, as people of faith, they will continue praying and engaging in street campaigns until they see results. As missional churches, Nigerian Pentecostal churches see themselves as 'called' to global evangelism and are convinced of their God-ordained role in reversing what they see as a trend of declining church membership and participation in the West. However, without contextualization, this aspiration to bring the 'intractable', formerly Christian, West back to Christianity will remain a challenge. As I suggest elsewhere,[8] power structures, beliefs systems, leadership styles and approaches to mission are important factors undermining Nigerian reverse missionary aspirations. As John Corrie[9] notes, maintaining familiar and traditional ways of thinking and using the tried and tested paradigm of mission, based on convictions and attitudes that seek to do mission as it had been done in the past, leads to lack of missional progress. This corroborates the views of some of the young participants in my study, who argue for 'a change of ideology, approach and agenda'. In other words, there is a need to adapt and adopt practices that resonate with others. As one SG participant noted,

> instead of focusing on the White generation of today, focus on some of my friends between the age of 18 and 30. Most of my Black friends who were raised from about the age of nine or ten in London/Amsterdam have almost the same attitudes to evangelism, Christianity, miracles, faith, as our White Dutch and English friends.[10]

A third and more recent focus of mission for NPCs is retaining their children (now grown adults) in church. Some SG participants express frustration at the continued 'Nigerianization' of these churches, describing some practices and liturgy as recycled religion. They express frustration and disappointment about the difficulty of effecting and influencing change and identify this as one of the reasons why young people leave Nigerian churches. This essay discusses ways of engaging the second-generation in mission, premised on the reimagination of mission and the construction of well-resourced systems and internal structures. This is aimed at suggesting ways that NPCs can critically engage with the SGs' lived realities to create new forms of epistemologies for mission. It gives a background of the involvement of European empires, colonizers and Christian missionaries in spreading the gospel in colonized Africa generally and its impact on the emergence of Christianity. Using the case of Nigeria, the chapter briefly discusses how Christianity came to Nigeria through the efforts of Western European missionaries and liberated slaves like Bishop Ajayi Crowther and how this history shaped, directly or indirectly, Nigerian Christianity in general and Pentecostalism in particular. Based on my ethnographic doctorate research,[11] the chapter discusses the beliefs of the first-generation[12] and second-generation[13] in relation to mission. Considering the limited success of reverse mission to date, I ask whether the SG could become instrumental in achieving the aspiration of Nigerian church leaders for multi-ethnic churches.

Empire and missionaries

According to historians, Protestant missionaries and churchmen were fatally compromised and corrupted by their dealings with slavery in the seventeenth and eighteenth centuries.[14] With the abolition of the Atlantic slave trade in 1807, colonial economies changed over to an economy based on the exportation of agricultural products – palm oil from Nigeria, groundnuts from Senegal and Gambia and cocoa from the Gold Coast (Ghana) – as well as importation of finished products from Europe.[15] By 1880, limited areas of Africa had come under the direct rule of Europeans, mostly along the coastlines to enforce the prohibition of slave trade. These gradually became outposts for European commercial interests and considerable influence and direct political control. In a rapid turn of events, between 1890 and 1910, almost 100 per cent of the world's second-largest continent had been conquered and occupied.[16] European governments scrambled to colonize African nations as their satellites, which was later formalized with the Berlin conference of 1887. However, prior to the conference, Christian missionaries had arrived and were active in many African nations.

In Nigeria, the Anglican Church Mission Society (CMS; the largest and most significant of the societies), the Wesleyan Methodist Mission Society, the Foreign Mission Committee of the United Presbyterian Church of Scotland, the Foreign Mission Board of the Southern Baptist Convention of the United States and the Catholic Society of African Missions of France (Société des Missions Africaines, SMA) were active. They established mission churches in many towns and cities between 1846 and 1855, which were run by European missionaries assisted by Nigerians and returnee liberated slaves from Sierra Leone.[17] In other parts of Africa the missionaries worked to convert the people by building schools like the Fourah Bay College founded in 1827 in Sierra, while schools were built in Ghana, Nigeria and other parts of Africa in addition to mission churches. These changes had hitherto posed no threat to the sovereignty and independence of African nations and until 1891, according to Jacob Ajayi, a dialogue was still possible between missionaries and the different communities and there was room for ideas and influence of different personalities on both sides. With increasing difficulty to dialogue, the relationship changed and resulted in secession from western mission churches and eventually, political independence.[18]

Towards the end of the nineteenth century, lay leaders broke away and started indigenous churches that had Nigerian leadership.[19] These set the pace for churches like Cherubim and Seraphim through the emergence of charismatic leaders like Moses Orimolade Tunolase and Joseph Babalola in the 1920s. These were referred to as '*Aladura*'[20] churches because of their focus on prayers. This movement produced the founders of most Nigerian Pentecostal Churches in their various forms, either directly or through the tutelage of these early founders.[21] As Adogame explained, 'The need for Christian expression which is influenced by African culture, traditions and experiences led to the development of some African theologies such as Liberation, African and Black theologies.'[22] These theologies shaped African spirituality in Africa and were 'carried along' by migrants to destination countries. Scholars note that similar continuity occurred in other African countries and enabled the preservation of traditional religious beliefs and practices such as spirit beliefs among Pentecostals. One example, according to Anderson, is the belief in an ontological world of spirits, witchcraft and manipulating forces that must be conquered through deliverance prayers.[23] This is a pneumatology that the SG in my study do not share and, as Nyanni articulated in the Ghanaian case, 'young people not only analyse events spiritually but also logically, adding that this differentiates their understanding and perception of the spirit world from that of their parents'.[24]

The empirical study

My doctoral research, which investigated NPCs' aspiration for multi-ethnic congregations, used three Nigerian *Yorùbá*-initiated churches – The Redeemed Christian Church of God, House on the Rock and Winners Chapel – as case studies. These denominations have their headquarters in Nigeria and maintain branches globally (the RCCG is reportedly represented in about 200 countries). A branch of each denomination was selected in London and Amsterdam for comparative purposes. This chapter is drawn from field work which used a qualitative approach and engaged with the views of church leaders and members (both the older FG and younger SG). The data presented in this study represents the perspectives of study participants and not necessarily all Nigerian/

Nigerian-British Pentecostals. Interviews, focus groups (with about 70 participants) and extensive participant observation were used. The aim was to gain an insight into their efforts to attract non-Africans, and the theological and social factors that shape their evangelistic practices. Geographical location, denominational differences, gender, generation, and member/leader status were taken into consideration. In addition, I observed patterns that emerged in participants' stories and, coupled with my observations and analysis, I endeavoured to present information that is as insightful as possible. As an analytical framework, André Droogers' three-dimensional model of power dynamics, where power is seen as present in any religious organization, was employed.[25] Data was thematically analysed and some of the themes are discussed below.

Nigerian Pentecostal beliefs, practices and conflicts

For Nigerian Pentecostals, prayer covers all areas of everyday life. To them, prayer is the act of turning to a higher Being (God) and petitioning him for something or someone. They see it as a two-way communication with God, with the total confidence that he hears and answers prayers. They support these assertions with some Bible verses[26] to show that not only is it God's commandment, but prayer is also important and efficacious and there are ways to pray. An interviewee said that, 'We [first-generation] pray vigorously, very loudly and very aggressively because we believe that is how prayers are answered.'[27] The RCCG includes praying as one of its practices, enjoining members that 'We are commanded to pray and not to faint, to pray without ceasing, to pray to receive all the goods "He" promised in "His" treasure for us and those who are unable to pray annoy God.'[28] Taken as transcendental, they describe it as the means to engage God in finding solutions to existential needs encountered in western societies and to establish relevance as individuals and minority communities. A pastor noted that 'a lot of the Africans within these churches are economic migrants with needs and their messages and prayers are usually focused on meeting those needs'.[29] SG participants also believe fervently in prayer but are critical of prayer styles and contents that concentrate excessively on addressing the existential needs of the majority FG congregation. Or deliverance prayers which are often presented combatively as a weapon for waging battles against (spiritual) enemies and their perceived diabolical influences on personal progress. However true the FG may believe this to be, SG participants contend that it has the potential to cloud the need to re-appraise other reasons – which may be non-spiritual – for lack of progress, whether in spiritual or secular endeavours. Missiologist Babatunde Adedibu asserts that occasionally it is an intertwining of Pentecostal and Nigerian traditional religious practices that often results in church communities that are centres for the 're-creation of *Yorùbá*/Nigerian/African dialectics'.[30] In other words, a theology of re-missionizing that presents God in a way that preserves Nigerian (Pentecostal) identity thereby restricting integration into British society. Nevertheless, prayer remains central to mission and while collecting data I participated in several virtual prayer meetings during the Covid-19 lockdowns (sometimes as early as 5.30 am) and ample time is often devoted to praying about the recruitment of new members.[31]

Worship through music and dance is another practice that Nigerian Pentecostals believe is divinely inspired to honour God. A common assertion is that when you pray, God hears and answers from heaven but when you worship and praise him, he comes down in your midst to 'inhabit your praise'. It is seen as an encounter with the divine presence and power of God. As observed during my doctoral research, worship involves singers and musicians leading the congregation in a series of gospel songs with dancing, usually for between 30 and 60 minutes. It is performed with exuberance and emotionality displayed through kneeling, jumping, crying, laughing and sporadic shouts. Participants argue that this follows the Bible pattern, which instructs believers to make a joyful noise unto the Lord (Psalm 100). One FG participant said that 'We older ones are being "touched" by heavy music because that is what we know.'[32] While participating in worship services, I observed congregants being encouraged to shout because praising God effectively requires noise and Christians should praise God with shouting.[33] Social behaviours are based on complicated socialization processes and this affinity for high volume was described as a transferred social behaviour from the Nigerian origin of members.

> [In Lagos, Nigeria], the horn is going, some people are shouting for customers, public address systems are blaring from loudspeakers' implying that [if you are not loud], 'the surrounding noise will overshadow what you are saying.[34]

This suggests the need for reappraisal and re-socialization since there are differences between the British and Nigerian contexts. Nienke (a White Dutch interviewee and partner of one Nigerian participant), recollected the first time she attended a RCCG worship service. She experienced the music more as a 'big noise' rather than singing.[35] SG participants agree that although they enjoy the music and dance, the choice of songs and high volume can be problematic, particularly for their non-African friends. While the cultural antecedents of the FG cannot be dismissed, there is need for inclusive practices within the British context. This calls for contextualization which demands creativity and intentionality in presentation so that even when directed by the Holy Spirit, the service appeals to different audiences while not compromising core beliefs.[36]

There is also the preaching of the Word, which Nigerian preachers often present as a message from God directly to the congregation thereby giving it a divine connotation. During an online message in 2021, the preacher was introduced as follows:

> Our daddy in the Lord, Daddy E. A. Adeboye will be bringing us the Word of solution from the throne of God, from above. [As you listen], the God of heaven will release solutions to you and your life will never be the same again.[37]

In the perception of SG participants and in a manner similar to prayers, the content and delivery are culturally influenced with messages oriented towards meeting the needs of the mainly older members. Imagery is vital in communication and the sermons often draw on the life-world and experiences of the dominant culture and cohort, which can sometimes exclude others. The SG attend and sometimes leave to become members of other churches like Hillsong,[38] which they claim is more youth friendly. For example, participants in a focus session compared the sermons at Hillsong to those of the Nigerian church of their parents and asserted that Hillsong had messages that were more practical.

> On our way home, we still think about things and discuss the issues raised, when I leave here [RCCG], I really do not understand the message. I think in Christianity you can also learn about life and how to approach it. In those churches [like Hillsong], they are very practical. I can relate to the message.[39]

The subjects that young people want addressed are not often given enough attention in Nigerian diaspora churches. Sade, a young undergraduate at the time, saw it as 'messages that are not often relatable to parts of the congregation and the context in which people live'.[40] Debby, another SG participant, said that, 'As someone who has been a Christian all my life, I frequently do not understand the sermons.'[41] Corroborating this assertion, one older participant, a senior leader in one of the case churches, agreed that discussing some of the issues confronting young people from Nigerian pulpits is 'almost taboo'. He gave an example of his experience when he visited a youthful church and what he found to be different.

> The pastor was talking about sex, and I realized that this is what the younger generation want to hear, whereas we would think that this is

not an issue to be talked about in a church. But this is what the young people are struggling with. The pastor afterwards told me they talk about three big things which most conventional churches do not talk about. These are sex, money and peer pressure.[42]

Additionally, the FG favour evangelism strategies that are people-facing or 'in-your-face',[43] such as street evangelism where church members stand at street corners preaching the gospel to passers-by, with or without loud-speakers. Leafleting (distribution of fliers which are promotional materials with a Christian message of salvation) and door-knocking (literally visiting and knocking on the doors of people's homes) are other forms. The SG in this study, on the other hand, conceive of evangelism in a relational sense, a process, not just occasional events. One SG participant of the London focus group argued that

> Conversations rather than leaflets [are more effective]. Speak to them first, find out how they are doing that day. I feel like we often rush into it [evangelism], like 'How many people can I evangelise today? Oh, I have done five, you have done six' but even one person [...]. Bring the church to them rather than them to the church [...]. We are going into the world to fish for men and that can be done. It is about restructuring the way that it is done.[44]

Evangelism should be complemented by social action or compassionate service within host communities in fulfilment of the 'Great Commandment'.[45] The huge financial resources and organization required for effective social action restricts this more to mega Pentecostal churches than small congregations.[46] The SG in my study, however, attribute the inability of small branches to engage in community action more to misplaced priorities.

> [The churches] are doing absolutely zero in that respect. We are in the centre of Amsterdam, which is the centre of smoking weed, teenage pregnancy and all; in the four years that I have been here, I don't think they've ever talked about smoking or pregnancy once, which is more important than tithe. If they talk about things like that, people around here will come because it is their everyday life.[47]

First-generation Nigerian church leaders that I spoke to for my doctorate insist that the inability to engage in social action is mostly due to insufficient resources. However, the SG view the limited engagement in social action as missed opportunities for evangelism, suggesting that churches may need to choose between expending available resources solely on pastoral care of members and other activities within the congregation or social projects externally within the community. The SG envision an expanded idea of mission that is holistic but also pays attention to the British context and contemporary societal issues. While acknowledging that many FG Nigerian Pentecostals are engaged in social action initiatives that pay attention to the British context, the SGs refer to smaller branches where they are members.

The struggle with power relations and leadership

In the preceding sections we have examined church liturgies and the impact on the missional success of Nigerian diaspora churches as they relate to the difficulty of retaining the SG and attracting White westerners. Clearly, there are inter-generational tensions between the SG and FG in terms of what mission is or should be, the approaches to reverse mission and the need to have more inclusive church liturgies. But what is the role of power and leadership in this call by the SG for contextualization?

Among Nigerian Pentecostals power in its centralized form takes a place of prominence, whether in administration and management of church institutions or for spiritual guidance of the congregation. Generally, in African societies, life and human existence are inextricably tied up with power and in such inherently hierarchic cultures churches reflect similar norms.[48] Among the *Yorùbá* people group, this power imbalance disproportionately affects women and young people, who are often at the bottom of the hierarchy. Pentecostal leaders argue, however, that administrative power and authority stem from Holy Spirit power. For example, the RCCG, using scripture citations in its Statement of Beliefs,[49] declares that the Bible commands believers to obey spiritual leaders and submit to them because rebellion is against the will of God and is punishable.[50] As discussed above, the traditional and cultural influences and spirit-oriented doctrines of diaspora churches, which are maintained by unbalanced power dynamics, were difficult for many second-generation Nigerian-British research participants to understand and accept. The problem is that it is theology that leaves little space for contextualization and adaptation of strategies because those who formulate the churches' vision statements are largely the FG, who are dominant in leadership. Although they define themselves as modern, enlightened and multicultural (which they are), many depend on Nigerian traditional and spiritual interpretations, based on certain core Nigerian Pentecostal beliefs and practices, in guiding diaspora congregations.[51]

The SG in my sample do not share a similar worldview because they are differently integrated, both educationally and culturally, within European societies. They contend that there is a need for attitudes and strategies that are relevant to their societies of birth/residence. This will require change to a leadership that is more representative of the followership. However, power relations within Nigerian Pentecostal churches remain controversial even among leaders. Pastor Agu Irukwu is the senior pastor of the RCCG Jesus House London and part of the first-generation himself, although more cosmopolitan.[52] He argues that the declining passion that is noticeable among young people is a result of lack of opportunity in leadership and he put it succinctly when he said:

> I realise that this institution [diaspora Pentecostal churches] was being suffocated by religion, traditions of men and culture; that this thing has become so strongly hierarchical that it has become like the civil service. If you served for a number of years, you moved forward. It was hierarchical, like a pyramid ... the way it had become, it had no room for young Davids and if it was so hierarchical, what chance do young Davids have except to join the queue but by the time it comes to their turn ... they were no longer young Davids.[53]

First-generation Nigerian Pentecostals in my sample view power as an attribute that is divinely bestowed on individuals by God for leadership. However, André Droogers suggests that sometimes leadership can be against the will of those who are led and rather can be for the achievement of goals that are often defined by the leader.[54] Contrary to the first-generation, the second-generation in this study argues that power structure characterized by hierarchical and patriarchal relations, which leaves policy and management decisions in the control of a few people, reflects the traditional Nigerian leadership style and is unacceptable in the British context. Relating issues of power management, ecclesiology (the nature and structure of these churches) and theology strictly to divine causality neglects the everyday lives of those with a different cultural background, upbringing and interpretations.

In addition to a change in power structure and the contextualization of beliefs and practices, the SG argue that Nigerian Pentecostal churches should engage with relevant societal issues. Rather than the liberationist theological antecedents of their parents, young people are interested in issues of social concern and social justice such as the environment, gender equality, human sexuality and racial inequalities. Additionally, a more pertinent theme for mission should be reaching and retaining young Nigerians who are steadily becoming disillusioned with aspects of Nigerian Pentecostal doctrine, rather than placing too much emphasis on intercultural mission. The SG would prefer to practise their faith in their birth countries as members of Nigerian congregations (because of the sense of belonging) but with the freedom to combine their spiritual encounters with their educational and technological exposures and trans-national social networks.

Conclusion: Innovative contextual missional insights and practices for the SG

This chapter focused on the challenges around church engagement of second-generation Nigerian-British individuals relative to the first-generation, and raised the question of how to empower the SG for more productive engagement in Christian mission in twenty-first-century Europe. The divergent views between the first- and second-generation on liturgy, mission, power and leadership discussed above emphasize the need for pragmatic suggestions. I conclude the chapter with the following suggestions based on my observations and interaction during my field work.

First, effective communication remains key to improved inter-generational relations. Lynne Lancaster and David Stillman (2002) explain[55] that a lack of understanding between generational cohorts, due to a lack of knowledge or appreciation of various cohort experiences, can create a generational gap in communication. This is exacerbated by the *Yorùbá* behavioural norm of respect for elders, which is seen by young people as an intimidating and subservient attitude. Additionally, it is a way of being that makes relating with their non-African peers difficult and antithetical to participation in non-African spaces. As Rijk Van Dijk found in his study of Malawian Pentecostal youth,[56] church activism that demystifies the spiritual connotations of power exercised by older people (geronto-cratic power) and lays a foundation for change is perhaps a way of creating channels of communication and encouraging exchange of ideas between church leaders and those they lead. In the opinion of the SG in my sample, directly addressing matters relating to leadership from the pulpit and actively training and appointing younger people to leadership are means of fostering better inter-generational communication. Further-more, investing in opportunities for young people to engage in intra- and inter-church discussions that address their lived spiritual realities in the context of Britain provides added value. This is because it allows space for them to generate and exchange ideas for reimagining mission in such a way that existing systems, structures and resources remain part of the solution.

Second, the mission practices that were effective when diaspora churches were founded are no longer as successful because of the change in demographics. In that period there was a regular flow of migrants from Africa who needed little convincing to become members because they found solace and support in the familiarity of African churches and community generally. Stringent migration policies within the continent and between Britain and continental Europe (since Brexit) have restricted the population of African migrants and reduced the pool of potential church members. There is therefore a need to broaden the search for new members from the host society who do not share a similar culture. The SG, who straddle both European and African cultures, are in a position to contribute to the development of strategies for creating multi-ethnic congregations, but as the SG in my study suggest, establishing them in the faith should be the first priority.

> [T]he fact is people are not born Christians and I think adults assume that because you have been raised in a Christian home, you are a Christian. You evangelise to people outside the church, but you do not evangelise your children just because they grew up with Christianity. That is probably the mistake the adults make.[57]

Third, although the SG are socialized in African culture, there are also conscious and subliminal influences which they imbibe from British society that affect their social, cultural and religious leanings. It could be argued that their religious worldview is neither exclusively that of their parents or even that of the society in which they grew up. The wider implications for the churches and for missiological discussions is the need to understand that the SG are quite westernized, with different religious and cultural expressions. Nigerian diaspora churches, and particularly the older first-generation members, do not seem to recognize that the SG are both indigenous Europeans and Africans. They have different religious and cultural expressions as enunciated in this chapter. Acknowledging this identity of young people will enable Nigerian and other African diaspora churches to equip them so that they can further the aspiration of reverse mission. As one participant advised, the work of the kingdom is inter-generational and is much bigger than any one generation and so the present generation of leaders should begin to prepare the next generation to finish what they, the FG, started very well.

Notes

1 R. Adebayo, 2018, 'The religion and spirituality of black churchgoing teenagers', unpublished PhD dissertation, University of Warwick; H. Kwiyani, 2019, *Our Children Need Roots and Wings: Equipping and empowering young diaspora Africans for life and mission*, Missio Africanus; T. Reynolds and E. Zontini, 'Trans-

national and diasporic youth identities: exploring conceptual themes and future research agendas', *Identities* 23 (4) (2016): 379–91.

2 C. O. Nyanni, 2021, *Second-Generation African Pentecostals in the West: An emerging paradigm*, Eugene, OR: Wipf and Stock.

3 A. Adogame, 'Engaging the rhetoric of spiritual warfare: the public face of *Aladura* in diaspora', *Journal of Religion in Africa* 34 (4) (2004): 493–522; G. T. Haar, 1998, *Halfway to Paradise: African Christians in Europe*, Cardiff: Cardiff Academic Press, p. 24.

4 R. Burgess, 2011, 'Bringing back the gospel: Reverse mission among Nigerian Pentecostals in Britain', *Journal of Religion in Europe* 4 (3) (2011): 429–49.

5 P. Freston, 2010, 'Reverse mission: a discourse in search of reality?', *Penteco-Studies* 9 (2) (2010): 153–74.

6 A. Adogame, 'African Christians in a secularizing Europe', *Religion Compass* 3 (4) (2009): 488–501; Asonzeh Franklin-Kennedy Ukah, 2009, 'Reverse mission or asylum Christianity? A Nigerian church in Europe' in *Africans and the Politics of Popular Culture*, Rochester, NY: University of Rochester Press, pp. 104–32; E. Morier-Genoud, 2018, '"Reverse mission": a critical approach for a problematic subject' in *Bringing Back the Social into the Sociology of Religion*, Leiden: Brill, pp. 169–88.

7 The period of the Enlightenment, most historians would agree, started in the early modern age, seventeenth to eighteenth century. It was an era of great technological and intellectual development, a shift of focus from faith to reason, from religious dogmatism to rationalism and from collectivism to individualism.

8 B. Adenekan-Koevoets, 'Nigerian Pentecostal diasporic missions and inter-generational conflicts: case studies from Amsterdam and London', *Mission Studies* 38 (3) (2021): 424–47.

9 J. Corrie, 'The promise of intercultural mission', *Transformation* 31 (4) (2014): 291–302.

10 Oyin, Amsterdam focus group (SG participants), accessed 26.08.2018.

11 B. Adenekan-Koevoets, 2022, 'Nigerian Pentecostals and "reverse mission" in London and Amsterdam', unpublished PhD dissertation, University of Roehampton.

12 First-generation are individuals born abroad with both their parents also born abroad and from the same country of origin. They tend to have either only foreign citizenship or have obtained European citizenship through naturalization. In this study, the FG are those born and educated in Nigeria and involved in Pentecostalism prior to migration, who came to Europe over the age of 25. I have identified them as such because having been involved in Pentecostalism in Nigeria, they have imbibed the beliefs and practices of Nigerian Pentecostal traditions and continue these in the European context.

13 Second-generation are individuals either born in the host country as offspring of at least one Nigerian parent or brought to Europe at a young age, who have undergone the European educational system, who did not participate in Pentecostalism in Nigeria and have not been exposed to Nigerian traditional and cultural norms and values. I also refer to them as Nigerian-British citizens because they are British nationals by birth but of Nigerian origin through their parent(s).

14 B. Gerbner, 2018, *Christian slavery: Conversion and race in the Protestant Atlantic world*, Philadelphia, PA: University of Pennsylvania Press; A. Ryrie, 2022, 'How Protestant missionaries encountered slavery', *Gresham College*, 9 May, https://www.gresham.ac.uk/watch-now/protestant-slavery, accessed 28.03.2023; A. Ryrie, 2021, 'The failure of the first Protestant missionaries', *Gresham College*,

22 September, https://www.gresham.ac.uk/watch-now/protestant-failure, accessed 28.03.2023.

15 For more on the economic implications of slavery and the slave trade, see E. Williams, 1975 (2021), 'Capitalism and slavery' in *Sociological Worlds*, London: Routledge, pp. 260–8.

16 A. Adu Boahen (ed.), 1985, *Africa under colonial domination 1880–1935*, Vol. 7, London: Heinemann; Berkeley, CA: University of California Press.

17 Jacob F. Ade Ajayi, 1965, *Christian missions in Nigeria 1841–1891: The making of a new elite*, London: Longmans, Green & Co., pp. xiv–13.

18 The struggle for the liberation of colonized African countries began in the middle of the last century and led to independence from the European colonizers. However, despite the decolonization, western influence through the activities of Christian missionaries, who had a symbiotic [but complex] relationship with colonialism, remained (see L.G. Sanneh, 2007, *Disciples of All Nations: Pillars of world Christianity*, Oxford: Oxford University Press, pp. 131–3). Notably some early Christian missionary activity in West Africa was carried out by African agents, in some instances independently of western missionary control, although there was diversity of approaches among different Protestant, evangelical and Pentecostal missions (see A. Hastings, 'African Christian Studies, 1967–1999: Reflections of an editor', *Journal of Religion in Africa* 30 (1) (2000): 30–44; J. D. Y. Peel, 2016, 'The three circles of Yoruba religion' in J. D. Y. Peel, *Christianity, Islam, and Orisa-Religion: Three traditions in comparison and interaction*, Oakland, CA: University of California Press, pp. 214–32). Presently, with only about a third of world Christians being White western, a considerable proportion of mission activities in its diverse forms continues to be from north to south particularly through developmental projects, laden with conceptually western theologies to the detriment of non-western voices. See Deji Ayegboyin and S. Ademola Ishola, 1997, *African Indigenous Churches: An Historical Perspective*, Greater Heights Publications.

19 E. Isichei, 1995, *A History of Christianity in Africa: From Antiquity to the Present*, Grand Rapids, MI: Eerdmans; O. Kalu, 2008, *African Pentecostalism: an introduction*, Oxford: Oxford University Press; O. U. Kalu, 2000, 'African Christianity: Its Public Role', Book review, *International Bulletin of Missionary Research* 24 (1) (2000): 36; L. Sanneh, 1983, 'The horizontal and the vertical in mission: an African perspective', *International Bulletin of Missionary Research* 7 (4) (1983): 165–71.

20 What eventually brought the *Aladura* Churches into prominence in Yorùbá land was the worldwide influenza epidemic of 1918 and the prevalent economic depression at the time. Leaders of these Yorùbá Churches started prayer and healing fellowships to battle the outbreak and its effects and claimed a measure of success over the epidemic, especially with the temporary exit of western missionaries due to the epidemic (L. Sanneh, 2008, *Disciples of All Nations: Pillars of world Christianity*, Oxford: Oxford University Press, pp. 191–2).

21 M. A. Ojo, 'Pentecostalism and charismatic movements in Nigeria: Factors of growth and inherent challenges', *The WATS Journal: An Online Journal from West Africa Theological Seminary* 3 (1) (2018): 5.

22 A. Adogame, 2013, *The African Christian Diaspora: New currents and emerging trends in world Christianity*, London: Bloomsbury Academic.

23 A. Anderson, 2018, *Spirit-filled World: Religious dis/continuity in African Pentecostalism*, London: Palgrave Macmillan, p. 8; B. Meyer, 'Make a complete break with the past. Memory and post-colonial modernity in Ghanaian Pentecostalist discourse', *Journal of Religion in Africa* 28 (3) (1998): 316–49.

24 Nyanni, *Second-Generation African Pentecostals*, p. 197.

25 A. Droogers, 'The power dimensions of the Christian community: an anthropological model', *Religion* 33 (3) (2003): 263–80.

26 See Romans 8.26; Hebrews 11.6; Colossians 1.9.

27 Interview D, London, 05.12.2017.

28 RCCG, 'Our Beliefs', *The Redeemed Christian Church of God*, https://www.rccg.org/our-beliefs/, accessed 28.07.2023.

29 Interview, Pastor Ade, 15.02.2018.

30 B. A. Adedibu, 'Reverse Mission or Migrant Sanctuaries? Migration, Symbolic Mapping, and Missionary Challenges of Britain's Black Majority Churches', *Pneuma* 35 (3) (2013): 405–23.

31 Researcher's Field diary, 08.05.2020.

32 Interview D, London, 05.02.2017.

33 Researcher's Field diary, 03.09.2017.

34 Interview T, London, 06.05.2018.

35 Nienke, Amsterdam focus group 26.08.2018.

36 Nyanni, *Second-Generation African Pentecostals*, p. 202.

37 RCCG, 2021, 'Pastor E.A. Adeboye Special service: It is time to fly', *Facebook*, 28 March, available at: https://www.facebook.com/watch/live/?v=2812298345686784&ref=watch_permalink, accessed 29.08.2023.

38 Hillsong is a megachurch which describes itself as a contemporary Christian church. It was founded by Brian and Bobby Houston in 1983 in the western suburbs of Sydney, Australia, and claims an average global weekly attendance of 150,000 people. It has lately been in a series of scandals and criticisms involving the founder and other prominent church leaders.

39 Amsterdam focus group, 26.08.2018.

40 Interview S, London, 07.12.2018.

41 Debby, Amsterdam focus group, 26.08.2018.

42 Interview, senior pastor O, Amsterdam, 29.08.2018.

43 R. A. Catto, 2008, 'From the rest to the West: Exploring reversal in Christian mission in twenty-first-century Britain', unpublished PhD dissertation, University of Exeter.

44 London focus group, 23.02.2018.

45 Matthew 22.37–39.

46 M. J. Cartledge, S. Dunlop, H. Buckingham and S. Bremner, 2019, *Megachurches and Social Engagement: Public theology in practice*, Vol. 33, Leiden: Brill.

47 Amsterdam focus group, 26.08.2018.

48 A. H. Anderson and W. J. Hollenweger, 1997, 'African Pentecostal churches and concepts of power' in *Africa Forum, Council of Churches for Britain and Ireland*, pp. 1–4.

49 Numbers 12.1–10; Hebrews 13.17.

50 RCCG, 2023.

51 B. Adenekan-Koevoets, 'Nigerian Pentecostals and "reverse mission"', p. 435.

52 Irukwu is one of the visible Nigerian leaders engaged in ecumenical relations and discussions as shown through his involvement in such organizations as Churches Together in England. He has also been able to involve leaders of British mainline churches, despite differences in ecclesiology and theology, in some activities of the RCCG like Festival of Life (RCCG, 2019)

53 Jesus House London, 'Jesus House ONLINE // Sunday Service 08-08-2021 // Pastor Agu Irukwu', 2021, *YouTube*, 8 August, https://www.youtube.com/watch?v=uri6w1tZfvQ, accessed 22.04.2023.

54 Droogers, 'The power dimensions of the Christian community', p. 265.

55 Lancaster, L. C., and D. Stillman, 2002, *When Generations Collide: Traditionalists, BabyBoomers, Generation Xers, Millennials: who are they, why they clash, how to solve the generational puzzle at work*. New York: HarperBusiness.

56 R. Van Dijk, 1999, 'Pentecostalism, gerontocratic rule and democratization in Malawi: The changing position of the young in political culture' in *Religion, globalization and political culture in the Third World*, London: Palgrave Macmillan, pp. 164–88.

57 Amanda, London focus group, 23.02.2018.

7

'Marginality' as Mission Priority: Decolonizing Theology to Participate in God's Mission

ELIZABETH JOY

Introduction

Cathy Ross, one of the two editors of the book *Mission in the 21st Century: Exploring the Five Marks of Global Mission*, introduces the book as a *Taonga*, which in Māori she says is difficult to define but is associated with wisdom, and applied to something that is very precious, cherished and can refer to anything or any person.[1] So 'mission' to me is *Taonga*, especially *missio Dei* or God's Mission. Contributing to this volume that brings together 'voices from across the spectrum of denominations in Britain in the first two decades of the twenty-first century',[2] I draw from my experiences working with the Council for World Mission (CWM) as the Executive Secretary of Mission Education from October 2002 to January 2011, as well as my experience with Churches Together in England as a National Ecumenical Officer representing my Church – the Malankara Orthodox Syrian Church (MOSC) – from 2013 to 2016, as a volunteer from 2015 to 2018, and as a Director/Trustee from 2018.

This chapter attempts to look at mission in Christ's way according to John 20.21–22. It addresses the postcolonial context from a theological perspective. It tries to find a way forward for mission today. Therefore it looks at the question, 'How can we participate in God's mission addressing Britain's problem of lingering colonialism bringing forth a new form of mission?' It uses material from CWM resources from 1975 to 1999, Statements and Rayan's article on 'Decolonisation of Theology'. It highlights two of the mission frontiers that need global attention and teamwork. It concludes that a Pentecost mission model will be a way forward. I start by defining some important terms.

Missio Dei

The word mission comes from the Latin word *missio* meaning 'a sending' with reference to what an individual or group wants to do or is convinced to do. We distinguish between 'mission' (singular) and 'missions' (plural). While the first term refers to the *missio Dei* (God's mission), that is, God's involvement with the world, the latter refers to particular forms, related to specific times, places, or needs of participation in the *missio Dei*. Ultimately God's mission remains indefinable, it should never be limited by our narrow confines. The history and the theology of early Christianity are mission history and mission theology.[3] The most we can hope for is to formulate some approximations of what God's mission is all about for our times, and the realities that persist today – these harsh realities that compel us to reformulate our response to God's presence in the world. However, what continues and amazes people of all generations through history is the depth of inclusiveness in Jesus' own mission. It embraces the rich and the poor, the oppressor and the oppressed, breaking down the walls of hostility.[4] The nature of God's mission can be understood both in 'apocalyptic' and 'eschatological' terms. Apocalyptic in the sense that there are current concrete irruptions as revelations of God's liberating activity in the here and now; and eschatological in the sense that we hope for a consummation of God's reign in terms of love, justice, and the equality of all humanity.[5]

Marginality as priority (MAP)

Theology supports mission and mission informs theology. Mission should spring up to meet the requirements in our contexts both local and global that seek justice from all sorts of oppression. Mission needs to recognize marginality as priority, that all may have life in all its fullness. Easter experience determined the early Christian community's self-definition and identity. Jesus' historic mission compelled the apostles to consummate and find their identity and self-understanding in, through and by the Easter Experience.[6] This experience is the experience of being liberated and challenged to oppose all injustice in order to proclaim the good news to all people, especially those in the margins. Therefore, 'marginality as priority' is for me both the road map and the key for the Church's mission and theology. We as Christians get it from Christ's mission mandate in Luke 4.16–20, originally from the book of the prophet Isaiah chapter 61, which Jesus read in the synagogue. I also take Matthew 25.31–46, which informs the criteria on which people will be judged on the last day. Marginality as priority calls for justice in relation to creation and the humanity within it as we do theology today.[7] Whatever you do to the least of these ... you do it for God. You see God continuing to suffer in the suffering of God's people (all people who suffer), and people are judged according to their response to the least. You need not necessarily be the one with more wealth, prosperity or status but you need to be moved and share your resources, however less they may be. It is easier for people at the margins to share what they have. They are engaged in God's mission.

Rayan's 'Decolonisation of Theology' and its impact on mission

Doing theology is a collective reflection on the community's faith experiences that will enable the Church to move forward in its mission. Samuel Rayan puts it very succinctly, connecting theology and mission:

> Theology is done by bringing faith-experience with its interpretations and symbols face to face with real life with its problems and suffering: by letting them meet, clash, question and challenge each other, illumine, and interpret each other and encounter God ... Faith experience will interact with situations of oppression and death till it becomes a call and a stimulus to fresh liberating and life enhancing action.[8]

Sharing the meaning of the word 'decolonization' from the Concise Oxford Dictionary (9th edition, 1995), Rayan challenges us as colonizers or colonized or participants in God's mission to be inclusive in a sensitive way when we look into the colonized perspectives. About the descriptions from this dictionary and its impact on both the colonized and colonizers, he says:

> These descriptions – 'new country', 'withdraw, 'leaving it', 'the mother country' – come naturally to the colonial outlook. For the people of the 'new country', however, to decolonize would be to make their territory independent by ridding it of the settlers who, more often than not, have been invaders, illegal immigrants or cheats. The Oxford definition, then, of decolonization needs decolonizing. We have little or no knowledge of colonists withdrawing except when thrown out ... Under Colonial domination, the exploited and marginalised people's creativity and resourcefulness deteriorate ...[9]

Rayan then reminds us, the people of India, especially the Christians on its West Coast, that long before the arrival of Vasco da Gama in 1498 and the colonial era there was a Christian church. It had its own theology expressed in its structure, worship and life, if not articulated in discourse.

My own church, the MOSC (Indian Orthodox Church) has its own long history which can be briefly paraphrased as follows:

> In its recorded history, the Malabar coast in southern India has had trade relations with West Asia since the Old Testament era. It was these trade routes that later enabled Christianity to reach Kerala through St. Thomas the Apostle, who arrived on the Malabar Coast in AD 52 near the present day township of Kodungallur. He preached the Gospel to the locals (which included Jewish settlers in Kerala), baptized many, ordained priests and founded seven churches. These seven villages later became epicentres of Indian Christianity and other parishes started evolving from these seven mother parishes. History records that Christianity along the Malabar coast existed under the leadership of a local head titled 'Archdeacon'.[10]

For the Orthodox Church, liturgy contains the theology of the Church. Through history, when other denominations tried to overpower the Orthodox faith it happened by using force, by burning the liturgy. However, the Church Fathers have been alert to affirming their allegiance to the Orthodox faith and reverted back to using the Orthodox Liturgy. One such event in history is the Koonankurishu (Bent Cross) Sathyam (oath) in AD 1763. The following narrative brings to light the renewal that took place.

> Mattancherry and Fort Cochin are two cities in Kerala where various civilizations of the world have created significant impact which led to cultural and religious synthesis. The Portuguese followed by the Dutch and later on the British ruled the cities and used them as their first trade hub till independence of the country. Cochin became a thriving commercial centre, and a major religious centre where various religious groups tried to establish their administrative supremacy ... In this regard, the St. George Church of Mattancherry, which still languishes in the historic memories of the legendary Koonankurishu Sathayam (Koonankurishu Oath) has played a significant role of its own, never to be ignored.[11]

Decolonizing theology is neither new nor confined to a particular nation. Ever more explicit efforts in decolonizing 'thought, theology and life' are seen in the theologies of liberation that have been articulated since the late 1960s. Rayan points to the historical fact that in America the first harvest was gathered in James Cone's A *Black Theology of Liberation* in 1970 and in South America, Gustavo Gutiérrez's *A Theology of Liberation* in 1971.[12] He also reminds us of the arrogant and immoral act of Pope Alexander VI, who handed over to Portugal and Spain for ever all the lands belonging to the East and West divided by an imaginary line in the Atlantic. The colonizers could dispose of all the natural and cultural wealth of these lands to be converted, enslaved or abolished. Rayan blames the teaching implied in this unscrupulous act for that which 'directly or indirectly infected most colonial missions and their theologies'.[13] If we bring forth new mission models they will for sure inform our theologies too, or if we change our theologies this will impact on our mission models. They are two sides of the same coin and mutually impact each other even when they are not nurturing mission. Rayan emphatically nails it when he says that 'colonial theology failed to see that the subjugation and exploitation of peoples effectively annulled the Gospel of freedom and divine filiation'.[14] These theologies made by the ruling class for the ruling class were conveniently carried on by colonial missionaries. Rayan strongly condemns this outlook, pointing to the errors of the colonial era that still linger. The following bold comment should steer us through to find the way forward:

> Operating from within the West's mercantile framework, the churches (from West Asia and Europe) saw themselves as bringing God and Christ in their ships to these godless shores. Colonial mission and theology committed the a priori error of taking for granted that God had never been here, that Christ had not preceded them ... that the Spirit has never been in liberating and life-giving dialogue and communion with the hearts and dreams of the men and women of this land.[15]

Rayan points to the fact that colonial mission and theology made the same error of taking for granted that God, Christ and the Holy Spirit were never present in the lands that they explored and exploited. He concludes with a realization which will throw more light on our venture to find a mission model for our time:

> Theology is thus always on its way. It never arrives. There is no definitive and normative theology. Theology is ever in the making. It is always to be remade and refined as struggles develop, as experience deepens, change follows change, and history keeps unfolding. It is ever on the move in the direction of the Truth symbolized by faith and mysteriously known in Love. Theology is a pilgrim of Truth.[16]

This observation and correction that God's presence is in the midst of people who suffer for want of an identity and the right to live as God's people leads us to the next section, which deals with the CWM and its role in exploring new mission models in the first two decades of the twenty-first century.

My journey as a missionary

Born in a traditional Lutheran Christian family in Bangalore and growing up as a daughter and a granddaughter of ministers in the India Evangelical Lutheran Church (IELC), I was brought up in good Christian faith. At the age of four I lost my vision in my right eye in an accident when a stone injured my eye lens. I never knew I had lost my sight in one eye, neither did I know that my face was disfigured. All along, my father used to tell me that the IELC missionaries in Bangalore at that time were praying fervently for me and consoled my father, saying that one day I would be a great missionary. I did not aspire to be a missionary nor expect that to happen – until I joined CWM and knew that, although we were executive staff, we were considered missionaries.

After my marriage my Christian faith in the Orthodox Church grew deeper. My faith and understanding of the 'communion of saints' deepened tremendously.[17] My vision and passion to include children as full communicant members from the time they were baptized became part of my mission which I promoted in the Mission with Children programme in CWM. I believe in liberating oppressed identities based on caste, colour, gender, age, region or religion. I was accepted as a member of the Orthodox Church although my church is not a member of CWM. My passion for people at the margins and witnessing to my faith through lived mission was seen through my work of building communities of women and men in mission, youth in mission, women in mission, and especially, mission with children, which I designed from scratch.

CWM's Strategic Framework 2020–2029

In its strategic framework for 2020–2029, CWM has moved beyond the 'Mission in Partnership' model to a mission model that is 'deeper, more outward-looking and more ecumenical in identity'.[18] The first two decades focused on devolving mission work, moving it to the margins and empowering member churches to find their mission priorities. However, twenty-first-century mission has yet to grapple with the issues that we as local, national and global communities confront in relation to making mission relevant today. The rest of this chapter will deal with just two aspects of it: the transatlantic slave trade, which has been abolished but not destroyed, and the human trafficking that continues as a form of modern slavery.

The transatlantic slave trade

Nineteenth-century colonialism replaced the slave trade with 'another form of exploitation, resulting in power and wealth for a few, and power-lessness and poverty for the majority. Colonial expansion threatened the integrity of mission, presenting missionaries with new challenges in seek-ing to respond to the powerless.'[19] The reason for the replacement was the Act of the UK Parliament passed on 25 March 1807 to abolish the slave trade in the British empire.

In December 2007 the World Alliance of Reformed Churches (now WCRC) and World Council of Churches jointly commemorated the Bicen-tenary of the Abolition of Trans-Atlantic Slave Trade Act in Jamaica. If we are to move forward in mission we need to hear the voices from these colonized nations. The WCC has been doing remarkable work, yet a lot is still to be done towards reparation and restoring human dignity. The concept paper for the bicentenary clearly spelt out the following, which describes the same position even now with very few changes:

> For its very logic, purpose, manner and continuing impact, the trans-atlantic slave trade, also often referred to as 'African holocaust', would perhaps remain as one of the most shameful wrongs in human history. For over four and half centuries, millions of Africans were transported to serve the economic interests of European colonial powers in their so-called 'New World'. It was not only a case of the combination of racial arrogance and greed resulting in a massive abuse, exodus and exploitation of human beings and natural resources, but one that stands as an unparalleled testimony to the human capacity to be diabolical in the pursuit of wealth and power. Its long-lasting legacies include the continued underdevelopment of Africa, the endless struggle for dignity and survival of the African diaspora in the Americas where African identity has been made an object of racial discrimination, besides the centuries-old psychological trauma of the slave trade which continues to haunt generation after generation.[20]

Although the cry for racial justice is growing after a long wait of hope and frustration, the truth of the concept paper is still hovering, echoing the following:

> The silence, reluctance, and tardiness of the colonial powers to own responsibility for this crime against humanity is indeed shocking! It was only recently that the successive powers admitted that it was a wrong: yet they stopped short of apologising for fear of reparations claims. Such calculated expressions of remorse and regret did very little

to undo the damage, let alone to support initiatives to outlaw today's forms of slavery. The demand for reparations has always been intellectualised, complicated, trivialised with rhetoric and empty promise, and addressing it avoided in any concrete way. Even as the world marks the 200th anniversary of the formal abolition of slave trade, the former colonial powers have fallen miserably short of repenting in such a way that would heal the wounds of the offended and right the wrongs of history.[21]

Having been associated with Churches Together in England since 2013, I have worked with the Black Churches in the UK and Ireland. One of the painful areas is the way in which these communities are still striving to get reparations in order to move forward. CTBI and Black British Christian Forums jointly organized a webinar entitled, 'I will repay: Church and Reparations', in Black History Month (October) in 2021, with the following three core aims:[22]

- To articulate the various Christian positions around reparations
- To equip the church to speak with confidence on reparations
- To help solidify the Christian work around reparations.

As part of the New International Financial and Economic Architecture (NIFEA) initiative, the webinar titled 'ZacTax: A Reparatory Tax System for a Just and Sustainable Recovery' was held on 25 June 2021.[23] The World Council of Churches, the Council for World Mission, the Lutheran World Federation, the World Communion of Reformed Churches and the World Methodist Council were co-organizers. Within this search for transforming communities through reparations, the NIFEA webinar has the potential to birth a new mission model for the twenty-first century.

Human trafficking

One of the continuing evils that has been addressed by the Council for World Mission (CWM) under the Mission Education Unit while I was its Executive Secretary is modern slavery. When the mission models moved from the giver–recipient model to sharing in One World Mission, which led to the formation of CWM in 1977,[24] the theme was 'From everywhere to everywhere'. Talents and resources were shared according to what one could give and receive. When CWM along with the Church of North India organized the Global Consultation on Combating Human Trafficking in Delhi on 2–7 March 2009, a statement was made to all CWM member churches. It called upon them to recognize human trafficking as a form of modern slavery, in order to uphold the dignity of creation. It recommended an action plan to offer prevention, protection and restoration to those who are vulnerable in our society at local, national and global levels.[25] It concluded with this powerfully affirming statement: 'Together we unite in solidarity as we stand with our brothers and sisters in the worldwide faith community, and we declare that human trafficking should occur from nowhere to nowhere.'[26]

Churches Together in England committed itself to 'Churches Combating Modern Slavery – Human Trafficking' (CCMS – HT) in 2016. Even now CTE participates in the UN meetings on social issues of modern slavery. Whether it is the cry for justice in the postcolonial and empire era or global communities aspiring to combat human trafficking, we need to remember that many parts of the world are engaged in this evil through demand, supply or transit of human beings for forced labour, bonded labour or debt labour, criminal exploitation, child exploitation, sexual exploitation, domestic servitude, descent-based slavery, organ harvesting or any other form of exploitation through force, fraud, coercion or deception. While people are exploited in these ways through modern slavery, the impact of colonialism means that the cry for reparations is hardly heard, keeping communities in every part of the world on the margins.

We have many writings that address mission with the margins, mission to the margins and mission from the margins. Irudaya Raj talks passionately about Jesus' mission as 'Revelation mission to the marginalized' and 'not divisive but unitive', a solidarity method that Jesus employed.[27] All these point to the need for marginality to be the hermeneutic key for theologizing today;[28] 'marginality as mission priority to be in God's Mission'.[29] Therefore we now turn to MAP as a methodology.

'Marginality as Priority': MAP as a methodology and a way forward

'Marginality as Priority' can be seen as a methodology for doing mission today. In 2022, the annual meeting of the Society for the Study of Theology (SST) in the UK focused on the theme of Racism, Freedom and Epistemic Justice. As one of the panellists I insisted that the three wheels – the content of theological education, the teaching and learning bodies, and the leadership and governance – should be in continual dialogue with each other, remaining open to new insights and challenges in order for SST to achieve the goal specified in its 2022 theme. I also listed the following three aspects as important for achieving this goal.[30]

1. The quest for freedom and justice means actively listening to the cry of the oppressed and marginalized.
2. Justice must be an epistemic priority in order to realize the urgency of committing to marginality as a priority
3. The content, method and curriculum of theological education has to reflect the goal of justice that guarantees freedom. Theological education will support Christian mission and Christian mission, through mission education, will in turn inform theological education, engendering liberative praxis theology.

CWM decided to share in many-sided mission on account of the 'multitude of human situations'.[31] CWM upholds mission and unity as inseparable, based on John 17.21. Rayan shows how the African delegates in the Catholic Synod of Bishops pressed for theological pluralism. Pope Paul VI stressed the need for theological unity. The African Bishops chose a theology of unity, saying, 'Unity presupposes pluralism.' Ten years earlier, Pope Paul VI spoke beautifully of this 'diversity in unity'.[32] His words are very powerful and bear outstanding witness to God's nature of mission and diversity in unity: 'Each nation received the Apostles' preaching according to its own mentality and culture. Each local Church grew according to its own personality, customs ... without harming the unity of faith ...'[33] Here the Church growing means growth in bearing fruit, growing in mission. The paradigm shift from 'church-centred mission' to 'mission-centred' church, and the growth of the Church from maintenance mode to mission mode, are very important. Even in its founding statement CWM affirmed boldly what it believed as it moved on from the Giver–Recipient model to Sharing in one World Mission:

> No particular church has a private supply of truth, or wisdom or missionary skills. So, within the circle of churches which we serve we seek to encourage mutuality. This is a recognition that to share in international mission every church is both a receiver of help and a giver of its talents.[34]

If unity presupposes diversity, then even the unity of faith presupposes diversity. If interfaith dialogue can have this as its bottom line of understanding each other, then harsh judgements can be avoided. Each culture and community will be open to correcting themselves in the light of what we understand and learn from others. Liberation theologies, be they Black theology, Dalit theology or Minjung theology, all point to the need for applying marginality as a methodological priority for both theologizing and mission.

According to the 1989 CWM statement, the importance of mission and unity is well stated in the following words:

> One without the other has no credibility. Mission without unity is a countersign of the gospel of Christ that proclaims that God wills that all humans are gathered together into one family in God. Similarly, unity without mission is dangerous for it makes the Church an end in itself and obscures the sacramental – the sign and the instrumental – character of the Church.[35]

The WCC's 2013 publication 'Together Towards Life: Mission and Evangelism in Changing Landscapes' (TTL) affirms and reiterates in paragraph 106 the fact that the global Christian gravity has shifted from the North and West to the South and East. This compels us to revisit our missional affirmations and reflections from the perspectives of the marginalized, oppressed and those that are in the global South and East. This provides more hope and confidence for Dalit theology, for example, to explore mission theology from a Dalit perspective. TTL paragraph 107 endorses and urges an articulation from a Dalit theological perspective when it says,

> We affirm that marginalized people are agents of mission and exercise a prophetic role which emphasizes that fullness of life is for all. The marginalized in society are the main partners in God's mission. Marginalized, oppressed and suffering people have a special gift to distinguish what news is good for them and what news is bad for their endangered life. In order to commit ourselves to God's life-giving mission, we have to listen to the voices from the margins to hear what is life-affirming, and what is life-destroying. We must turn our direction of mission to the actions that the marginalized are taking. Justice, solidarity, and inclusivity are key expressions of mission from the margins.[36]

TTL 109 affirms that the gospel of Jesus Christ is good news in all ages and places and it is the centrality of the incarnation, the cross and the resurrection that accelerates the need for evangelism.[37] Finally, TTL 110 reiterates the need for building relations of respect and trust between people of different faiths.[38]

Pentecost mission model as a way forward

The Pentecost event as we find it in Acts 2.1–21 pictures communities from around the world gathering in Jerusalem where the apostles and a mixed community of disciples of Christ are gathered together in prayer.

The prophecy according to the prophet Joel happens. The empowered Church goes out to different parts of the world renewed in the Holy Spirit and engages in God's mission. The Pentecost mission model is explored briefly here from the Orthodox understanding of the 'liturgy after Liturgy'.

Ion Bria puts the Orthodox faith succinctly when he writes:

This liturgical concentration, 'the liturgy within the Liturgy,' is essential for the Church, but it has to be understood in all its dimensions. There is a double movement in the Liturgy: on the one hand, the assembling of the people of God to perform the memorial of the death and resurrection of our Lord 'until He comes again.' It also manifests and realizes the process by which 'the cosmos is becoming ecclesia.'[39]

The cosmos needs to become a place of worship where our worship and liturgy prepare us to go and serve the world with love that witnesses to God's love.

As described earlier, the MOSC (the Indian Orthodox Church to which I belong) came into existence in AD 52, being established by St Thomas, one of Christ's twelve disciples. Our Church came into existence because of St Thomas's missionary activity. Moran Mar Baselios Marthoma Paulose II, Catholicos of the East and Malankara Metropolitan enthroned on the Apostolic Throne of St Thomas, affirmed in 2020:

Inspired and ignited by the love of God revealed in Jesus Christ, the mission of the Church is to share this love. The missionary activities of Malankara Orthodox Church are apparently the reflection of this mission.[40]

'The liturgy after the Liturgy', which is an essential part of the witnessing life of the Church, requires the following:[41]

1. *An ongoing reaffirmation of the true Christian identity, fullness and integrity, which have to be constantly renewed by the eucharistic communion.*
2. *Enlarging the space for witness by creating a new Christian milieu, each in his or her own environment (family, society, office, factory, etc.), is not a simple matter of converting non-Christians in the vicinity of the parishes, but also a concern for finding space where Christians live and work where they can publicly exercise their witness and worship.*
3. *The liturgical life has to nourish the Christian life not only in its private sphere, but also in its public and political realm. One cannot*

separate the true Christian identity from personal sanctification and
love and service to man (1 Pet. 1.14–15).

4. *Liturgy means public and collective action and therefore there is a*
   sense in which the Christian is a creator of community; this particular
   charism has crucial importance today with the increasing lack of
   human fellowship in society.

Fractured and marginalized identities are given, imposed or reclaimed/
retrieved identities. Lived mission through the Pentecost mission model
aims at transforming identities, overcoming inequalities and liberating
the oppressed and the oppressors so that they can sit together around
the table as we find in Luke, where people from North, East, West and
South (NEWS) will sit around the table as equals at the feast in God's
kingdom. Unless we repent and embrace socio-economic transformation
(RESET), moving beyond the barriers caused by age, gender, ethnicity
and status (AGES), we will not be able to implement the Pentecost
mission model (DRIVE), where the prophecy of Joel is fulfilled with a
diverse community waiting in prayer. The barriers of the acronym AGES
are overcome in this Pentecost event. The old will dream dreams and the
young will see visions. The old and the young need to come together in
lived mission. The experience and dreams of the old can be made real
only if the young have vision/s. The mission is seen as we look back in
history to the apostles, but without a vision from the young people and
their input the future mission will not be accomplished. Therefore the
old and the young need to DRIVE where dreams reaffirm integrity and
visions empower to make NEWS happen – the good NEWS of transformation both from the oppressed and oppressive. So DRIVE overcomes
discriminations based on AGES and creates Good NEWS where people
can come together and sit as equals at the feast table in God's kingdom
or reign. Thus DRIVE NEWS overcomes AGES. This is the Pentecost
mission model for lived mission.[42]

Conclusion

If marginality is a hermeneutical key for theologizing today, then marginality also becomes the priority for mission and unity. Our mission is that
of reconciliation and unity. The current WCC Assembly Theme, 'Christ's
love moves the world to reconciliation and unity' should open our eyes
and hearts to welcome people of all faiths and no faith to realize this
theme, bringing about a transformation especially in the context of these
dividing realities. It is not just in Christianity that we find such a call to
serve others with love. God's love that sent God's only Son into this world,

supporting and strengthening us through the Holy Spirit, empowers us to love our neighbours truly. Here the love of God the father, the life that Christ brings into this world that we may have it abundantly, and the truth that the Holy Spirit continuously leads us into will help us. Thus we can expand our horizon of understanding marginality as a priority for doing theology and mission in today's contexts. Love, Life and Truth (LLT) as the sign of the Trinity that is in *perichoresis* will lead us in this journey to meet with our neighbours so that we may be in discussion and dialogue with people of all faiths and beliefs.[43]

The Pentecost Mission Model will take us forward in our mission of work and witness. It will transform our churches and communities in Christ's way, by overcoming discrimination based on AGES and the obligation to DRIVE helps us to opt for marginality as our mission priority. I conclude that we can address the pitfalls of colonial mission by redefining the concept and continuing to discern God's will in changing situations to bring transformation.

I would like to conclude with this hymn which I composed on 24 November 2002:

Once again, we thank and praise you
God the source of life and love
For your goodness, blessings, all new
We adore and thank you now.
For your calling that demands us
To opt for all poor, outcasts
May your love which for ever lasts,
Help cross barriers that oppress.

Death strikes through hunger, ill health
Wars and weapons of great wealth
Wipe away your peoples, nations
In the name of religions.
May your word confront, convict us
Convince, convert and comfort.
That we may in our life spell out
Your life for all creation.

As we're called to do your mission
May we hear your voice – deep sigh
Through pain, agony of people
Through earth's groaning and loud cry
Bring your life and liberation
Bring forth new Mission Model

Through our life fulfil your vision
Bring glory to your Mission.
(Hymn: Once again we thank and praise you
Tune: Joyful, Joyful We Adore Thee)

Notes

1 C. Ross, 2008, 'Introduction' in A. Walls and C. Ross (eds), *Mission in the 21st Century: Exploring the Five Marks of Global Mission*, London: Darton, Longman and Todd, p. xiii.

2 B. Aldous and V. Turner, Introduction to this volume.

3 D. Bosch, 1991, *Transforming Mission: Paradigm shifts in theology of mission*, Maryknoll, NY: Orbis Books.

4 Bosch, *Transforming Mission*, p. 28.

5 E. Joy, 2004, 'Mission in the 21st Century' at World Mission Conference, UCZ Theological College, Zambia.

6 Bosch, *Transforming Mission*, p. 40.

7 E. Joy, 2023, 'Marginality as hermeneutical key for theologizing today, a paper presented on 21 March 2023 at the Research Institute for Systematic Theology (RIST) in King's College, London,

8 S. Rayan, 1998, 'Decolonisation of Theology', *Jnanadeepa: Pune Journal of Religious Studies* 1 (2) (1998): 149.

9 Rayan, 'Decolonisation of Theology', p. 140.

10 Diocese of UK-Europe and Africa, 'A Brief History', *Diocese of UK-Europe and Africa. Indian (Malankara) Orthodox Syrian Church*, https://indianorthodox uk.org/the-church/church-history, accessed 04.09.2023.

11 The Malankara Orthodox Syrian Church, 'Koonan Kurishu Pilgrim Centre', *The Malankara Orthodox Syrian Church*, https://mosc.in/pilgrimcentres/coonan-cross-pilgrim-centre, accessed 05.09.2023. The Koonan Cross Oath (Koonan Kurishu Satyam in Malayalam language), taken on 3 January 1653, was a public vow taken by members of the Saint Thomas Christian community of modern-day Kerala, India that they would not submit to the Jesuits and Latin Catholic Portuguese dominance in ecclesiastical and secular life.

12 Rayan, 'Decolonisation of Theology', p. 141.

13 Rayan, 'Decolonisation of Theology', p. 143.

14 Rayan, 'Decolonisation of Theology', p. 143.

15 Rayan, 'Decolonisation of Theology', p. 145.

16 Rayan, 'Decolonisation of Theology', p. 154.

17 Elizabeth Joy, 2016, 'St Mary and Samoa: Reflecting on September 2009', 20 September, *elizabethtjoy87*, https://elizabethtjoy87.wordpress.com/2016/09/20/st-mary-and-samoa-reflecting-on-september-2009/, accessed 10.06.2024.

18 Council for World Mission, 2021, 'CWM Strategy Framework 2020–2029, Rise to Life: Confessing witness to Lie-flourishing communities', 22 April, p. 9, https://www.cwmission.org/wp-content/uploads/2021/04/2020-2029-Strategy-Framework.pdf, accessed 05.06.2023.

19 CWM, 1996, 'Missionary Training Module: Being a Missionary Vol I', p. 41.

20 World Council of Churches, World Alliance of Reformed Churches and Council for World Mission, 2007, 'Abolished, but not destroyed: remembering the slave trade in the 21st century', 31 July, *Oikoumene*, https://www.oikoumene.org/

resources/documents/abolished-but-not-destroyed-remembering-the-slave-trade-in-the-21st-century, accessed 11.06.2024.

21 WCC, WARC and CWM, 'Abolished, but not destroyed'.

22 Churches Together in England, 2021, 'I Will Repay: Church and Reparations webinar series', *Churches Together in England*, https://cte.org.uk/i-will-repay-church-and-reparations-webinar-series/, accessed 02.06.2023.

23 World Council of Churches, 'NIFEA Webinar: ZacTax: A Reparatory Tax System for a Just and Sustainable Recovery', *Oikoumene*, https://www.oikoumene.org/events/nifea-webinar-zactax-a-reparatory-tax-system-for-a-just-and-sustainable-recovery, accessed 02.06.2023.

24 Missionary Training Module (MTM) 1, p. 44.

25 CWM and SARC, *Combating Human Trafficking* (Delhi, India, 2009), pp. 17–18.

26 CWM and SARC, *Combating Human Trafficking*, pp. 17–18.

27 R. Irudaya, 2007, *Mission to the Marginalised*, Chennai: Sri Venkatesa Printing House, pp. 142–275.

28 Joy, 2023, 'Marginality as hermeneutical key for theologizing today'.

29 E. Joy, 2023, 'In God's Mission with Evangelical Migrant Christians: Prospectives from an Orthodox Perspective in UK Context'.

30 Plenary Panel at the SST annual assembly.

31 MTM 1, p. 44.

32 Rayan, 'Decolonisation of Theology', p. 153.

33 P. Echo, 1977, *Bulletin of White Fathers, 1964:2*; A. Shorter, *African Christian Theology: Adaptation or Incarnation?*, New York: Orbis Books, pp. 150–2.

34 R. O. Latham and B. G. Thorogood, 1975, *Sharing in One World Mission: Proposals for the Council for World Mission*, London: CWM Publishing, p. 6.

35 D. P. Niles, 1999, *World Mission Today*, London: CWM Publishing, p. 9.

36 WCC, 'Together Towards Life: Mission and Evangelism in Changing Landscapes', *International Bulletin of Missionary Research* 2 (38) (April 2014).

37 WCC, 'Together Towards Life: Mission and Evangelism in Changing Landscapes," https://www.oikoumene.org/resources/documents/together-towards-life-mission-and-evangelism-in-changing-landscapes, accessed 21.07.2024.

38 WCC, 'Together Towards Life'.

39 I. Bria, 2013, 'Liturgy After the Liturgy', *Orthodox Christianity*, 26 April, https://orthochristian.com/61078.html, accessed 05.09.2023.

40 Baselios Marthoma Paulose II, 2020, https://mosc.in/uploads/2020/01/Kalpana-No.-184-2020-Mission-Sunday-English-1.pdf, accessed 03.06.2023.

41 Bria, 'Liturgy After the Liturgy'.

42 Elizabeth Joy, 2023, 'Sermon on the Day of Pentecost Feast at St Thomas' Indian Orthodox Church, London' (28 May).

43 Elizabeth Joy, 2023, 'Marginality as hermeneutical key for theologizing today'.

8

Beyond Breaking Point:
Responding to Brokenness in
Rural Scottish Parish Churches

HEATHER J. MAJOR

Introduction

The existing model for mission and ministry in rural Scottish parish churches is broken. Many rural churches are being crippled by ageing congregations, a lack of resources (both human and financial), inaccessible or impractical buildings and a lack of support from denominational structures. Churches in rural areas are faced with closure or assimilation into clusters of churches covering ever-increasing geographical areas. The question 'Is there a future for our church?' echoed through my PhD fieldwork and subsequent conversations with rural churches and church members.[1] It was a cry for honesty about the lived realities of rural churches and a desperate appeal for hope in the midst of despair. As I attempted to wrestle with the complexities of my experiences, I reflected on the importance of perspective in exploring potential possibilities for a creative and sustainable future for rural Scottish parish churches, while acknowledging the underlying hurt, pain and brokenness. In this chapter, I propose that church leaders, mission and ministry workers responding to brokenness in their local contexts need to listen, lament, learn and leap in order to find glimpses of hope beyond the breaking point.

Background

The theme of this book is 'lived' mission, so it is important to establish the background context and setting of my lived experience before embarking on a more detailed discussion of the implications. In early 2016 a small Scottish presbytery established a partnership with the University of Glasgow to offer a PhD studentship in Practical Theology, Rural Church and Mission. The brief was to spend an extended period with two case study churches in the Scottish Borders, carrying out ethnographic field-work and contributing to the life and ministry of both churches in an active capacity while investigating the complex realities of rural mission and ministry. I adopted a mixed method approach to my research, using autoethnographic[2] fieldwork with multi-sensory participant observation and action, influenced by and based in practical theology and Christian theological reflection. Choosing to use a pragmatic approach to my field-work allowed me to engage honestly with the lived reality of day-to-day life in the Borders, building my knowledge and awareness of the challenges facing rural ministry and mission through personal experience and rapport with local people.

In October 2016 I embarked on a journey of discovery as I immersed myself in the messiness of accompanying people through the daily life of small parish churches and villages. Over the following 27 months I participated in Sunday services, special events, community activities, church meetings, group discussions and countless conversations as I attempted to answer the question, 'Is there a sustainable future for mission and ministry in rural Scottish parish churches?' based on my experiences and observations. Using an autoethnographic approach gave me the freedom to focus on the particularity of the local culture, relationships, behaviour and attitudes, recognizing the value of stories and experiences in generating theories about the future of mission and ministry in rural Scottish parish churches, while simultaneously giving me a structural framework for evaluating the results of my research.

Although my research focused on the local experience of two small rural churches, I needed to understand the broader context of the Church of Scotland as a national parish church which is Presbyterian in structure and polity. At a local church level, a congregational board made up of members and elders addresses practical or financial matters, while a kirk session of elders is responsible for worship and pastoral care. The minister is the 'teaching' elder, ordained to a ministry of Word and Sacrament, while the elders of the congregation are ordained as 'ruling' elders with responsibility for consistent spiritual oversight within the church.[3] Representatives of local kirk sessions, usually the session clerk and minister, attend the regional presbytery meetings, which offer support and accountability for local churches, addressing concerns about practical and spiritual matters within the region. On a national level, the General Assembly, made up of representatives from presbyteries and local churches, meets annually to discuss matters such as policy, procedure, mission, ministry provision, training and so forth, supporting the work and witness of local, regional, national and international representatives of the Church of Scotland. In addition to these governing structures, the Church of Scotland has a central office in Edinburgh with employed staff members who serve on various councils and committees, supporting the work of the Church of Scotland at every level, contributing to the generation of resources, management of buildings, guidance on legal matters and administrative requirements of a national organization.

Setting the scene

Against the background of my research model and the broader context of the Church of Scotland, I intentionally focused on the lived realities of two small local churches. My case study churches, which I will call Braedubh and Riverglebe to preserve the anonymity of my research participants, are historic parish churches set in small rural villages. There were parallels and similarities between both churches, but as my research progressed I became more certain that exploring the specific local contextuality and uniqueness of these churches and their people was essential. What might the future look like for mission and ministry in *these* parish churches? How might their contextual particularity impact my interpretation and recommendations as I understood Braedubh and Riverglebe as 'places'?[4] I needed to consider the physical presence, space and location of the churches and villages, the types of people and their relationships with each other and the history of the churches in relation to their local area.

To begin, Braedubh was a large village of approximately 1,450 people, viewed as a 'town' by many of the smaller neighbouring villages. Riverglebe, on the other hand, had a much smaller population of around 240 people. Both villages had a primary school but, while Braedubh also had several local amenities in the form of shops, pubs, a Post Office counter run by a local shopkeeper, a few small businesses and a village hall, Riverglebe only had one small hotel/restaurant and a number of holiday homes.

Braedubh had several active community groups and regularly held activities or classes in the village hall, as well as larger outdoor events designed for family participation. There were also regular school events or activities, including end of term services held in Braedubh parish church. Although Riverglebe also had school events, there were limited opportunities for community investment in the first year of my fieldwork. However, Riverglebe village underwent significant transformation during my time in the area as a new village events group was started, along with a community choir and several special interest groups. In both Riverglebe and Braedubh I found that many church members were active participants or leaders in community groups, reflecting the common perception that 'the same five people are involved in everything' while others were more passive.

In terms of physical presence, both churches are positioned on the edges of their respective villages. They are historic churches in ancient stone buildings standing in graveyards with Commonwealth War graves and bearing witness to previous generations and the continuity represented by the parish church. Both churches are, by far, the largest community spaces in their villages, with the capacity for seating 400+ people comfortably, although regular Sunday attendance at Braedubh averaged between 15 and 22 people per week while Riverglebe typically had between 8 and 18 people attending services twice each month. Despite their size and seating capacity, both churches had poor accessibility and limited facilities, impacting their potential functionality. They also had a variety of maintenance or refurbishment costs related to the buildings and surrounding property.

During the period of my research, each church was linked with one or more neighbouring churches in a 'charge' or 'linkage', overseen by a minister or an interim moderator (where the church was in vacancy). Services were led by ordained clergy, either full-time stipendiary ministers or retired clergy providing pulpit supply, and were generally limited to an hour in length so that they could travel between the churches in their charge. This was often complicated by additional service elements or special services, for example a baptism or Remembrance Day observance. Many of the churches across the presbytery were heavily reliant on retired clergy who lived in the region to ensure the regular provision of Sunday worship.

In addition to this somewhat simplistic summary of the immediate context of my case study churches, it is important to introduce myself. When my fieldwork began, I was a single woman in my thirties with no young children and I did not travel to a larger population centre for work, which made me something of an anomaly. Everyone I encountered wanted to know something about me and what I was doing in the area. When it came to church services, I was a singer who knew many of the hymns, so I sang with confidence. As a result, I was immediately noticeable in churches where the average member was in their late sixties or early seventies, struggling to hear the organ and read the words from the small hymnbooks. While the physical shape and history of the churches remained constant, from the moment I arrived, I had an impact in the local context. As my fieldwork progressed, I became more invested in the local church and community, participating in local initiatives, attending local events, facilitating church gatherings and contributing to services as required. This, in turn, gave me opportunities to walk alongside people and listen to their stories, perceptions and challenges.

Listen to the story

As I intimated in the introduction, the first place to start in responding to brokenness is to listen. It can be tempting to look for ways to 'fix' perceived problems and things that are difficult without taking time to understand the underlying challenges, hurt and pain. This is especially true for those who are entering a ministry situation in a local church with a set of assumptions about the context, their own personal bias and a set of expectations from the local church or a denominational mandate or agenda. As Mary Clark Moschella notes, 'listening is difficult because it requires us to give up the role of expert, and become a learner again.'[5] I was in the privileged position of understanding my role as that of a researcher and investigator, which meant that I began by observing and listening. However, although I viewed myself as a participant observer, when I first arrived in the local area church members saw me as the outside 'expert' who would help them restore their churches. There was an underlying expectation in Braedubh that I would be a catalyst for change who would provide vision and energy. As a result, it was necessary to continually remind them, and myself, that my role was to come alongside and understand the situation and the people rather than create programmes and plans.

During my fieldwork I intentionally prioritized building relationships as I attempted to explore and examine the challenges and opportunities facing these churches. There were many complex interpersonal relationships present in both churches and their villages. My fieldwork highlighted the complexity and messiness of people's lives and perceptions of church, mission and ministry. Every person who participated in my research had their own story and perspective. I quickly discovered that everyone had an opinion about the local church and ministers past and present. One village resident articulated their resentment towards a previous minister's lack of engagement with the local community by describing the minister as 'an odd fish' who 'never said hello when [they] walked past' and 'refused to participate in community events'. For this resident, the way the minister behaved influenced their perception of church as a place that was unwelcoming.

Over the months of my fieldwork, I spent time talking with people when I saw them on the street or met with them over a cup of tea. As I did, I began hearing stories of hurt, pain and brokenness. I heard from people who grieved the loss of younger generations in local churches. I heard stories of resentment or anger, disillusionment and perceptions of abandonment. On several occasions I was approached by individuals who asked, with quavering voices, 'Will there still be a church here for my funeral?'

I found it easy to be overwhelmed by the challenges facing both churches. I became absorbed in the weekly stresses and strains of looking to the following Sunday or considering how to mop up the water running down the wall. I heard stories of concerns over building inaccessibility and frustrations about music or the length of sermons. People told me of interpersonal conflict and tension between church members and office bearers which had left lasting effects. Throughout these conversations I heard a common thread of concern and frustration about external circumstances or issues. Each became an excuse for the state of the church, distracting church members and office bearers from the big picture of the future of mission and ministry.

After 27 months of fieldwork, I concluded that the established models and approaches to local mission and ministry were unsustainable. The familiar patterns relied on dwindling resources, both human and financial, as members ceased to attend regularly due to age or lack of mobility. Treasurers observed that Sunday offerings were small and the largest financial contribution to church funds came from legacies left to the church by individuals following their death. Funds that were held by the churches were rarely released for mission and ministry purposes, often prioritizing the financial costs of maintaining or insuring the building and properties. Braedubh had limited finances, with little anticipation of more. Riverglebe was in a very comfortable financial position due to the proceeds of selling their manse and a large legacy; however, the terms of the legacy were clear that it was for the building and property rather than the broader work of the church in the community.

Both church buildings were deteriorating and largely inaccessible for those with reduced mobility. For these people, much of the discussion around the future of rural churches involves consideration of accessibility and provision of appropriate facilities for ensuring inclusion.[6] As one elderly church member with a visual impairment and limited mobility said, 'It's painful to sit in church. The sun streams in those big windows by the pulpit and I can't see anyone but if I move closer it hurts my neck to look up [at the minister in the pulpit].'

The problems with accessibility in both churches were a poor indication of care and hospitality for people. The physical location of the church and its place in the community were closely related, particularly for those with little understanding of the Christian faith who attended the church for special events or family weddings, baptisms and funerals. For these individuals and families, the condition of the building and its facilities was a witness to the priorities of the church. As the non-Christian spouse of one church member said during a rare visit to the building after a community spring cleaning: 'It feels a lot more welcoming now. It's like people care and the church is alive instead of festering in dust and cobwebs. It was like a horror film in here before!'

The costs of maintaining, heating and insuring the buildings were regular topics of board and kirk session meetings. Exterior lighting was problematic for both churches, impacting the possibilities for evening meetings. Braedubh had a good church hall, but it was under-utilized. Problems with the roof and leaks rendered a portion of the church unusable, causing difficulties with damp and mould and concerns about electrical wiring. The interior, exterior and access to Braedubh needed significant updating but there was no available money in church funds for the extent of work required. Riverglebe also required work to make it fit for purpose by updating the interior, improving accessibility and providing toilet facilities and a servery. Despite available funds, delays with council planning permission, utilities and tendering for work meant that during the period of my fieldwork the process had not progressed beyond discussion of possible plans. The church's raised position in a historic graveyard meant that excavation of the path to facilitate disabled access would not be possible, further limiting its potential as a community space.

During my fieldwork I found a dependency upon ordained clergy, stipendiary or retired, for all aspects of mission and ministry. Prior to the arrival of the new minister in Braedubh several church members commented on their anticipation of a minister who would change things. My suggestion that the time of transition could be productive rather than static was greeted with resignation and reluctance. As I discussed the situation with an interim minister, they said, 'I can't do everything on my own!' and, in the same conversation, admitted that it was often easier to do it alone rather than 'trying to wrangle people' into doing things. Suggestions from church members about change or development, such as the creation of a pastoral care team, were not implemented because the local culture of the church expected such initiatives to be led and organized by the minister. Those who offered their perspectives and abilities were discouraged and frustrated by the lack of engagement among the elders and congregation.

In Riverglebe, anything that might be viewed as traditionally 'ministry' related or connected with spiritual or religious conversations was reserved for clergy. Church members who suggested new initiatives focused on social or community events with little association with church life and worship apart from using the building. I witnessed and participated in new initiatives with significant social benefits, but they were not designed to be evangelistic or concerned with faith development.

As I asked questions about denominational identity or affiliation, I found a common theme of isolation among church members, who felt their church was neglected and lacking support from the presbytery or the national church represented by 121 George Street, Edinburgh. When I spoke with elders and church members they used evocative words and phrases to describe the situation:

'121 is out to get us.'

'They don't care. They just want to close us down.'

'It's a behemoth of an organization – an outdated dinosaur.'

'121 is only interested in city churches.'

'It's cold.' 'It's unfeeling.' 'Obstructive.'

I found that local churches and church members focused on their own experiences and the immediate challenges of the present, often to the exclusion of considering the wider community, other churches and planning for the future. I regularly heard people talking about the past days of the church, often tinged with a sense of despair or resignation that the time had passed and the church was no longer the same. As a church member in their mid-sixties who was born and raised in the church remarked: 'I remember when we needed to use the galleries every Sunday. All the young families came to church and the organ was always used ... Haven't seen kids here for years. I'm not sure what we'd do if any ever came!'

This inward and backward perspective created difficulties for constructive conversations about the future. People were quick to tell me about the challenges, barriers and obstacles, but struggled to see potential opportunities. When they did speak about dreams or ideas, they were often discussed with the same attitude as I might talk about winning an Olympic medal: a glorious dream with no hope or realistic expectation.

Lament the brokenness

After listening to the stories and establishing good relationships with local people, I began to reflect on the importance of lament as a step in responding to brokenness. I use that word intentionally, drawing on the Hebrew Bible/Old Testament theological foundations of lament as well as the more common definition associated with the term.[7] In secular terms, lament is an expression of grief, hurt, sorrow, disappointment and complaint or regret. In other words, it is about naming the truth of a situation in all its messiness and giving voice to any associated emotions. Authentic lament leaves no place for superficial or dismissive reactions to lived realities. In a theological sense, lament moves beyond expressing emotions into a void or creating a culture of negative complaining and grumbling by appealing to God on the grounds of a covenantal relationship.[8] Authentic lament leaves no place for superficial or dismissive reactions to lived realities. When I engaged with lament as a response to the situation in these churches, I was specifically acknowledging my belief that God cared about Braedubh and Riverglebe. As a result, I could weep over the challenges, but I could also let go of situations that were beyond my control.

As I walked alongside Braedubh and Riverglebe churches, I listened to the cry of church members who were desperate for hope. They were afraid of what the future might hold and grieving the losses of the past. Although there were those who were positive about the possibilities, many were overwhelmed and intimidated by the thought that their church would not be the same. For many churches, church members and clergy, there is a tendency to either dwell in a negative cycle of endless complaint or attempt to cover up the messy realities of underlying tensions by moving on to something new. Neither is healthy or helpful when it comes to addressing complex and multi-faceted challenges in churches or ministry contexts. To borrow an analogy from medicine, it is imperative to clean a wound and treat any underlying infections before applying a dressing. In the same way, it is often essential for churches to engage in individual and corporate lament, giving voice to their experiences and emotions, before they are in a good place to consider what the future might hold.

For example, several members of the Riverglebe congregation had joined the church when their own church (Kingriver) had been closed by the Presbytery after their minister retired. While there were those who recognized the impracticality of maintaining their previous church building, they were heartbroken over the lack of recognition or acknowledgement that they were grieving. There was minimal communication about the legacy of their church building and no clear indication of what they should do with the physical trappings of generations of ministry in Kingriver village. Instead, Riverglebe church and church members focused their attention on the possibilities for the future. As a result, there were underlying tensions between members that made it difficult to plan constructively for the future. During a phone conversation with a church member about an upcoming meeting, the church member (an individual in their late seventies) took the opportunity to pour out their grief and anger over the poorly handled closure of Kingriver and 'forced union' with Riverglebe:

'Kingriver should never have been closed. Do you have any idea how important the building is for history? I wouldn't mind so much if it had been taken over by Historic Scotland but it's a crime that it's being neglected.'

'Was that the plan?'

'That's what we thought. We never would have left if we thought it was just going to be abandoned, but Presbytery doesn't care.'

'Did you know I still have all the communion silver, the altar cloth and even the Christmas tree? No one's ever asked about them. What am I supposed to do with them?'

'Have you spoken to the minister?'

'When am I supposed to do that? [The minister] is always busy with other things. You know I can't get to church much since I gave up the car.'

'Would have been nice if Riverglebe folk had asked about Kingriver things though. I know they have their own traditions and ideas but it should be our church too.'

Learn

Listening to the stories and lamenting the painful realities are a good way to begin responding to brokenness; however, it is also important to engage in actively learning together as preparation for action. As Vaughan Roberts and David Sims argue, there is a need to think about how stories are told and what consequences or actions may be influenced by the process of shaping the stories. Many church stories 'enshrine the negative' or '[demonise] somebody, often the minister, and sometimes the denominational body' which is what I found during my fieldwork.[9] Learning from the stories includes learning from the past, actively reflecting on the present and learning from others as churches look beyond their own immediate experiences or contexts. In my experience, one of the most effective tools for learning about the past and present was to ask the question, 'Why?' as I reflected on the challenges and opportunities facing my two case study churches.

When I arrived in the Scottish Borders I needed to attune and adapt to local accents and colloquial phrases. Many Scots phrases which are common to the Borders are colourful, with layers of nuance that required me to develop my awareness of the local context and relationships. 'It's aye been', or the shorter 'aye bin', is a multi-purpose phrase that indicates relation to the past. Although simplistic, the basic translation of the phrase is: 'It has always been this way.' The phrase also includes an element of implying: 'It *will* always *be* this way.' Essentially, 'It's always been this way so why change it.' It can be applied to activities, groups, people, individuals, villages, local government.

There is a range of meanings attached to each use of the phrase, dependent on context, tone of voice and the relationships between people. The most common and generalized interpretation is the idea of being 'stuck' in the past. For example, during a conversation with a village resident at the local café in Braedubh, I asked about a local initiative and was informed, 'It's a nice idea but ye ken they'll nae go fer it. They're aye bins.' As the above example demonstrates, the phrase is often used to speak of others in a derogatory or dismissive way. This can include comments in media or newspapers on the traditions which have been maintained in Border communities for several hundred years, or local people speaking about others who appear uninterested or unsupportive of change and new initiatives. However, the phrase can also be innocuous, simply stating a perceived fact about particular practices or activities. There is much to be learned from 'aye been' and the phrase itself provided a colourful way of reflecting on present situations in local churches.

After being introduced to the concept I began questioning what the phrase really meant. I examined the traditions and practices of the churches with an overarching question in mind about how 'aye been' might affect both the short- and long-term future of mission and ministry in both churches. I found that 'aye been' often either referred to practices or traditions which originated within the living memory of church members or was a way of saying, 'I don't know where this started, or why, but I can't imagine it changing.'

As I asked, 'Why?' I discovered that many people had not stopped to think about the purpose of traditions and rituals. Many had never felt able to ask the question and had just accepted the status quo. As L— said, 'I never thought about why we stand when the Bible is brought in. It's just "aye been"!' They were fascinated by the history behind the tradition as I retold the story of how the practice began in the Church of Scotland as a way of honouring the primacy of God's word. Learning about the past and reflecting on the present gave them some insight into the purpose of the practice and how it related to the purpose and identity of the church.

A leap of faith

Taking time to listen to stories, lament the hurt and pain and learn from the process is of limited value in a missional sense unless it is accompanied by some form of action. I have chosen to call this a leap of faith because it often requires confronting fear without assurance of results. As I engaged with Braedubh and Riverglebe, I found evidence indicating that fear was one of the primary barriers to change or implementing new initiatives. Interestingly, it appeared to be less about fear of trying something new and failing than it was about the possibility that the change might mean a permanent departure from previous practices with no room for reflection, revision or discussion. In other words, that changing something would create a new 'aye been' that would remain for the next 60 years.

James Hopewell's book *Congregation: Stories and Structures* presents a convincing argument that 'narrative can be a means by which the congregation apprehends its vocation'.[10] One of the challenges facing Braedubh and Riverglebe was a crisis of identity and purpose that hampered their ability to engage in meaningful local mission. By encouraging church and community members to reflect on the reasons for the actions and traditions of their churches, I provoked emotional responses ranging from defensiveness to confusion or relief as people engaged with questions of purpose. Several people were suspicious of a possible ulterior motive for my questions. Was I trying to trick them into changing things? Surely it was better to just leave things alone! After all, the church was still open and Sunday services were still happening. The appearance of familiar forms and models reinforced their sense of security in the face of uncertainty about the future. The fact that some of the traditional practices of the church no longer fulfilled their purpose was less important than their familiarity.

As I talked with research participants, I noticed a tendency towards focusing on the individual details and challenges of their immediate situations, often to the exclusion of other options. When faced with questions about a vision for the future or about evaluating the potential changes which might be made in each church, people based their answers on their personal experiences.

In response to a proposal about offering tea and coffee after the service: 'We tried that years ago and it didn't work so why would it work now?' In response to a suggestion about changing the interior furnishings and layout: 'Oh no, we can't remove the pews! There was a big church fundraiser to get the material for the pew cushions and it would be disrespectful to the church ladies who worked so hard to make them!' (The big fundraiser had happened 18 years previously.) When asked about the possibilities for a Bible study group: 'There was one years ago but it was just a gossip group made up of the minister's cronies. The people who went were the "inner circle". I don't think anyone would be interested in another one.'

While this gave me insight into their perspectives, it limited their view of possibilities. In such cases I found it helpful to look beyond the borders of my case study churches into the neighbouring parishes.

One neighbouring parish, which I call Ellieneuk, underwent significant change within a matter of months as they engaged in radical reform. Ellieneuk was a tiny parish church that was given three years to change, or the building would be permanently closed. Beginning with a congregation of between four and six people who attended the monthly service, within 18 months the church was meeting every week with an average regular attendance of between 30 and 45 people. There was an intentional shift towards local, contextualized and active relationship building and mentoring, led by an interim moderator who invested in building meaningful connections with local people, inviting church and community members to participate in church initiatives. There was a clear purpose that looked towards the future, dreaming about long-term goals and taking steps to communicate those dreams to the people involved at multiple levels. I saw a programme of teaching and instruction that equipped local church members with tools and opportunities to develop their gifts and understanding of the Christian faith. Entrepreneurial leadership and hard work inspired local people. Welcoming and encouraging people to invest their natural interests and gifts in the work of the church made it possible for individuals and families to feel valued, knowing their contributions were shaping the church.

Towards the end of my fieldwork, I arranged a meeting with Ellieneuk church members where I intentionally asked them what would happen if the interim moderator was incapacitated or left the church at short notice. I was curious about their response in light of the fear and anxiety expressed among church members in Riverglebe when faced with my questions about their minister's future retirement. After a short pause each member indicated their conviction that the work that had started would continue.

> '[The interim moderator] is like a Jack Russell terrier, tenaciously visiting and giving us opportunities for training as elders and leaders.'
> 'It's been modelled for us, this way of believing there's a future for [Ellieneuk].'
> 'We just had 6 weeks of services led by church members where [the interim moderator] was just a support and didn't have anything to do in the services.'
> 'I'd never led a service or prayed in front of people before but [the interim moderator] gave me a lot of freedom to try different things.'
> 'We're all in this together. Everyone wants it to succeed.'

It might change and look different, but they all expressed confidence that the church would survive and continue to move from strength to strength because they had all invested in the developments within the church. Each person felt their voice was being heard and they had grown in their abilities and confidence. They all acknowledged that it would be a loss and they would grieve that loss, but it would not stop the growth and development of mission and ministry in their local area and beyond. Although the interim moderator had initiated the transformation of Ellieneuk, the people who found a sense of belonging there were fully committed to the vision of being a transformational Christian community rooted in their particular place.

A living example

Although Ellieneuk was, in many ways, a pioneer ministry that began from a small seed after reaching a point of no return where their only options were to change or close, it was precisely that ultimatum that gave them the necessary impetus to leap out in faith. My two case study churches were still considered to be viable by the Presbytery, hence my presence as a researcher. In reflecting on the four components I have highlighted in this chapter, I am reminded of a series of memorable conversations and encounters in Riverglebe which demonstrate the depth of pain and hurt that can be associated with churches in local areas as well as offering a glimpse of possibilities for reconciliation.

When I first arrived in Riverglebe I found a church and a village struggling with a lack of identity and community spirit. One local villager, who was also a church member, described Riverglebe as a place which had 'lost its heart'. Although there were additional socio-historical or cultural reasons for this, I was particularly interested in my perception of a relational disconnect between the church and the village. By establishing communication and taking the time to listen, I found that I was able to uncover deeply rooted elements of brokenness that stretched back over generations.

Like many of the small towns and villages in the Scottish Borders, Riverglebe has an imposing war memorial. Inside the church there is a lengthy 'Roll of Honour' detailing the names of those from the local area who served in World War One and World War Two. For such a small village, the list is extensive and a few older members of the community attributed the disconnect between church and village to the involvement of the parish minister as the recruiting officer for World War One:

> Ye ken it was the days they thought the war would be done by Christmas. Everyone was so proud to serve. The ministers [of the parish church and a neighbouring Free church] were both recruiting officers. It was their job to get the boys to sign up and they made it a competition to see how many they could each recruit.

> They went to war with their friends and they never came home. Or they weren't the same if they did. My mother blamed the minister. Said he shouldn't have pressured her brother and her cousins to go. Only one of them ever came home.

As a result of the recruiting effort, virtually every family in the area was directly impacted by devastating losses of life and physical or psychological trauma associated with the war. This, in turn, led many families to resent the minister, the church and, by extension, the God who demanded the lives of their men.

While it was important to acknowledge the pain of the past as it was identified by these participants, intriguingly, despite the historic role of the church in encouraging young men to go to war, Remembrance Sunday was the most consistently attended service apart from Christmas and frequently saw the congregation triple in numbers. I was certain that attributing the lack of connection between church and village to World War One was only part of the story. As I continued to ask questions, I discovered that subsequent years reinforced the perception of villagers that the church was unconcerned with their daily lives and struggles. Local villagers felt that ministers in more recent years had neglected opportunities for investing in the community or engaging in relationship. As a result, the church, which was physically on the fringes of the village, was also increasingly marginalized by failing to meet people on their terms.

During my fieldwork I witnessed small steps being taken to address the issue. One of the most visually striking revolved around one Remembrance Sunday when the church invited the village to join them at the war memorial for the act of remembrance. Although it was traditionally observed following the service, as church people arrived for the service they noticed local villagers gathering at the memorial. After some discussion among the elders, the church members left the church building to join the villagers and begin with the act of remembrance before returning to the church building for the Sunday service.

'Nice to see lots of people out.'
'It's too cold to be standing out here for long.'
'Well, you could always come into the church after for a cup of tea or coffee after the wreath and join in the service.'
'Is it actually warmer in there?'
'It's usually warm for the choir practice.'
'That was very good. [They] did an excellent job.'
'I'm so cold.'
'Are you coming up?'
'No, no, that's quite enough church for me this year.'
'Might as well get the full experience. We'll come up.'

As a result of the interaction at the memorial, several local people chose to come to the Sunday service who had not previously attended. Although the circumstances were less than ideal, their perception of the church's willingness to adapt and move to meet with the people made a positive impression that offset the problems with communication and expectations about timing. Church members were willing to give up 'aye been' because they recognized the potential of meeting local people where they were. Despite evidence of historical pain and resentment, Remembrance Sunday presented one of the most important opportunities for missional engagement with local people in their context.

Glimpses of hope

One of the most difficult aspects of responding to brokenness is finding hope. The position of both churches during my fieldwork was precarious and unsustainable. As I looked at my case study churches and the perspectives of many church and community members, I saw a combination of resignation, apathy, despair, exhaustion and desperation. Attempting to continue the existing patterns and traditions without implementing change would lead to the closure of my two case study churches within a decade. However, my fieldwork also gave me insight into potential opportunities for change.

The geographical or territorial nature of parish ministry in Scotland *should* indicate that decisions about the future of churches should be made in relation to their locality. A contextually appropriate missiology is essential.[11] Each church has a particular story, purpose and identity that has a direct impact on their sustainability. In Braedubh and Riverglebe I found people who were deeply attached to *their* church as a building and a place that represented the ebb and flow of their lives.[12] Despite poor attendance for regular services, the church building was a place for people to gather for school or community events. Even for those who did not regularly attend, it was a visible representation of the witness of the Christian Church, by which I mean the Church universal rather than a denomination.

By engaging in a process of listening, lamenting, learning and leaping, I believe that churches like Braedubh and Riverglebe have the potential to become missional communities. As I spent time building relationships with participants in the churches and villages, I paid attention to their spoken and unspoken assumptions and core beliefs. Although I found anxiety, insecurity, exhaustion, discouragement, fear, frustration, hurt and anger, I also found hope, longing for purpose, caring hearts and dreams or desires for the future with little understanding of how to implement change. Many people had little knowledge or understanding of the goal or purpose of mission and ministry beyond Sunday services, but they were gradually exploring possibilities as they actively considered the lived realities of their local context. As they moved beyond the breaking point, they began getting glimpses of hope.

Notes

1 H. J. Major, 2022, 'Living with churches in the Borders: mission and ministry in rural Scottish parish churches', unpublished PhD thesis, Glasgow, University of Glasgow.

2 Autoethnography is an approach to research and writing that seeks to describe and systematically analyse (*graphy*) personal experience (*auto*) in order to understand cultural experience. See Carolyn Ellis, Tony E. Adams and Arthur P. Bochner, 'Autoethnography: An Overview', *Forum: Qualitative Social Research* 12 (1) (2011): 1.

3 Although this is the official structure, as my research shows there is significant discrepancy between this and the practical understanding of roles and responsibilities at a local level.

4 Philip Sheldrake, 2001, *Spaces for the Sacred: Place, Memory, and Identity*, Baltimore, MD: Johns Hopkins University Press, pp. 22–32.

5 Mary Clark Moschella, 2008, *Ethnography as a Pastoral Practice: An introduction*, Cleveland, OH: Pilgrim Press, p. 142.

6 The Arthur Rank Centre (ARC) has developed a toolkit to help rural churches with accessibility. Arthur Rank Centre, 'Accessible Welcome', *The Arthur Rank Centre*, https://arthurrankcentre.org.uk/mission/accessible-welcome/, accessed 17.03.2021.

7 Further discussions of lament are widely available. The following selection represents significant contributions to the practice of lament within church or ministry settings. Walter Brueggemann, 'The Costly Loss of Lament', *Journal for the Study of the Old Testament* 11 (36) (October 1986): 57–71; Paul A. Baglyos, 'Lament in the liturgy of the rural church: an appeal for recovery', *Currents in Theology and Mission* 36 (4) (August 2009): 253–63; Sally A. Brown and Patrick D. Miller (eds), 2005, *Lament: Reclaiming Practices in Pulpit, Pew, and Public Square*, Louisville, KY: Westminster John Knox.

8 Both of Pemberton's books offer a way of engaging with lament that is both pastoral and practical. Glenn Pemberton, 2012, *Hurting with God: Learning to lament with the Psalms*, Abilene, TX: Abilene Christian University Press; Glenn Pemberton, 2014, *After Lament: Psalms for learning to trust again*, Abilene, TX: Abilene Christian University Press.

9 Vaughan Roberts and David Sims, 2017, *Leading by Story: Rethinking church leadership*, London: SCM Press, pp. 44–6.

10 James F. Hopewell, 1988, *Congregation: Stories and structures*, ed. Barbara G. Wheeler, London: SCM Press, p. 193.

11 Liam Fraser's treatment of contextual missiology in Scotland reflects many of the distinctive elements of Scottish churches. Liam Jerrold Fraser, 2021, *Mission in Contemporary Scotland*, Edinburgh: Saint Andrew Press, pp. 203–24.

12 John Inge refers to this as the temporal connection to the past. John Inge, 2003, *A Christian Theology of Place*, Aldershot: Ashgate, pp. 123–39.

9

Witnessing as Mission: Powerlessness as Prophetic Discipleship in the Hostile Environment

TOM HACKETT AND VICTORIA TURNER

Victoria Turner: Hi Tom, thank you so much for joining me today. So maybe to get started, if you could just introduce yourself and tell us how you started volunteering at the detention centre.

Tom Hackett: My name is Tom Hackett. And yeah, as you said, I'm a volunteer at a – technically named by the UK government – immigration removal centre. But, in reality, they are detention centres because people are detained for a long time with no time limit.

I volunteer with a small charity based in Crawley near to Gatwick called GDWG, which is the Gatwick Detainees Welfare Group, and they visit people in two immigration removal centres, which are right by Gatwick Airport. So Brook House and Tinsley House, and I've been volunteering there now since 2017. So, six years.

And I got involved when I first moved nearby, and I heard about the charity. But actually, when I think about it more carefully, it really stems from when I did a voluntary year in the Netherlands after I finished university. It was with something called the Mission House, which was run by the Council for World Mission and the Protestant Kirk in the Netherlands. This house was for young people from around Europe to live together for a year to do voluntary work and live together in a community. We lived in this house together but then worked in different social projects around Amsterdam, and one of the projects that I helped out at was the detention centre outreach at the airport. We used to go in weekly as a group and hold drop-in sessions and social times in the centre where people could come. It was having the experience of that project that made me think about the situation in the UK.

I mean I knew that the situation in the UK wouldn't be great, because we know that immigration for a while has been a big political issue in the UK. So when I returned from ten months in Amsterdam, I found that we had very large detention centres, usually based near to different airports. From there I managed to find GDWG from kind of researching a bit online.

And I think that that's part of the problem as well, that detention is a hidden issue. People aren't aware that immigration detention centres exist, and this particularly – about the fact that we have indefinite detention, so there is no time limit at which people can be held there. The UK is the only place in Western Europe that does not have a maximum time limit. So yeah, that's why I got involved when I started my current role as Children and Youth Development Officer for the URC and moved to London, I was accepted as a volunteer by this charity.

Victoria: Right, and what maybe some people might think is that the people in the detention centre are like criminals who've been denied right to remain in the UK. Maybe you can explain what kind of people you do find in the centres? Because the media often makes us think they are dangerous, like terrorists, right?

Tom: Yeah. Well it's definitely not … It's not all terrorists, even despite what some of the media maybe may try and portray. And it's not all criminals either, despite what the government would say as well. So the breadth is amazing, it's a real range of people that can end up in detention. But essentially, anyone who would not have legalized status and the right to be in the UK could potentially be held in detention through the capacity that the government policies would say that they would not have a legal right to be in the UK, and that they would be removing them from the UK.

The detention centres were designed as short-term centres where people will be there for a very limited amount of time before being removed. But, in reality, people end up there for a long time, particularly if they're from countries where there's a dispute about whether someone could safely be returned. So, if the Government, the UK Home Office, is trying to return somebody to a country but there's a challenge in that it might not be safe to return, people can end up in detention for a very long time. It's like a limbo or a purgatory place. And if, for example, people do not have connections or an address to be able to release to in the UK as well they get stuck there. And there are some people with criminal convictions who are in detention, but not everyone has in the same way. So, in the UK, anybody who has a prison sentence of 12 months, or more than 12 months, who is a foreign national, then the UK has the right to deport you. So sometimes there are people there who have served long prison sentences. But then, they have served their time and gone through the criminal justice system, and at the point where they will be released, they are moved to an immigration detention centre. So they get no chance of rehabilitation. And then this is often immediately at the time of them finishing that prison sentence as well.

I believe the hostile environment is criminalizing people too, or it is designed to. For example, people seeking refugee status in the UK, when people are claiming asylum, in the time when they are waiting for the decision, when it is being processed, they do not have the right to work in the UK. It is illegal for them to take on employed work, which often people find surprising, because a lot of the right-wing media, that's one of the big things that they would use to say that people are coming to the UK – to live off our benefits – that people are not wanting to work, that people are lazy, but actually it is illegal for them to work, and they're not able to. So they're forced to live off a very small amount – £5 a day. Many of them want to be part of society and have a job, but that is criminalized. So sometimes, when people are not able to survive on the support that they have, they do turn to working illegally, and that can actually be a reason that they end up in detention because of working illegally, or if they get a prison sentence for that, that might be the thing that they get a 12-month prison sentence for – for trying to survive and the hostile environment has forced them into doing that.

People can also be in prison for entering the UK illegally, maybe for using false documents, which, again, might be something that they are forced to do because of their situation. It could be classed as fraud but necessity meant that was their only feasible way to escape whatever they were running from.

Victoria: That word 'illegal' gets thrown around and misused quite a lot, doesn't it? So the idea that somebody can't go back to their home country, because it's not safe, makes me think like well, maybe they should have been accepted for asylum? It's almost as if these detention centres are like holding pens for 'illegal' people, but of course, a person cannot be illegal – but it's a way to not give them the rights that they should have.

Tom: Yeah, absolutely. And I think, people that I have met with experience of detention, they definitely feel dehumanized and stigmatized during, and still after it. And also that detention is part of a wider web. Since Theresa May had spoken about the hostile environment, the language masked that people are held indefinitely, and tried to divide it into a 'them' and 'us' from a fear of attention on this situation. Being detained was also designed to discourage people from – well – what the government would say, coming here – to stop 'illegal' migration. But it is always legal to enter a country to claim asylum. It is a right that everybody has. So yeah, it's interesting. The language and the dehumanizing language that people have.

And yeah, you say about rights. If you look at the UN Human Rights Declaration, it does say that nobody will be detained without a time limit. I can't think of the exact language, but it's around arbitrary detention.[1] Nobody should be detained arbitrarily. And this, actually, is exactly what is happening in detention. GDWG worked with somebody who was detained for ten years in detention. They've now been released, but were detained that long without having a criminal conviction too!

Victoria: It's crazy. So I imagine that the atmosphere in these centres, that if people are either just going to be held or sent to somewhere that they escaped from, is quite hopeless?

Tom: Yeah, definitely. And I think, the key job you have as a volunteering visitor is just to be someone who can try and bring that hope to the individual, which can be very difficult when people are in such challenging situations and environments.

People do lose hope, particularly if they don't really know what is happening. They might not be aware of detention if they've just arrived in the UK. They might not realize how long they're going to be held there, and it's only when they speak to others that they find out. You can normally see a change, particularly when someone's been in detention for a few weeks. So if you compared to when they first arrived, where that hope is at its most, you see it leaving the person as they start to realize that they could be there for longer, and the fact that they don't know how long it's going to be, and they don't know what the situation would be, whether they're going to be returned or whether they would be released back into the UK, or even given to another country, which maybe yeah may be somewhere dangerous for them as well.

It's the indefinite nature of it which is the issue. So, like in prison, where people have a release date to focus on, you would count down the number of days and it gives you motivation. In detention centres however, many people when you say, 'How long have you been here?', they don't actually know exactly how long they've been there, whereas others count the days religiously because that's all that they can do.

Victoria: What would be the situation where someone would be released back into the UK? Can you appeal yourself being in the detention centre?

Tom: Yeah, there can be different cases. And actually, there have been a number of cases where people have legal representatives [who] have appealed and people have been found to be detained unlawfully, and the government has been taken to court because of that. There was a big thing in 2018 with the Windrush scandal that was in the papers, where those from a descendant of the Windrush community, who had lived all their life in the UK, were then detained and deported. That got big media attention. But that also happens quite regularly for people.

And yeah, people also may, for example, on health grounds be able to appeal their detention. So, often if somebody is not in a physical or mental state to be able to be in detention, they can appeal. I've seen people with severe mental ill health, who are held for a long time, who, according to the Home Office rules, should not be detained, but their appeals aren't being processed or listened to.

Often people can't be released from detention even when their appeal is passed, or they're cleared, because they have been in there so long that they no longer have an address to be released to. So they would have to wait, whether that's Home Office accommodation, asylum seeker accommodation, or trying to get in touch and find friends or family who are able to act as a security for them staying in the UK.

Victoria: And so I think maybe this is a point because you brought up Theresa May. I think it's been in the past about seven years, it's got to the point today, like when they literally have signs saying, 'Stop the boats'. Do you feel, because you do advocacy and campaigning around this as well? Right? Do you feel like it's hard to talk about the rights of asylum seekers and refugees? Or do you think that's more of like a grassroots uprising that is resisting their treatment and so it's easier to talk to people?

Tom: Yeah, I think definitely the severity of the hostile environment has increased. The media is especially to blame. But it has always been there. A lot of these policies were actually brought in under the Labour government as well, but I do think that yeah, it has got worse recently, and that the government is playing into the media and what they believe voters would want in terms of wanting to look like they are taking action against refugees. So you see the current Illegal Migration Bill and the Rwanda policy, where it is about processing people's claims, they're changing it so people are being held in detention but offshore in that detention, and also being detained in a second country.

The proposed offshore detention centres as well, I was talking to other friends who volunteered in the Netherlands in recent years and it did remind us both of the situation in the Netherlands, where it was a detention boat that we used to visit.[2] There is something very specific about the situation when people are being held outside of the land and on the water. Where you're not physically allowed to be in the country while you're being detained. So yeah, there's a big shift in the UK.

But there are also many people who are speaking out. GWG's campaign is focusing on detention, and particularly for an end to indefinite detention, and we see more people joining those campaigns in terms of wanting to speak out about the injustice. So it's been really encouraging, particularly this last week. We've just come to the end of Refugee Week. I think it was the twenty-fifth anniversary this year, which is a week every June where we raise issues around refugees, but also support arts and culture and stories alongside campaigning. And this year we were thinking of compassion and extending compassion to others and our neighbours wherever they are from.

I went to a talk for Refugee Week, and it was around those grassroots responses that you spoke about, and it was about Kilburn Street in Glasgow in July 2021 when we were still in lockdown. There was a dawn raid that was happening from the Home Office, where they would basically come to people's properties – so their homes, in early morning to take them to the detention centres. But the community around there responded when that dawn raid was happening, and they actually surrounded the Home Office van and managed to prevent those individuals from being taken.

And I remember seeing that during lockdown, it got a lot of media attention, but nobody talked about the amount of work that it takes to get to that point so it can look like a real spontaneous thing. And it was like the solidarity of neighbours coming out, but a lot of that, and the fact that it was so effective was the work between all the organizations about building those links and building that sense of community. So that when that happened, lots of people made lots of calls to others to say – you need to be here. And more and more people gathered in support because of that. But, yeah, it takes a lot of grassroots organizing to do that.

People may feel really overwhelmed, thinking, well, what can we do about that situation? But actually, it was those small things about people knowing and standing up for their neighbours in their local area that had that big impact.

Stories like this counter the media that is promoting the hostile environment, promoting separation. We know that actually, it's those human connections that challenge those quotes you read in the *Daily Mail*, that 'there's not space here', 'they're all dangerous' and those things.

But if it's someone within your community that this is happening to, you can really change a person's perspective. And I've seen that even with people that I know agree with the most anti-refugee anti-migration articles, but when someone in their community is facing that, they completely change their mind. The rhetoric turns into – 'Well, this person's lived here all their life', and it's almost 'We don't mean *those* refugees.'

When you see the really high figures quoted with big graphics and front page news – they dehumanize the experiences, the stories, the memories and relationships and make it a distant issue. Whereas actually, when you see them as just complicated human beings like us, it builds up that connection. So helping people to see refugees and asylum seekers as neighbours, that's the first step to change this system.

Victoria: It feels like we're at a point at the moment where it's like, if you agree or disagree about whether they should be allowed to stay here for ever, in these intermediate periods – whether that's when they're stuck on the shore trying to come over or whether they're held in a detention centre – you should care how they're being treated.

Tom: Yeah, absolutely. And I think that's where the government's policies and the media, the hostile everything and the dehumanizing policies, that distance between people is what is relied upon. It's the myth of the competition for resources and so the ideas go that 'Oh, it's not that I wish any harm to the others, but we need to support our own people.' First, we just need to expand our perception of our neighbours and our own people, but also we need to understand that these policies are designed to build that hostility between all people – because whenever we put people into different categories and boxes and decide how much less than the normative person they deserve, it's unfair and racist and harming us as one people.

Victoria: What role is the Church currently playing in advocacy for refugees and asylum seekers? And what would you like to see them do?

Tom: The Church can have a massive role in raising awareness and campaigning for the rights of these people. You know, obviously what the Bible says in terms of things about loving others, loving our neighbours, exploring that 'who is our neighbour' and thinking about our global neighbours and the fact that we're called to model the way that Jesus spoke out about injustices that were happening in his time. We need to be changing that narrative from the hostile to the welcome. I'm encouraged in the URC. You know, many churches are speaking out, even Archbishop Justin Welby in the House of Lords, and work by the Joint Public Issues team that works ecumenically. I think a lot of denominations are taking campaigning against the hostile environment and those policies as priorities, but also taking actions to create a more welcoming environment for others.

Yeah. You hear people saying that the church should not get involved in politics. But for me, if we look at what Jesus did, he was getting involved in those social justice issues, and that is political. I think there's a difference between being party political and political. So we should be speaking out and challenging those in the position of power to be acting in a loving way to all, regardless of which party is in power.

Victoria: And you first got involved through the mission house in Amsterdam – do you think your faith pushed you into this?

Tom: Yeah, my Christian faith for me personally is what leads me to act in this way, and the reason that I got involved in Mission House in the first place, and that led me to doing this kind of voluntary work. GWG itself is not a faith-based charity. People who volunteer there are from all faiths and none, and they would work with people of all faiths and none, and particularly in detention centres.

In the six years that I've been visiting I've met people of so many different faiths and learnt so much from them.

So the motto of the Mission House was 'Where words and action meet'. So I ask myself the question: What am I actively doing in order to live out my faith and that call to love and to love others as well?

And also, what I do is quite normal, like accessible. It isn't a chaplaincy service that we are offering. It is social visits, and just being there with people. So I wouldn't talk directly about faith unless they brought it up because the visits are for, and therefore are led by, the individual that we are visiting and it wouldn't always be appropriate to be talking about faith. But actually, I've seen for many people faith is important and continues when they're in there. When we talked about hope, a lot of people will say that their faith is a real lifeline. There are chaplains, and you see staff from different faiths, and there is space where people are able to worship.

One of the things I often talk about with people is how we can't change the situation. When they're in detention you can't physically remove them. That's ultimately down to the Home Office, and we have no power in anything like that. But we think together about what could be the things that will help make the real difficult situation easier, and talking through what they find helpful. And for many people it is that space of worship in the place that they can go in the community there.

I'm not going into the visitors' room with a view of converting people to become Christians. But I do see that it is me following the examples of Jesus and how he worked in the society he found himself in.

The aim of why I am going into detention is to maybe bring a little bit of hope to the people that are there, so that they know that there are people out there who care – despite the narrative that they often see of hate.

Victoria: That lack of power that you feel when you're there, and like having to just kind of be with someone and not actually being able to tangibly change the situation. That must be like …

Tom: ... really infuriating. It can kind of wear you down. It can be really frustrating. I think it's something you have to learn to carry. I remember in the induction that they made that very clear. I remember Anna, who's now the director at GDWG, her saying in my induction that if you are somebody who is a campaigner and an advocate and you are here because you want to change those structures, then the role of visitor may not be for you, because actually yeah, you're not able to change the situation for that person legally, you're not allowed to offer any legal advice to that individual. So if they ask questions about their immigration status, that can only be answered by a legal representative. I mean, I don't have the expertise to be able to offer that advice, so I wouldn't be wanting to, but if they ask questions about things that you know you might be able to answer or find out, you have to resist. We don't want the Home Office to stop the listening service.

And yeah, if you see things or hear things that might be happening in the detention centre, we can't damage the relationship with the centre, so we can't be calling out the staff while we're there. But that's why we do campaigning in other ways, so GDWG partners with Refugee Tales to be raising awareness about the issues.

But it's hard, to not be able to help in that time when people are really disempowered, and it is those structures of the Home Office that you cannot change by the nature of being in detention. They completely rely on legal representation to have any kind of voice.

Their phones are taken off them when they're in detention, and mine too, you can't take anything in – smartphones are taken off. They're just given an old phone that can do calls and text messages. So all of those connections that you have and the ways that you may be able to prove your story as well, you don't have access to while you're in there.

But actually, it's great that once people have been released, we can then get onto campaigning to bring an end to the indefinite detention for ever, and many people say they want to campaign afterwards because they don't want others to go through that same situation.

So Refugee Tales is a project that shares the stories of those who've got lived experience of immigration detention to call an end to indefinite detention. And it's in campaigning for that time limit. It is about countering that hateful rhetoric and explaining how hard it is to be in a place you haven't chosen to be without an end date.

We have a main event each summer where they do a walk over five days, and each day people can join. We walk together as a community of walkers, including people with lived experience of the detention. So we walk together and build that community. And each evening someone will tell some refugee tales, and these are events where the stories of those who've experienced detention are shared. We gather in a local town that is on the walking route, people will be invited to join us, to hear those stories, and to campaign. And again, I think that that is a really effective tool for building those relationships and raising awareness. So that people have that connection, because often people say they have no idea of the situation. You find that after hearing the stories, people tend to want to know more about immigration detention and then they might campaign, but also again, it is about that building, that sense of community which is what is stripped away when people are held in detention and the hostile environment.

Often, people struggle once they are out of detention too. They are dispersed across the country, so they will be sent to places where they don't have connections, and will regularly be moved around the country, so that they can't build up a community or connections to support them. Refugee Tales can build a lot of bridges and help people find support.

Victoria: I joined a project where I spent a week with a bunch of young people and a bunch of refugees and asylum seekers, and we went walking in the Yorkshire Dales, and it was like the most transformative week of my life. I think, just walking with someone and sharing their stories and hearing their stories. But I also found it really, really hard to listen. And heartbreaking.

Tom: It is yeah. It was like very moving. It can have a real impact on those who joined. So it builds power in that it connects and builds community for those who have experienced this, but also for people who are listening as well. It is not easy to hear those stories, but it's important that we do. But we also need to be aware of holding people too tightly in that narrative. For some, the impacts of detention are more long term and very much further than the walls of the detention centre. So even though someone said they were there for around three months, still now, several years afterwards, they're still processing the impact of it. So we need to be aware of not trapping people in that narrative that yes, there are individuals that say that they want to advocate, and they are comfortable sharing their stories, but for others they don't want to be trapped in that narrative of a detainee and having to be somebody who, yeah, has to be sharing one experience that they had all the time.

So it's about finding the appropriate ways of raising awareness and not just using people as case studies when you need to prove a point. Or yeah, just using those dramatic experiences too but actually about sharing that hopeful narrative as well, and showing that sense of community.

Victoria: Maybe you can talk us through a normal day in a detention centre, like what does your role look like in that normal day?

Tom: I'm always very aware that I only see one small part of the detention centre. I only see the public spaces that they want me to see. The realities of somebody who is in there 24 hours a day can be very, very different.

I visit two different detention centres in the UK. So, as I said, GDWG work at Brook House and Tinsley House, which are both for Gatwick Airport, but Brook House is based on a category B prison. So essentially when you see it, it looks like a prison. It's an H block and it's essentially cells. Where people stay, their rooms are the would-be cells, people are on wings, but within that there are bits that I visit – like the social room.

It's something like over ten locked doors I go through in terms of signing into the visitors reception centre to be able to get into the visits room. You have to book and the day before bring your ID to be able to be registered there and registered with a photo. You can't take anything in, so phones and anything you leave behind. You're escorted through different rooms until you reach the visitor room which can have up to 16 people visiting. You would normally have low coffee tables, and you have a row of free seats one side, because someone can have up to three people visit them at the time, and a single seat the other side of the table, and you're not allowed to move those seats or tables. People have to sit the opposite side. So when I was there last week someone came, and it was a friend that they were visiting. They automatically sat next to them on the row of free seats. They were told, 'No, you have to be separate.'

Everyone is searched as well on the way into the visits room, and when they leave as well. So often, when I'm there as a GDWG visitor, if there's other people in there it will be friends, families, and domestic visits that are taking place, and essentially that happens two times a day – different times for the two centres. So normally in the afternoon from 2 until 5, and then there's a break for them to have their meals, and they have to do a roll call – which is a lockdown where they check the numbers, which again sounds like a prison, and then afterwards I think, 6.30 till about 9, they have that but in Brook House, from 9.30 pm it is essentially locked down where they all have to be back in their rooms in their cells until the next morning, like 7 am, when they would be released for breakfast. During the day they're able to move around within their wing so they can interact with others during meal times. And there are some activities but essentially, it's that same pattern every day which people can become institutionalized to as well – in the same way of prison. They have access to a gym. They have access to sports activities as well. So often when I arrive, I can hear people playing football in the outside area, but that essentially is behind a big fence with barbed wire all the way around it. You often see loads of the balls caught in the razor wire at the top.

There are sometimes workshops and classes that they can go to. So there's a library. Sometimes people find that helpful for them to go to the library and sometimes there are art classes that take place where people can go and be creative. It's sometimes actually really hard for people to take the step to go and do that, particularly when people are struggling with their mental health, and where people may be very depressed as a result of the situation. It can be difficult to engage with those things that would be helpful for them.

There is something called the community kitchen, that runs where people, I think, once a week, can request food from their own culture and have space to be able to cook it themselves. People say that that's something that's really helpful. But there's only a limited capacity to be able to do that. It can be small things that help break up and bring that hope within that situation as well.

Essentially, though, it is modelled on a prison, and it was never designed to be a place where people would be held for long periods of time, so actually, it can never be really an environment where people would want to be there for a long time.

People tell you stories as well, and it's the same threads that come through. So, for example, a lack of adequate healthcare. People who have existing medical conditions, that have been there a while, often health-care is delayed or prescriptions aren't offered. People often talk about two paracetamol, that whenever they go to the doctor all they are ever given is two paracetamol.

I think I've seen changes recently where things are starting to be better. Often people complain about the food being very, really bad in there. And that's actually why they value the cultural kitchen so much, because it's a chance for them to have food from home, but also there's something about sharing around food and stories flow from food.

Some can also have a job when in detention, in the centre. So that might be helping in the kitchen, or cleaning, and they say that helps pass the time. But they are aware that in doing that job they get paid one pound an hour. Yeah, how can that be legal? The fact though that it gives them something to do is valued.

Victoria: OK. Wow. That's horrible … So maybe we could end with a more theological question. So thinking about your experiences, what do you think Christian mission in the twenty-first century should prioritize, or should ideally look like?

Tom: I think, for me, personally, it is about building relationships with others. So I believe that it has to be relationally based and rooted in the loving and caring for others. I believe that hospitality is a form of mission, so that when we're being hospitable to others that is the first step towards us building relationships. So that when we know the people around us, when we are hospitable, and when we have those relationships with them, we are able to serve them better and bring justice for others as well. When we look at the examples of Jesus, often his thing was spending time with people in the places where they were, so within their own context, and getting to know people so that he would know about the issues that they were having. But also he would eat with people, he would meet them where they were. So I think that spending that time with people, even in those really hard places, that enables us to be aware and respond to issues that people are facing and then speak out about them and campaign for those issues.

I don't know if what I do is like a theological method, but because you're meeting people, and they're disempowered so much in that situation, I always feel like, even though there is actually nothing I can actually do, it is just witnessing and being there that is helping. Like kicking up a fuss and trying to change everything for them actually won't help anything – and that's such a hard situation to be in. But I also really believe that it would be where Jesus would be. It's a privilege I have really to be able to listen.

Notes

1 'No one shall be subjected to arbitrary arrest, detention or exile. Arbitrarily detaining nationals of other countries, depriving them of any of their rights and subjecting them to ill treatment or punishment can never be justified.' See United Nations Human Rights Office of the High Commissioner, 'Body of Principles for the Protection of All Persons under Any Form of Detention or Imprisonment', *United Nations*, https://www.ohchr.org/en/instruments-mechanisms/instruments/body-principles-protection-all-persons-under-any-form-detention, accessed 12.06.2024.

2 See update since the interview was undertaken: Lizzie Dearden, 2023, 'Bibby Stockholm: What life aboard "quasi-prison" barge will look like for asylum seekers', *The Independent*, 7 August, https://www.independent.co.uk/news/uk/home-news/bibby-stockholm-barge-inside-portland-migrant-b2388754.html, accessed 12.06.2024.

10

Befriending the Elderly Stranger: Lived Mission and Older People

JAMES WOODWARD

It is the purpose of this chapter to explore some of the issues and questions that are associated with our understanding of age and older adults within the context of society and faith. Older people in western society experience both poverty and marginalization. In an imperial and capitalist culture their relative lack of economic and social traction has left them overlooked and even silenced. We both fear age and the often-used descriptor, 'an ageing church' has become symptomatic of an ecclesiological and institutional anxiety about survival.

I write as a middle-aged white man whose lived experience of practice has been wholly within England. Within the context of this volume, I am aware of both the strengths and weaknesses of some of my horizons of thinking. I will argue that a radical reconstruction of priorities in mission and lived mission in and among older people will inevitably result in some fundamental epistemic disobedience. It will challenge some cultural assumptions about power and ecclesiology alongside models of ministry for mission.

The chapter is organized into four sections. The first section invites us into a closer attention to experience. Three stories from my own experience illuminate elements of the nature, challenge and opportunity of attending to the narratives of older adults.

This is followed by a brief examination of the social context within which our views and practices relating to age and ageing are shaped. I ask the reader to note the power and pervasive realities of ageism that shape our views and relationships.

The third section offers an overview of some of the thinking around the spiritual lives of older people from several writers and researchers. I draw upon the work of Gutmann, Carstensen, Thornstam and Coleman. This work illustrates how and in what way older adults become more spiritual and open to the religious questions that faith holds before us. Finally, section four discusses the nature of paying attention in pastoral ministry as a way of modelling lived mission drawing on the work of Andrew Root.

Paying attention to experience

Colin Woodward – a story close to home[1]

During the planning and initial research for this chapter, my father collapsed and died. Despite his mature age (of 85) he was in reasonable health thanks, in part, to the care of my siblings and the village where he had lived and worked all his life. By some of today's comparisons it was not an easy life – sent to work at 15 down into the depths of a coal mine where he laboured for over 40 years. It was characteristic of him to support my mother during a devastating diagnosis of dementia to be able to live and die at home. The geography of life shifts and there are new and surprising things to navigate, not least a deep and profound reminder of mortality together with the complicated emotions of grief and sorrow. This is part of my story but elements of it are universal. We age. We work. We retire. We live with both the possibilities and limitations of our bodies and health. Eventually all of us will die. This is my own fragment of narrative, and the story of its consequences is still being written. It is however also a universal narrative. Each of us must travel through the stages of life towards maturity, old age and death. This lived life is the substance within which we make meaning, aspire for the best for our families and communities and hope that the course of our journey is reasonably pain free.

I think it would surprise my father to imagine that he might be the subject matter for a chapter on mission. There was, in him, some deep ambivalence about the church. His views of those who participated in the life of the local church were informed by years of recognizing the gaps between participation and practice in Christian discipleship. His life story and working-class roots were shaped by the mining industry and its fortunes. During the Thatcher government he articulated some fundamental questions about the purpose of the church and where its preference and bias might be rooted. While Bishop David Jenkins offered a robust defence of the miners from the pulpit during the 1980s, Dad echoed a strong belief that English Anglicanism was essentially deeply disconnected from the working classes.[2] Marginalization, injustice and meaningless ideology were part of the purposes of established religion in his world view. Lived mission meant very little to those who were cast aside in the free market.

Sister Margaret – a challenge from the other side of the world

Over 20 years ago I made a visit to Sydney, Australia to discover more about their provision of housing and care for older people. The range and scope of their provision across the city and suburbs was impressive. Some of these retirement villages were run by Christian charities. A great deal of thought and investment had gone into the design and purpose of the variety of space and approaches to support and care for older people. I was especially impressed with the space provided for those living with dementia and memory loss. The attention to quality of the environment and especially their sensory gardens were clearly transformative for the flourishing of those living there.[3]

In one home I was privileged to spend some time with a Roman Catholic sister who has dedicated much of her life to working with older people, especially those living with dementia. Over tea one day I asked Margaret why it was that we were so seemingly incapable of thinking about age and older people through a more generative lens. Her reply has shaped much of my thinking ever since: 'I think that most of us, James, have still yet to befriend the elderly stranger in ourselves.'

The state and story of things? Explaining and accounting for where we are and what we look like

One of the gifts of my present work is a very wide variety of contact with the local church across denominations.[4] It is always good to see how community works and especially the resilience, honesty and energy that has gone into coping with the pandemic and building back in the service of others, especially those in need. In the places where we have had the opportunity to gather and reflect together on the present gift and the future possibility of Christian witness and mission there is one recurring theme. Sometimes it is expressed as a passing matter of fact but more often it is a judgement on the shape change has taken in a particular place. Here is what is said: 'Look at us – we are all getting older'; 'We are worried about the future – the church is growing older and ageing rapidly.' Occasionally it is put too sharply: 'There are just too many older people in this place.' These are some starting points for this chapter to explore what we might discover as we listen to the narratives of older people. As we listen, we become aware that there is complexity, limitation, truth, prejudice, revelation and wisdom.

Paying attention to the context – an ageing society?

We are experiencing a revolution in human longevity. There has been a steady increase in life expectancy in recent years. In 2014 there were 10 million people in the UK over 65 years old. By the year 2030, this figure is projected to rise to 15 million. Although there are some indications of a slowing down of life expectancy, some estimate that by 2050 the number will have nearly doubled to 20 million.[5]

Today there are more than one in ten people who are over 60 years old. The number of very old people grows even faster. All this has significant implications for the way any society organizes its wealth and provides benefits and pensions. While the UK might not be representative of a global picture of age and ageing, all political and economic systems face the challenge of ageing populations for health, welfare and social insurance systems. In this gift of modernity we also face the paradox that we seem either unprepared or lacking economic will to make appropriate provision for older people.[6]

The statistics have long posed financial and political challenges to how we care for older adults, particularly those who do not have the financial resources to support themselves with appropriate housing and care in third and fourth age. Successive governments have failed to make appropriate decisions to support the most vulnerable of older adults in our society. The more politicized the discourse has become, it seems, the less able we are to place these challenges and opportunities into a broader historical and cultural horizon. In the pandemic, for example, one of the main groups that were most affected were older people. Many died in care homes and the sheer variety and diversity of provision of care across this country was laid bare. A lack of consistent and reliable social policy left many vulnerable people at severe risk.[7]

It is fair to point out that there have been many attempts to solve the challenges of funding for social care for older adults, but none have been adopted. In the present financial situation there is a justice issue in achieving the right balance between individual responsibility and publicly funded provision.[8] Lived mission must always be aware of the ways in which a particular context, inheritance, class or economic status shapes the lives of those who find themselves less advantaged within society. Lived mission is always shaped by geography, human prejudice, economics, class and culture.

Language shapes the way we think and act. Culture can have a powerful and abiding influence on how we think about ageing. The World Health Organization defines ageism as the way stereotypes of older people affect how we think and feel both towards others and indeed towards ourselves. This has and can shape how we act, which may be a form of discrimination. It follows then that if we internalize negative stereotypes about the shape age takes in individuals we run the risk of devaluing and discriminating against older people. In this sense ageism can intersect with other forms of disadvantage including sex, race and disability.[9]

There may be several consequences to our fear or prejudice about our own age and ageing process alongside older adults in our families, communities or organizations. There may well be part of all of us that fears older age in such an acute way that it has a detrimental effect upon our well-being and flourishing. This may impact on our health and longevity. It may also erode solidarity between generations.

Several agencies and research units have engaged with ways in which ageism might be combated. The work of the Centre for Ageing Better has offered several resources to enable discrimination and inequality on the basis of age to be challenged. Educational activities can work in enabling people to consider the way in which some of the language around age and older people perpetuates inaccurate information and stereotypical judgements. Work across the generations can also help reduce stereotypes and prejudice.[10]

There is some further work to be done in engaging with ageism in religious organizations. In this area those working in and between world faith traditions may have much to learn from the ways in which Islam, Hinduism and Judaism make provision for older people within both their theological thinking and pastoral practice.[11]

Paying attention to the lived experiences of older people

Ageism has the potential of both overlooking and marginalizing the importance of older people and their ageing journey. Ageism perpetuates negative stereotypes and may even act to prevent us from some of the inner work of befriending age in others and ourselves. The 'spiritual' may be obvious, but it may also remain hidden and unarticulated. There are many people who are spiritually curious but have to discover places, communities or languages within which this curiosity can be expressed and explored.

Erik Erikson's concepts of 'generativity' (the capacity to give of oneself to the next generations) and 'integrity' (acceptance of life in the face of death) are influential in the shaping of some literature in the area of spirituality and ageing. We should note that these concepts were formulated more than 50 years ago but have yet to be put to work in deepening wisdom about our human condition and developing learning through research.[12]

Accounting for such views and understanding the complexity of how we make truth claims especially in our understanding of human nature is a key part of our theological task in the practice of mission. Perhaps in the area of ageing we might seek to defend and encourage interdisciplinary engagement and dialogue as part of a conviction that all knowledge is unitary, not separate, and disciplinary. The late Michael Argyle, who was one of the few practising Christians in the Oxford University psychology department, once told an audience, provocatively, that most people who studied psychology did so because they wanted to obliterate their religious upbringing and any lingering traces of religious hold on their thought and emotions. Psychology offered the prospect of an alternative understanding of human nature in which religious faith would be superfluous. It seems that psychology, along with other disciplines, has a deep discomfort of religion.[13] This is often a much-overlooked area of reflection on the nature of missiology and the practice of mission. It may not be an exaggeration to suggest that much of our language of mission remains obtuse, intangible and, for some, simply irrelevant to modernity. Theology may need liberating from its own internal anxieties and psychodramas. Lived mission might take as its starting point a contemplative attention to how others hear and see who we are, what we do and what we say.

In Erikson's well-known account of the life cycle, he demonstrates his commitment to, and sympathy for, religion. He describes religious faith as the mature adult virtue, which grows out of trust. In this country, Peter Coleman and his work at Southampton University has engaged in some fundamental questions relating to the widespread existence of spiritual experience and its consequences for the person's life.[14]

The challenges and complexities of growing older

The last decades have seen the apparently triumphal entry into human history of the 'Third Age', a time of life when people are free to be themselves, to pursue their own chosen interests, not necessarily for selfish ends. Given reasonable health and economic conditions, this can be the optimum time of life. US studies on self-esteem across the lifespan demonstrate that the seventh decade of our life, our 60s, is the peak time of high self-satisfaction. For many people the third age can begin in the 50s and continue well into the 80s and perhaps beyond if they are fortunate. But the third age comes to an end, often abruptly as the result of a severe health event like a stroke or a key bereavement such as the death of one's spouse. Older people are often not prepared for the dramatic changes in their lives and, perhaps because the preceding period has been so positive, the latter stages of life, the fourth age, when control is increasingly taken away from the individual, can be experienced very negatively. The sense of loss of meaning and purpose that this engenders can cast a shadow over the preceding years as people begin to envisage a bleak future.[15]

Human culture has failed to keep up with changing life expectation.[16] As a result, the negative features of ageing have been enhanced rather than counteracted. Comparatively speaking, we live at a period of history when ageing has lost much of its earlier dignity. Perhaps we sense that an older culture gave dignity which we have lost and not yet replaced? Although older people were a small proportion of the population in previous societies, they were a significant part of most cultures that have existed in historical time. It may be the moment for our missional culture to recover the voice and experience of older adults.

Although it is misleading to paint an over-idealized picture of the past, there is strong evidence that in traditional societies older people had more valued roles as tenders of the family, community and culture, and their mental health was better as a result.[17] But the more important point is that personal well-being, the pursuit of individual happiness, was not the objective of such cultures; rather it was the well-being of society as a whole, and in this older people were seen to have a vital role to play. One can depict biological change as the natural enemy of ageing seen as 'fulfilled growing old', with its greater appreciation of the double-sided character of experience, a friend in disguise who awakens us, by means of the problems and pains it brings, to give more attention to the spirit. Culture, on the other hand, has always been the natural friend of ageing. Culture has provided the social and environmental means whereby older people have been enabled to continue functioning and contributing at a high level.[18]

The failure of western post-enlightenment culture to adapt to the rising tide of older people in its populations could also be understood as a failure of religion. Some authorities have even attributed the problem to Christianity. Christianity, of all the great religions, gives apparently little significance to ageing. Partly this is because Christ died in early adulthood at an age that came to be seen as the perfect age, and also because Christianity – compared with Judaism – gives much more attention to continued life beyond death. The length of one's life ceases to be important. Wisdom also is no longer the prerogative of the old. This argument is crudely put – and it is important to recognize the witness that older figures such as Simeon and Anna do give in the New Testament, and that Christian churches, like most other social institutions, have functioned as gerontocracies up to the present day. But the relative lack of privilege given to age by Christian churches deserves further consideration.[19]

The increased importance of religion with age

The evidence provides a consistent picture of the increasing importance of religion with age. Religious beliefs, behaviour and experiences that reflect spirituality all increase with age. The only exception is diminished attendance at religious services among the very old and this is understandable in terms of reduced health and mobility, but this is often compensated by increased rates of other forms of religious and spiritual activity. Moberg emphasizes that this pattern of results has been consistently found over the last 50 years as successive generations have aged and died, despite the predictions that it would diminish as secularization swept through society.[20]

How might we discover and nurture meaning and purpose in older age? The work of Gutmann, Carstensen, Thornstam and Coleman

It is David Gutmann's psycho-anthropological work in traditional societies that opened up the importance of religion in the life of some older people.[21] In a series of longitudinal studies in societies around the world, he demonstrated the important role of transmission that older people played in demonstrating religious practice and communicating religious injunctions. There seemed to be a moment of transition, particularly in older men's lives, when they came to take on the role of elders, often dressing and shaving differently, spending more time in prayer, ceasing to be involved in practical matters. By their change of behaviour and their more passive orientation they became persons of greater respect and even awe. Carstensen and Tornstam both build on and develop this research.[22]

Carstensen and her team reach several perhaps surprising conclusions about older people. This work is part of a movement away from decline models of ageing to a lifespan developmental model, which considers how particular processes and strategies facilitate adaptive ageing. We note a contrast between a picture that demonstrates decreased biological, physiological, and cognitive capacity alongside evidence that suggests that people are generally satisfied in old age and experience high levels of emotional well-being. Carstensen offers a view of ageing as adaptation, which sheds significant light on resilience and well-being across adulthood. We note that older people are less likely to experience persistent negative emotional states and can regulate their sense of equilibrium and well-being. In other words, older adults can embrace complexity, paradox and ambiguity in the experience of life. Older people were more able to experience poignancy of both positive and negative emotions.

We should note these challenges to older people's flourishing alongside the significant contribution by Carstensen to gerontology: the argument that we should be freeing ourselves from the presumption of decline. The research work of Tornstam in gerontological sociology originated in Sweden in 1973. The model of gerotranscendence suggests that human longevity includes the potential for a transcendent movement away from the materialistic and rational point of view common in the first half of life. His research suggests that successful completion of such a shift is accompanied by an increase in life satisfaction. In this respect it sits with and complements the work of Carstensen. Put quite simply, this research suggests that older people become more open to the transcendent and the spiritual in older age. This has the capacity to help us all to age well.

The theory of gerotranscendence grew from the decades Tornstam spent making careful observations of people living in old age. Tornstam argues that in older age there is a process of discovery, of coming to terms with the complexity of life and self. There is a decrease in self-centredness and a movement from egoism to altruism. Associated with these findings is a mapping of the changes in relationships. Older people become more selective and less interested in superficial relationships. There is an increased need for solitude. There is a distinction between oneself and one's role. Attitudes to wealth change. There is less acquisitiveness and a greater awareness that possessions can ensnare and confine a person.

The combined work of Carstensen and Thornstam challenges us to reconsider the spiritual prospects of older age and to see within our life-span the possibilities of creativity and power. We will remain ignorant of the depth and breadth of this potential and power as long as we insist on simply comparing youth to age. These findings bear out much of my own pastoral experience over the last three decades. Many of our churches are populated with older adults because they become more aware of the spiritual and religious dimensions of their lives in the third and fourth ages. They bring into our ecology a lived experience that can be used to deepen wisdom and build community. Older people are our elders holding wisdom and spiritual treasure.

Peter Coleman has argued that we cannot understand religion's influences on positive psychological processes or promote such processes if we do not understand the phenomenon of being religious.[23] Psychologists, he argues, must learn from religious practitioners themselves about the nature of religion, its function, and the costs and benefits of membership.

There are several key findings from Coleman's research that we might bear in mind when considering the nature of meaning and purpose in later life through the lens of lived mission.

1. Death and bereavement are a major challenge to coherent meaning and mental health. The pattern of bereaved spouses, following them from the first to the second anniversary of death showed more uncertain and unsupported belief being associated with poorer outcomes in terms of depression and low levels of personal meaning.

2. Participants were asked to describe their own experience of religious institutions. The findings of Coleman's study confirm that, for this generation of British older people at least, personal spiritual experience appears more significant and indeed more frequent than communal church life, and spiritual questioning increases.

3. This greater individualizing or rather personalizing of faith is accompanied by greater need for spiritual education. Coleman discovered that many older people hold significant reservations about many of the tenets of the Christian creed.

There are some important organizational and even ecclesiological implications for Christian communities considering Coleman's work. We note the reality of the spiritual uncertainty, questioning and lack of rootedness present in many British older people as reflected in this research. Within the frame of our commitment to mission we certainly need to explore further the question of how we understand the ways in which faith is transmitted. The traditional model suggests that the older person (among others) is a reliable transmitter of religious models of thought and practice.

Conclusions: building inter-generational communities of spiritual friendship?

1 Building friendships across the generations

There is an increased acknowledgement of some of the implications for individuals, families and communities of what might be described as a loss of the relational and pastoral as a serious threat to our human flourishing. Some of the work at a national level on loneliness[24] reminds us that friendship is one of the most indispensable requirements of life, indeed a necessary means of and for our flourishing.

We have already noted the destructive possibilities of ageism and we would do well to explore the extent to which ageism in the churches has contributed to what Coleman describes as 'a period of history when ageing has lost much of its earlier dignity'. We need each other and have much to learn from one another as friendship is nurtured and we share our desire to support, engage and deepen wisdom for living.

2 A renewed interest in spirituality and religion?

Experience here in this community of learning, at Sarum College, shows us that there is no loss of interest or energy in a spiritual quest today. There may be some loss of confidence in aspects of institutional religion and organized church, but both individuals and groups are no less spiritual. Their search and journey continues. There are many individuals who, given the right context and relationship, wish to narrate their journey of faith and explore the spiritual dimensions of their lives. A new enlightenment may be dawning. It may be that we need to be in a position where curiosity is nurtured and a different kind of religious journey offered. For too long religion has been over-dominated by a combination and process of binary arguments about either proving or disproving truth, whether outside or inside the church. In this consumerist and often superficial culture of doing, we have lost the ability to engage with the idea of mystery or wonder – quite simply, 'curiosity'.

3 Who and what sustains the spiritual?

The wider European and especially Russian narratives offered by Coleman may be a pointer to what sustains and deepens the spiritual. When we consider some of the brutalities exercised during the Communist era it is significant to note that there is a life-changing strengthening of faith when it is under fire. One of the lessons to be learned here might be how we nurture a sense of the spiritual that can carry individuals at points of crises in their lives – when there is greater uncertainty and adversity. Any theology for lived mission needs to engage with pain, loss, vulnerability, the hope for wholeness, the reality of death, and doubt and uncertainty. Popularism and superficiality may have some power in attracting new adherents to faith but are we nurturing a faith that can sustain some of the more problematic and challenging experiences of living?

We might remind ourselves that the themes of love, friendship and social trust are fundamental to what older people need from both life and religion. Could it be that the more complicated life becomes in this modern age of fragmentation and the breakdown of community, the more religion might have to offer in these areas?

4 Good and bad religion?

The ways in which religion might be destructive to human well-being need to be articulated and explored. What are the legitimate objections to belief as it shapes an individual's self-image and sense of destiny? Is religion enabling a fundamental self-love? In relation to our work with older people, does religion help them cope with diminishment, change and death? There is some research which suggests that there is plenty of evidence that religion has a positive contributing influence on well-being. In the light of this, is it possible to make a distinction between good religion and bad religion? Might we learn from older people themselves and their experiences of community, faith and pilgrimage as we gain a greater sense of the limitations and possibilities of religion?

It may be very hard to overestimate the sheer effect of the decline of religious affiliation. The 1980s and 1990s therefore became a very significant period of difficulty in relation to the shape and influence of religion over people. Churches must bear some responsibility in the strategies that they have employed to cope with this decline – especially in the emphasis on work among young families and children. Is it possible to be objective about the marginalization of older people because of these mission and evangelistic strategies?

Finally, despite this decline there must surely still be some measure of authenticity about the kind of spiritual questions people ask in old age. There are of course interesting issues about whether religion in the end answers our needs and yearning and spiritual questionings. Do we need to liberate religion from structure and institution into a more radical counter-cultural movement? Will it ever be possible to do this without the baggage of ideology and fundamentalism?

Paying attention to pastoral presence in the practice of lived mission

Andrew Root in his exploration of pastoral ministry argues that that we must connect and be in relationship with others as the basis for lived mission:

> Our relationships are the very field, the very place, where God is encountered. Pastoral ministry can be nothing more and nothing less than making space for people to encounter the very presence of God. Space is created in the sharing of relationships of persons.[25]

It follows that the pastor is invited to join in God's continued action in the world. In this framework of relationality, Root reminds his reader that the pastor is a storyteller performing and protecting the stories of his people. This chapter argues that in the life of lived mission we ought to attend to those stories that are so often ignored or overlooked. We have noted an increase in religious and spiritual awareness in older adults which has generative potential of sharing wisdom and faith. Too many of our cultural norms in Christian communities nurture and perpetuate age-ism. We should examine therefore what shapes the values and practices of missional engagement. What would a commitment to older people look like for lived mission? How far would it challenge any model of evangel-ization that colludes with the dominant culture and power structure of both society and church.

Root draws upon the work of Giddens who has explored the develop-ment of independence and relationship within a developing culture, arguing that relationships with other human beings became not a neces-sity but an individual choice.[26] We live in a culture where we have become obsessed with ourselves as autonomous feeling subjects and so our relationship with other people and indeed our dependence upon them has shifted. Technology has both liberated us and imprisoned us in what Root describes as an obsessiveness and a 'therapeutic self-help conscious-ness'. Self-help is soaked deeply into 'an unquenchable individualism'.[27] It may therefore not be surprising that within this cultural, social and relational change the realities of age and the numbers of older people in our families and societies have ceased to become a priority for our time and organizational life as Christian communities. In this picture, ministry is turned into a system of programmes of intervention that are designed to draw people into membership. In an anxious and declining ecology, a commitment to older adults is either marginalized or overlooked.

Lived mission might explore support and engagement that would en-able people to connect with their spiritual life. This mission would recover a valuing of age and older adults as teachers of wisdom, examples of spiritual generativity, embodied faith bearers. The adults can be a space for people to rest in relationships as human person to human person. Being and listening are profoundly affirming and bear much fruit. We are our lived relationships. We are no longer objects or statistics but people and persons.

Root goes on to develop how lived mission might be essentially con-nected with sharing in the life of others. In this context we need to recover how our engagement with older people at a deeply personal level can explore what human flourishing might look like in the face of change, fragility and human vulnerability. It is perhaps only in such relationality that we ourselves can really be ourselves. In this life we understand, grasp and name the grace of relationship as we always open ourselves up to the other as a place of the indwelling of God's grace. This is inextricably linked with power participation in the incarnation. We cannot share in the life of others if we refuse to connect and engage with them. This is true of all pastoral ministry and mission. That mission, that lived mission may be compromised if there are people or groups that are simply over-looked. Root concludes, 'We cannot share in the life of others if we refuse to act for them. We are given the gift of our personhood by action done with and for other persons.'[28]

Pastoral presence might be defined as the exercise and commitment to empathy. It is the experience of feeling that helps to make us a person. Empathy is the spiritual reality that takes us into, that moves us towards, another. Empathy is the surest lens of seeing each other in all our limitations and vulnerability. What do we see when we look and attend? How might lived mission develop this empathy as imaginative feeling? Lived mission is perhaps then the facilitation of empathetic encounter. We might be called into creating space that allows for gentle, slow, attentive sharing in others' lives. This is about becoming human within the context of God's encounter with us.

It is an observation that may be both subjective and limited, but there is a sense in which organized religious life in these post-pandemic times seems somewhat at a low ebb. Anecdotal evidence suggests that a significant number of people have not returned to churches, which may result in increased anxiety about sustainability for Christian witness and mission. It is within this context that we need to ask, where do we place older people? How do we relate to older people? What do we see as we look at one another's faces? Where do we see transcendence in each other's personhood? How might lived mission nurture encounter, creativity, depth and compassion?

Within this relational commitment there is a culture change both for the theology and practice of mission. This chapter may have opened with a simple definition of lived mission as our support of enabling stories to be heard. There is a radical spirit in a commitment to giving voice to those who have been marginalized by our functional and capitalist spiritual ecologies. In this story is the hook of a deeper and personal connection. Listening to each other and the range and complexity of human experience can help nurture gratitude and deep and emotional intelligence. Root shows us that sharing is the heart of a pastoral ministry and in this sharing of each other's humanity we are joyously celebrating the very sharing in the life of God.[29]

Notes

1 This chapter is dedicated to the memory of my father, Colin Woodward 1936–2023.

2 LBC/IRN, 1984, 'David Jenkins sermon on miners strike', *Learning on Screen*, http://bufvc.ac.uk/tvandradio/lbc/index.php/segment/0010800203004, accessed 10.10.2023. The Bishop of Durham, David Jenkins, makes his inaugural sermon (1984) on possible solutions to the miners' strike, suggesting National Coal Board Chairman Ian MacGregor should step down.

3 See Forward with Dementia, 'Gardening and people living with dementia', *Forward with Dementia*, https://forwardwithdementia.au/news/gardening-and-people-living-with-dementia/ for evidence of innovative practice of support and care for people living with dementia, accessed 12.06.2024.

4 For further information about the work of Sarum College, see https://www.sarum.ac.uk/.

5 See Veena Raleigh, 2018, 'What is happening to life expectancy in England?', *The King's Fund*, https://www.kingsfund.org.uk/publications/whats-happening-life-expectancy-england, accessed 12.06.2024; B. Bytheway, 2011, *Age and Time in Unmasking Age*, Bristol: Policy Press.

6 For a global perspective, see World Health Organization, 2022, 'Ageing and health', *World Health Organization*, https://www.who.int/news-room/fact-sheets/detail/ageing-and-health, accessed 12.06.2024.

7 See the Report Covid-19: Neglect was one of biggest killers in care homes during pandemic, BMJ 2021;375:n3132 and from the Quality Care Commission, 2024, 'Publication of statistics on deaths involving COVID-19 in care homes in England: transparency statement', *Care Quality Commission*, https://www.cqc.org.uk/publications/major-reports/publication-statistics-deaths-involving-covid-19-care-homes-england, accessed 12.06.2024.

8 See H. Small, 2007, *The Long Life*, Oxford: Oxford University Press; P. Thane, 2000, *Old Age in English History, past Experiences, Present Issues*, Oxford: Oxford University Press; A. Tinker, 1997, *Older People in Modern Society*, 4th edn, London: Longman.

9 Bytheway, *Age and Time in Unmasking Age*.

10 See Centre for Ageing Better, 2021, 'Challenging Ageism', https://ageing-better.org.uk/sites/default/files/2022-01/Challenging-ageism-guide-talking-ageing-older-age.pdf, accessed 12.06.2024; B. Bytheway,1995, *Ageism*, Maidenhead: Open University Press.

11 O. Valins, 2002, *Facing the Future: The provision of long term care facilities for older Jewish people in the United Kingdom*, Institute for Jewish Policy Research; D. A. Friedman, 2008, *Jewish Visions for Aging: A Professional Guide for Fostering Wholeness*, Woodstock, VT: Jewish Lights Publishing.

12 L. J. Friedman, 2004, 'Erik Erikson on Generativity: a biographer's perspective' in E. de St. Aubin, D. P. McAdams and T.-C. Kim (eds), *The Generative Society: Caring for future generations*, American Psychological Association, pp. 257–64; E. H. Erikson, 1950, *Childhood and Society*, New York: Norton.

13 From a personal conversation in Oxford, November 1987.

14 See P. G. Coleman, 2011, *Belief and Ageing: Spiritual pathways in later life*, Bristol: The Policy Press.

15 H. R. Moody, 1994, *Aging, Concepts and Controversies*, Newbury Park, CA: Pine Forge Press; H. R. Moody, 1996, *Ethics in an Aging Society*, Baltimore, MD: The John Hopkins University Press.

16 P. B. Baltes, 'On the incomplete architecture of human ontogeny: selection, optimization and compensation as foundation of developmental theory', *American Psychologist* 52 (1997): 366–80.

17 See D. Gutmann, 1987, *Reclaimed Powers: Towards a New Psychology of Men and Women in Later Life*, New York: Basic Books.

18 S. Tilak, 1989, *Religion and Aging in the Indian Tradition*, Albany, NY: University of New York Press.

19 J. Woodward, 2008, *Valuing Age: Pastoral ministry amongst older people*, London: SPCK; C. B. Mitchell, R. D. Orr and S. A. Salladay, 2004, *Aging, Death*

and the Quest for Immortality, Grand Rapids, MI: Eerdmans; S. Hauerwas, C. B. Stoneking, K. G. Meador and D. Cloutier (eds), 2003, *Growing Old in Christ*, Grand Rapids, MI: Eerdmans.

20 M. C. Bateson, 2010, *Composing a Further Life: The age of active wisdom*, New York: Vintage Books; V. L. Bengston with N.M. Putney and S. Harris, 2013, *Families and Faith: How religion is passed down across generations*, Oxford: Oxford University Press.

21 D. Gutmann, 1987, *Reclaimed Powers: Towards a new psychology of men and women in later life*, New York: Basic Books.

22 L. Tornstam, 2005, *Gerotranscendence: A developmental theory of positive aging*, New York: Springer Publishing Company; L. L. Carstensen and C. R. Hartel (eds), 2006, *When I'm 64*, Washington, DC: National Academies Press.

23 P. G. Coleman, C. Ivani-Chalian and M. Robinson, 'Religious attitudes among British older people: stability and change in a 20 year longitudinal study', *Ageing and Society* 24 (2004): 167–88; P. G. Coleman, 2011, *Belief and Ageing: Spiritual pathways in later life*, Bristol: The Policy Press.

24 Age UK, 2017, 'Jo Cox Commission on Loneliness', *Age UK*, https://www.ageuk.org.uk/our-impact/campaigning/jo-cox-commission/, accessed 12.10.2023.

25 A. Root, 2013, *The Relational Pastor*, Denver: IVP, p. 10.

26 A. Giddens, 1992, *The Transformation of Intimacy*, Stanford, CA: Stanford University Press.

27 Root, *The Relational Pastor*, p. 36.

28 Root, *The Relational Pastor*, p. 77.

29 Root, *The Relational Pastor*, p. 215.

Consequences

11

Mission and Racial Justice: Ecumenical and Millennial Perspectives

LISA ADJEI AND SHERMARA FLETCHER

Shermara's story (race and the Church)

'Race, Race, go away, come back another day! In fact, give me a break!'

I never defined, considered or subscribed to the social construct of being a 'Black Christian' until I started to attend a culturally White British denomination and the exigencies of the environment demanded that I knew who I was. This realization particularly increased when I was invited to meetings. At some point I always knew that I would be asked a question about race or expected to be the spokesperson for all UKMEC communities in a way that my colleagues would not.

Initially, I was not offended by people's questions that stemmed from a place of curiosity and sometimes fear. However, I was when they came from a position of ignorance, a lack of personal will to read about the nuances of race relations, and the expectation that those with lived experience of oppression would do the intensive intellectual labour of explaining their experience while being at risk of micro aggression and gaslighting. My tolerance also faded whenever there was an attitude of denial in understanding how complicit many were in upholding systems of oppression that yielded personal, communal, social and economic benefits. Over time I developed representation fatigue.

Within this denomination, I also noticed and was shocked by how often Black African, Caribbean and South Asian Christians would speak about race and share their dilemma of being vocationally called into a space that did not always affirm it. It was disconcerting to know that the freedom offered in Christ was not always translated into the spaces dedicated to worshipping him and that they felt stifled in contributing to God's mission because of personal and institutional prejudice and racism. There was also a sense of frustration about the lack of representation in the leadership and the constant promotion of leaders that did not reflect the diversity of the community they served. This was not my experience growing up.

This was alien to me, or was it?

Context matters and it's important to locate myself in this theological reflection and share that my perspective is shaped by my Black British Caribbean heritage. I grew up in a Black Majority Caribbean Church where I saw Black men and women occupy leadership roles and drive missional initiatives at a national, regional and local level. I am the daughter of an area bishop who exercises responsibility for several churches across Birmingham. I am also the daughter of a mother who is a National Women's Director in the church and has a successful secular career. The women's department also pioneered a national missional initiative for women called *Connect*, which encourages women to start missional communities with women in their local area around topics of common interest such as exercise, motherhood and careers. It was inspiring to see Black women impact communities with their missional activities and to see these activities help women from diverse backgrounds come to faith, share their stories in the annual retreat and connect to a local church.

Autonomy, creativity, mission and leadership by Black Christians was normal for me and I have always been near Black leadership. The Black majority space, as I remember it, was affirming in terms of race, full of opportunities and the famous exaltation spot in a Sunday morning service prepared you to speak before any crowd by the age of five. However, as I started to reflect on my perspective of autonomy and affirmation after my experience in a predominantly White British cultural denomination, I started to question if my shock, frustration and racial ambivalence was due to my third-generation Jamaican diasporan and millennial privilege.

The reality was my grandparents and their peers from the Windrush generation would not have shared this perspective. I believe they would have been acutely aware that they were Black Christians living in a hostile society well before Theresa May's Home Office policy. I not only experienced racial ambivalence due to the confidence and joy of who God created me to be as a beautiful Black woman, but also because of the sacrifices and battles the Windrush generation faced and overcame. I was living in their promised land.

Immigration, the Windrush generation and the Black majority church

Between 1948 and 1971 an influx of Caribbean men, women and children responded to the invitation, as Commonwealth citizens and British subjects, to help rebuild a decimated Britain in recovery from the Second World War.

This Caribbean migration saw many come with a burning desire to live out their faith and contribute to the British mission field. However, stories would be recounted about the pain and rejection that many faced as they were asked to not return the following week to some of the same historic churches that sent their missionaries to evangelize them in the Caribbean. While this was not the only narrative and experience of Christians in the Windrush era, it was a predominant one.

Despite the frosty reception, many first-generation migrant pastors emerged, planted their own churches and refused to let their missional pursuits be hindered. My grandad, Stanford Fletcher, was one of them. He was a Windrush pioneer who came to the UK in the 1960s and despite the obstacles that he and many others faced, he gave his life to Jesus and passionately pursued his missional journey. With others, he fundraised across many pubs in Birmingham on chilly winter nights to help gather the finances to build one of the largest Black majority churches in Birmingham. He also faithfully served as a deacon under the leadership of Bishop T. A. McCalla, who pioneered and inspired many Black men and women to lead churches in the UK and abroad. He then became pastor of a community church in Quinton in the city of Birmingham and fundraised for a community church van to fulfil missional activity to children in the local area and parents who were often financially struggling.

There were also many other pioneers in the Black Caribbean Pentecostal community who started Black majority congregations and organizations in a time of racial hostility. The first of these was Calvary Church of God in Christ, which started in London in 1948. The New Testament Church of God followed shortly, which held its first service in the YMCA in Wolverhampton in 1953, and the Church of God of Prophecy was established in the same year.

The Wesleyan Holiness Church was then founded in 1958 and New Testament Assembly was founded in 1961, to mention a few.

These churches still operate today and contribute to the religious, spiritual, missional and social life of the UK. It is also important to note that while many of these churches have a Black majority presence in the UK, they are also connected to international headquarters in the United States and are a part of a global communion of churches and Christians from all races and ethnicities. A second generation of Caribbean Pentecostal churches with British headquarters also started in the 1990s, which were contextual, visionary and entrepreneurial, such as Ruach Ministries founded in London in 1994, Christian Life City founded in 1996 in London and many more.

In the 1980s to 1990s, the Black majority church landscape also evolved through migration and the emergence of new African churches who followed the call of reverse mission to re-evangelize Britain.

Some of these churches are the Church of Pentecost founded in London in 1988, the Redeemed Christian Church of God (RCCG) also founded in London in 1988, Trinity Baptist Church founded in South Norwood in 1988, Kingsway International Christian Centre (KICC) founded in London in 1992 and others. Intercultural theologian Israel Olofinjana interrogates the efficacy of the reverse mission movement with his observation that, 'I discovered that some of them portray an international image through their names, flags and church materials, but in reality, they were mono-ethnic churches, that is, churches with one dominant ethnicity or nationality.'[1] This observation still raises questions and contentions today.

The sustainability of the Windrush generation and Black majority church's missional journey is an example of the encouragement in Genesis 20.50 that although, 'You intended to harm me, God intended it for good to accomplish what is now being done, the saving of many lives.' Babatunde Adedibu affirms this claim through his observation that, 'The Christian landscape in Britain now has a definitive imprint of African and Caribbean Christianity and is best described using the metaphor of Joseph's "coat of many colours".'[2]

As I reflect on my context and space of spiritual formation, the Black majority church, I have come to realize that migration, racial injustice and inequality, as well as self-determination and agency, have been some of the foundational drivers of this diaspora's missional movement. I could no longer detach race from my faith.

The Landscape – George Floyd (say his name!) and millennials

If coming outside the Black majority church space made me consider my faith and race, the killing of George Floyd made it imperative to understand the implications of being Black and Christian, for the sake of my salvation and identity. On 25 May 2020, the world witnessed the horrific death of George Floyd, shocking us into confronting the racial injustice experienced by Black Americans and Black communities across the world. Global protests rejecting the abuse of black bodies were televised, and most notably in the UK we witnessed the pulling down of the statue of the slave trader Edward Colston, who proudly towered over the people of Bristol. George Floyd's murder forced a re-evaluation of our most fundamental beliefs, institutions and theologies and inaugurated a cultural epoch of change.

Within Britian, many millennials of all races and faiths took to the streets and were leading voices in Black Lives Matter marches across the country. This global protest had a prophetic edge. The protest's righteous indignation became an act of mission from the world towards the whole Church which demanded that the Church wake up and renounce any ambivalence and complicit silence towards racial injustice. 'Wisdom really cried from the streets' (Proverbs 1.20).

I also believe George Floyd's murder provoked many millennial Black Christians in the UK into a crisis of faith and prompted them to question what it meant to be Black and Christian in the UK today. These were questions that could no longer be ignored, and the frustration of unanswered questions manifested in the exodus of people who left their churches or the Christian faith altogether. While writing from an American context, minister Dante Stewart offers a contemporary and personal insight into this attitude. He shares:

> I have learned that many of us have not given up on faith, just the way our faith has been used to oppress others. We have not given up on the Bible, just the way it has been used to marginalize others. We have not given up on Jesus ... we're not becoming less spiritual or religious. It's just that we have learned to put up with less, much less. Today many people talk a lot about people leaving churches, giving up on Christianity, and rejecting Jesus. In reality, they have given up on the white supremacist brand of Christianity that cares more about power than Jesus, that does not care enough to take either our bodies or our futures seriously. Like James Baldwin, we are holding on to Jesus while also living with our fear, trauma, doubts, and hope. Our story and the story of Jesus are bound together in faith, hope, love, and community.[3]

To reach young Black adults in the UK, I believe our missional strategies cannot exclude race. They also cannot romanticize race and race should not be used as a paternalistic weapon of control and condescension. Missional narratives should tell the truth about the intersectional identity of Jesus and his cultural background, that global majority heritage peoples fill the pages of the Bible and that their stories have played a prominent role in the biblical narrative before the Great European Migration, which saw Europeans at the end of the fifteenth century to the middle of the twentieth century moving into other parts of the world such as Africa, Asia and Latin America.

This truth-telling must also go beyond hermeneutics and become a historic fact in the understanding of western and British mission. Furthermore, the voices of Global Majority theologians need to inform how mission is conducted in Britain and they should not be typecast in the theological areas of race, liberation, or Black theology.

The emergence of the distinctively Black British Church is a phenomenon that has tried to address the discontent with faith ignoring the Black reality and experience. Independent churches such as The Arc Network of

Churches, led by Pastor Peter Nembhard, and The Tab, led by Pastor Mike White, are examples of this mission.

These dynamic inter-generational churches distinctively represent the hybridity and nuance of Black British culture. They are inspiring a generation of conscious Black British millennials and Gen Z churchgoers who may have parted from traditional African and Caribbean churches due to a cultural and inter-generational disconnect. They are also connecting with those who have parted ways with intercultural, evangelical churches that didn't always honour their blackness – especially in the wake of the Black Lives Matter movement.

These Black British BMCs make use of media and social media and have a distinct, culturally relevant message that is not afraid to speak theologically into the issues facing a generation who are often university educated and have grown up in an era of postmodern secularization, relativism and pluralism.

Another interesting social observation at the time of George Floyd's murder was of some of the inter-generational tensions. Older generations that lived through the Brixton riots of 1985 and the murder of Stephen Lawrence in 1993 showed their resistance through apathy or were cautious due to the measured belief that protest without strategy could damage the hard work that had been done to build race relations in Britain.

The perception that younger people had only just joined the struggle yet were having the biggest platforms and loudest voice without proving their resilience was a frustration during this time. Also, the commitment to engage with a racial injustice that took place outside Britain was another growing frustration and played into the narrative that the British experience of racial oppression is less important and valuable than that of their American counterparts. Where was the same energy for the UK's George Floyds: Stephen Lawrence, Mark Duggan, Rashan Charles, Kevin Clarke? And what about the women? There were also constant reminders on social media that brutal racially aggravated murders have also happened at the hands of British police officers and that state killings were also a British problem. The most recent being that of Chris Kaba, which will be explored later in this chapter.

The political landscape in the UK

It is important to understand the political context in which the mission in Britain has been operating over the last five years and how public attitudes and opinions towards race have shifted because of migration, populism and the pandemic.

Division in the UK has been heavily characterized by Brexit. This political epoch has exposed the political underbelly of the nation and has fuelled a culture war that has been compounded by the influence of social media in the digital age.

While social media is not the only contributing factor to social division, its algorithms give it the power and speed to socially engineer certain beliefs, perceptions and actions that have helped to create an insidiously social and political 'other' and 'enemy', creating sharp divides between communities.

The culture wars are also shaping the way forms of social abuse are 'called out' and held accountable. For example, issues such as misogyny, racism, climate change and sexism are often labelled as cancel culture, being 'woke', being a 'snowflake' with the assumption that you are a social justice liberal eroding the fabric of society and free speech. On the other hand, elite liberalism can be accused of dismissing nuance and the reality that people have different opinions, worldviews and intellectual autonomy while engaging in the same dictatorial tactics. They denounce others to get their points across. This in turn can create rigid binaries that fuel an unforgiving 'cancel culture'. There can also be scepticism about the liberal elite speaking on behalf of marginalized groups while enjoying and benefiting from the structures that perpetuate their marginalization.

The culture wars have also built momentum through the political scape-goating of migrants and those arriving in dinghy boats, which threaten to overwhelm the UK. Ever-changing and socially engineered attitudes towards migration have exposed polarity, division and civil unrest.

Why does this matter for mission? Because the gospel and the Christian faith has largely spread through migration and diaspora communities. Different understandings and revelations of the faith as seen through the New Testament and the Pauline epistles have come through diaspora communities and travel. I believe missiologists in Britain need to consider what a clampdown and changing attitudes towards migration fuelled by racial tension and political agendas means for the spreading of the gospel in this country.

Resistance and the ecumenical landscape – the work churches across England are doing

Going back to the aftermath of George Floyd's murder, I observed many public statements of support for Black communities across the ecumenical landscape of England. I also saw many denominations, from the Catholic Bishop's conference, Lutherans, Anglicans and Methodists to Pentecostals and others, express profound commitments to sustained efforts to eliminate systemic racism and actively work on promoting racial justice. Many millennials and other generations across the ecumenical landscape took to social media as a form of catharsis and demands for accountability. They demanded that the Church speak out, stand against racism, and deconstruct white supremacy in society and the Church.

Public apologies of lament were also issued, most notably from the 105th Archbishop of Canterbury, Archbishop Justin Welby, and the General Synod of the Church of England. On 11 February 2022 they voted to apologize for racism experienced by Black and minority ethnic people in the Church of England since the arrival of the Windrush generation. This apology led to an admission of their links to the transatlantic slave trade through the Queen Anne Bounty Fund and the Church Commissioners committing itself to investing in a better future by addressing its past wrongs. To establish this commitment, they announced a £100 million fund in perpetuity to be delivered over the next nine years, commencing in 2023, to a programme of investment, research and engagement.[4]

Quakers in Britain also issued a public declaration of repair. At their 2022 yearly meeting they agreed to make practical reparations for the transatlantic slave trade, colonialism and economic exploitation. This decision was influenced by the powerful evidence that was presented about the Lancaster Quakers in the eighteenth and nineteenth centuries, who profited from the enslavement of people. They also heard the personal stories of prejudice, discrimination and racism that members of their meetings had experienced.[5]

Black majority churches also had a responsibility to respond to the concerns of their members and the wider Black community about their past silence on issues of racial justice. They did this by joining the global call for reparations.

On 12 November 2020, three of the largest leading Caribbean Black churches in the UK, the Church of God of Prophecy (UK), the New Testament Church of God and the New Testament Assembly, collaborated with the University of the West Indies to host a series of Symposia on the 'History, Heritage and Identity' of people of Caribbean descent living in the United Kingdom, which explored the impact of centuries of neo-colonial exploitation.[6] This was a powerful statement of self-determination and organization in the face of generational trauma.

Parachurch organizations, such as Churches Together in England, also responded to racial injustice by constituting a national racial justice group in 2020. This group brings together racial justice representatives from across 44 member churches along with several CTE Trustees, a representative from Churches Together in Britain and Ireland (CTBI), and others with specialist skills and knowledge.

The three key focus areas are: the criminal justice system and specifically working with the Dea-John Reid campaign for jury reform; theology in partnership with Christian Aid; and music and liturgy to assess how to create cultures of racial equality. The hope is that these three strands will help foster deep relationships and ensure that Global Majority diasporas living in the UK find safe, equal and equitable spaces to flourish in British society.

They have also launched a national social media campaign called The Candle of Justice and have partnered with Christian broadcasters to help the Church to pause, reflect, pray and recommit to acting against racial injustice. CTE's racial justice working group has also contributed recommendations to the UN Working Group of Experts on People of African Descent, one of the Special Procedures of the United Nations Human Rights Council.

Why is addressing racial injustice important for mission?

The mission of God (*missio Dei*) is about helping to bring relief from suffering, and racism is a cause of suffering for both the perpetrator and the oppressed. In the New Testament, Jesus' sacrificial death reveals that the relief of suffering was a principal function of his ministry, as demonstrated in his miracles: from feeding 5,000 hungry people to relieving the suffering of a homeless, neglected and afflicted man in a cave who was isolated from the community.

The stain and sin of racism, discrimination and prejudice should not reside in the attitudes and hearts of Christians and the twenty-first-century Church, but unfortunately it does. While I use racism, discrimination and prejudice interchangeably I should highlight that they are different things. Prejudice deals with the negative attitudes someone has towards a particular group; discrimination is when these negative attitudes are acted upon. Racism goes beyond hurting one's feelings or having a negative attitude, it's about power. It is when these negative attitudes and actions have become embedded in society, when laws, systems and structures uphold them and impact someone's quality of life.

However, this is not a new issue and prejudice, discrimination and racism were experienced by Jesus as a member of the occupied and oppressed Jewish community living under Roman imperialism and was even perpetrated among his disciples and in particular Peter. Peter was a church leader who had earned his theological stripes in Judaism. And if that wasn't enough, he had even spent time with Jesus in the flesh, had walked on water and basked in forgiveness for denying Christ, yet he had a narrow, prejudiced and discriminatory attitude towards the gentiles, which fluctuated depending on the crowd and its level of importance (Galatians 2.12). We can learn a lot about God's attitude towards racism, discrimination and prejudice through Peter's story. God was not interested in all Peter's accolades, church accomplishments or even that he would establish this global church movement. He directly called out

Peter's prejudiced attitude through a vision and made it clear that he should not call any man common or unclean (Acts 10.15, 28).

This revealed a universal gospel that was radically inclusive and intolerant of any form of antagonism towards different peoples coming into communion with God and flourishing. The recording and correction of Peter's attitude shows that it's possible for Christians and the Church to be prejudiced and that it's not acceptable to perpetrate prejudice masked by theology, culture, church establishment, wilful ignorance and positions. Peter's correction and revelation also provides hope for perpetrators of prejudice, discrimination and racism that change is possible, and that God is also lovingly concerned about their deliverance and the condition of their hearts.

Prophetic hopes for the future

As I finish my reflections on race as a millennial and its implication for mission in England, my key hope for the future is that Christians, the Church and society will cross the bridge of personal prejudice, silence and fear. That we will not make the awakening of racial injustice a cultural moment, but will be propelled to continuously work for an equitable society where all can flourish.

Over the last two years I have seen an increase in employment, the releasing of funding, conferences, podcasts, reviews of leadership teams and a bolder confidence to call out injustice. For instance, the United Reformed Church released a statement on the racism faced by African students in the Ukraine war. However, I've also seen Christians and churches who did not speak out and who fiercely disagree that racial injustice is an issue. Instead of doing the theological work as to why racism mars the *imago Dei*, some churches and their leaders intentionally and unintentionally got distracted with tearing down the social movement of Black Lives Matter and forsook the real issue that people on their pews and in their communities were suffering.

In the face of racial injustice, do we have the confidence and determination to resist the temptation to remain passively silent and maintain the status quo in our society and church communities? Jesus condemns the religious rulers of his day for this kind of passivity in Matthew 23.23, stating:

'Woe to you, scribes and Pharisees, hypocrites! For you tithe mint and dill and cumin and have neglected the weightier matters of the law: justice and mercy and faithfulness. These you ought to have done, without neglecting the others.'

It's interesting that Jesus doesn't hold to account the politicians, guards or tax collectors, but explicitly speaks to the religious leaders of the day. What is he saying to us today? Jesus' condemnation also challenges Christians, the Church and its leaders to take seriously their responsibility to implement an inclusive environment where all equally flourish and challenge injustice in the world and Church.

This raises the critical question: what are we focusing on? Are we solely focusing on shiny six-point missional church growth strategies, how we can sustain our church, ecumenical and Christian cultures, and income, while neglecting the weightier concerns of unjust laws and social ideologies like racism that deplete people's lives? The impact of standing up and dealing with the weightier matters of the law, and pursuing justice is evident in Queen Esther's life and timeless declaration: 'If I perish, I perish' (Esther 4.16). Esther's decision to resist the temptation to remain silent saved generations from genocide and ethnic cleansing motivated by prejudice, discrimination and racism (Esther 3.8). Esther forsook her privilege and societal benefits and used her power to benefit nations and call out a corrupt, racially motivated government policy of her day.

Finally, I leave you with this proverb by Kwame Anthony Appiah to reflect on: 'Sticks and stones may break my bones, but words, words that evoke structures of oppression, exploitation and brute physical threat can break souls.'[7]

What will this mean for British mission and race?

From micro aggressions to overt racism, Kwame Anthony Appiah's words come up time and again for those who work in racial justice as well as the wider Black community. Words can break souls and do harm, but a new generation of millennials will not be silenced.

Lisa's story

Like Kwame Anthony Appiah, I am also an Ashanti of the Akan people of Ghana in West Africa, and a millennial who will not be silenced. I was born in the United Kingdom but spent the first five years of my childhood in Kumasi, Ghana. I returned to the UK with an inability to speak English and I started my first day of primary school in the UK in culture shock. My parents were based in Stockwell in south London, a very diverse and multi-ethnic community. My school resembled something of a United Nations meeting, with children from all around the world attending. On my first day, I was grateful to have another child in my class who was of Ghanaian heritage and could speak both Twi and English. He was assigned to me for a whole year and would translate the lessons as I started to learn English. These early memories shaped me more than I could realize at the time, as my world was one of diverse ethnicity as the norm. This continued throughout secondary school, when I attended a diverse comprehensive school in Clapham South, with the black students being a racial majority in the school. Even the large black church we attended as a family, with over 2,000 members, was over 90 per cent Ghanaian in its demographic. My world was black. Much of this has shaped my formation and worldview, my ability to interact with people from a wide range of backgrounds and how I read the Bible.

Unbeknown to me at the time, the multicultural and multi-ethnic bubble in which I had been raised was in for a rude awakening as I moved into university accommodation in the town of Guildford, Surrey. Guildford was completely different to London in so many ways, but the lack of ethnic diversity was a glaring reality. It was the first time I felt like a minority. I was so aware of my blackness, and things I had taken for granted and assumed were the norm I now began to miss. The way people of the town looked at me as I shopped on the high street, the children who would stop and stare at me in restaurants or queues, the questions about my hair and the presumptive touching of it, the assumptions about my upbringing in London and so much more were slowly becoming my new norm.

It was Revd Rene August, a South African theologian, who taught me that, 'If you take the text out of context, all you're left with is a con.' This quote has made me giggle many times but has remained etched in my mind. As those who seek to follow the example of Jesus, we must keep in mind his context, so that we don't miss the depth of what he taught and the way that he lived. A Palestinian Jew. A brown man, born to a young and poor carpenter family. An ethnic group under the colonial rule of the Roman Empire. This is the context Jesus Christ is born into (Luke 2). In John 1.47, 'Nathaneal said, "Can anything good come from Nazareth?"' This question gives us a glimpse into some of the societal prejudices of the town of Nazareth and its people. This is the town that Jesus is raised in. Christ is present here and it has implications for our formation. The entrance of Jesus into the world is intentional; he positions himself at the site of political, economic, geographic, religious and ethnic struggle rather than its power centre. Nothing about where and how he enters the world is easy or comfortable.

Racism is defined in the Oxford dictionary as 'Prejudice, discrimination, or antagonism by an individual, community, or institution against a person or people on the basis of their membership of a particular racial or ethnic group, typically one that is a minority or marginalised.'[8] Empires throughout history have always dehumanized those they saw as 'other' in favour of seeing themselves as superior. The Roman Empire would not have differed from this in its racial oppression of the Jews at the time that Jesus walked the earth. The interactions of Jesus with Samaritans throughout the Gospels resists the status quo and the prejudice held by his ethnic group, the Jews, towards the Samaritans. If we think about the Samaritan woman at the well, the ten cleansed lepers where only the Samaritan comes back to say thank you, and the story of the good Samaritan, all these stories portray those with Samaritan ethnicity positively – they are the heroes of the stories. The late Archbishop Desmond Tutu, resisting an apartheid regime in South Africa, stated that 'to treat a child of God as he or she is less than this is not just wrong, which it is; it is not just evil, as it often is; not just painful, as it often must be for the victim; it is veritably blasphemous, for it is to spit in the face of God.'[9]

In Chinua Achebe's book *Africa's Tarnished Name*, he speaks of the importance of narrative, how European literature was used as a tool to justify further oppression because it dehumanized those who were being colonized or trafficked in the Transatlantic Chattel Slave Trade. He goes on to demonstrate the findings of Dorothy Hammond and Alta Jablow, whose academic work shows, 'How a dramatic change in the content of British writing about Africa coincided with an increase in the volume of the slave trade to its highest level.'[10] Writers at the time went so far as to call the abhorrent slave trade 'a mercy to poor wretches, who would otherwise suffer from the butcher's knife'. Jesus shifts the narrative for the Samaritans he encounters, but rather than devaluing them he reinforces their intrinsic worth and value. In our own discipleship with Christ, we must be led on a journey towards racial justice and affirming the humanity of others. Through his life Christ navigated rejection of the racial oppression of the Romans while also subverting the prejudice against the Samaritans, and in so doing set a pattern for us all to pursue racial justice, regardless of whether we are resisting systemic racism or giving away unequitable inherited power due to race.

Some years ago, I had the honour of working with some inner-city young people at a Saturday school as they prepared for their GCSEs. I was asked to work with a young guy named Tyrone (I've changed his name to protect his identity). The main group were working on trigonometry, and he seemed to be struggling more than the rest and distracting the others. As I took him aside, I thought to myself, 'Let's go back to the basics and see where the problem is.' We went as far back as his times tables and long division. As I gave him some sums to calculate and he began to count on his fingers, it became more than apparent that he was so much further back than he should be. We spent the day working on long division and multiplication, and he was so surprised that he was able to grasp it – the joy on his face as he said, 'I'm not stupid', was priceless. Our spiritual formation can be similar to that of Tyrone when it comes to racial justice. There are gaps in our formation that make it difficult for us to have a meaningful conversation and understand. Like Lego, we must build block by block.

In 2020, the world watched a black man named George Floyd be publicly murdered on the side of a street in Minneapolis, USA. The dehumanizing act was fuelled by the colour of his black skin. This injustice, caught on a stranger's mobile phone, went viral, shaking many black and brown people all around the world to the core. It became evident that the UK churches were not prepared for the conversations that were to follow. Some buried their heads in the sand and retorted, 'Let's get back to the gospel', others listened to the painful experiences of their black and brown members but failed to follow up with any meaningful action. And others ignored the conversation altogether. I believe that, like Tyrone, the foundational blocks were missing for so many. Racial justice, lament and multi-ethnic equity had been left out of the formation of many people, churches and ministry teams. What happened to our theology around *imago Dei* and the sanctity of all life? What about our theology of the Trinity? A relational triune God? Or even the voices of the prophets in the Old Testament who speak again and again about justice, how we treat strangers and warn against the abuse of power? This led me on a pursuit to discover what faithful racial justice looks like in the Church. Out of this quest, Sankofa Collective was born.

Sankofa Collective

Sankofa is a word from the Akan tribe in Ghana; *SAN* (return), *KO* (go), *FA* (look, seek and take). The name Sankofa means we should reach back and gather the best of what our past has to teach us, so that we can achieve our full potential as we move forward. Whatever we have lost, forgotten, foregone or has been stripped away can be reclaimed, revived, preserved and perpetuated. We are an ecumenical community seeking to pursue racial justice as part of our spiritual formation. Our key pillars as a community have become opportunities for deeper spiritual formation. I will expand on them in this section below.

Formed in truth telling

I completed most of my education in the UK and have been able to graduate with a PhD in Biochemistry and Physiology. Most of the people who have heard me speak will hear me say often that, until 2019, the sum of my knowledge of British history was Henry VIII and his many wives, the Battle of Hastings, the Egyptian mummies and World War One. There is so much that we did not learn in the curriculum at school. This has created a huge knowledge gap that makes it difficult to be formed by the racial justice arc because many are genuinely unaware of systemic racial injustice in their own history. James Baldwin warns us that, 'Not everything that is faced can be changed, but nothing can be changed until it is faced.'[11] We must be formed in truth-telling around our history; this will require courage to tell the whole story and to teach future generations about the injustices of the past. The stolen generation of indigenous people of Australia, the colonial schools in Canada, the opium war in China, the scramble for Africa – there is much to face. In facing these histories, we should keep close the question, 'How were we formed here?' This will allow us to interrogate the thinking and ideologies that led to these grave injustices and examine how these same ideas are still in our midst today.

Formed in repentance and lament

Repentance takes us beyond facing wrongdoing, but rather requires us to deeply acknowledge wrong, to confess, 'This is broken, this harms us as human beings and we must walk in a different direction.' In the year 2020, we heard many 'I'm so sorry' statements from individuals, communities, churches and organizations. But many of these were not accompanied by a change of action. When we look at the repentance of Pharaoh in Exodus, it provides us with a warning that our repentance must be deep and be genuine (Exodus 5 – 12). How deep does our repentance go? What does it look like for our repentance to be true? These are questions we must ask ourselves and our communities. In the Exodus story, Pharaoh has many moments of what some might call 'repentance'. He vocalizes his remorse towards God and Moses for the oppression of the people. But ten plagues and ten apologies later, we see that this softening of heart was short-lived each time. As soon as a particular plague ends, the consequence and judgement of his actions, the frogs, the flies, the hail, etc., as soon as it stops Pharaoh's heart hardens again. It's important for us in our journey that our repentance and change of heart goes much deeper than a vocal apology. Deeper than just saying the words, 'I'm sorry'. Pharoah repented but then quickly returned to oppression, held on to power and still centred around his own comfort. If we are truly repenting, our actions always follow.

On 5 September 2022, an unarmed young black man named Chris Kaba was shot by the police in south London, UK. His death was a painful reminder that not much had changed. A UK police leadership finally admitted what many of us already knew, that they were institutionally racist. As a black community, we are losing our young mums during childbirth at four to five times the rate of white mothers. The 'adultification' of our young people at school, with cases like Child Q, highlights that this systematic racial oppression starts early and is not limited to our young black boys. Our hostile immigration laws that criminalize and dehumanize those who seek asylum or refuge in the UK. We have much to lament. In 2023, young black men are nine times more likely to be stopped and searched by the police. This means I don't know a single young black man that has not been stopped and searched by the police. These happenings are not a thing of the past or strategies of oppression found in the United States of America alone. These examples are present here in the UK and are happening now. We have much to lament.

As I meet with people, either within the Sankofa community or in local churches across the British Isles, I'm often asked something along the lines of 'When can we move on or forget?' This question has always struck me, because we often struggle with the practice of lament, suffering and pain in a western context. We are often too eager to move forward to some form of positivity or victory. However, our lack of lament actually points to how deeply broken we are as a society. Our inability to sit with one another in pain reveals that the fabric of our social connection as communities of people is deeply fractured. Many asked me and other black people, 'Why did the murder of George Floyd hurt us so much?'; but the more pertinent question is, 'Why did it not hurt them?' The ability to watch a man die, for it not to scar your soul or cause you to mourn, is a sign of our disconnectedness.

Formed in giving away power

The asymmetry in the distribution of power has created so many unequitable tables in so many spaces, including the Church. Racial justice is more than a social media post or black square on your Instagram page. It must move beyond the apologies, written or verbal. The real shift is to give away power. Walter Brueggemann said, in *The Prophetic Imagination*:

> Jesus of Nazareth, a prophet, and more than a prophet, practised in the most radical form the main elements of prophetic ministry and imagination. On the one hand he practised criticism of the deathly world around him. The dismantling was fully wrought in his crucifixion, in which he himself embodied the thing dismantled. On the other hand, he practised the energising of the new future given by God. This energising was fully wrought in his resurrection, in which he embodied the new future given by God.[12]

What Brueggemann points to here is that the new way that Christ comes to reveal and show us starts with the dismantling of a world system that doesn't work. The prophetic imagination emerges from an abandonment of the status quo. Millennial leaders have been bold in walking away from structures that no longer work and seeking to be missional in new ways both near and far.

As millennial leaders it's time for us to build new 'times tables' that will serve future generations. To reimagine the mission field and missional approaches in a way that honours the treasures handed down to us and cuts away at the packaging that no longer fits. We are the hybrid generation, often belonging to more than one nation. Raised at home in one culture and schooled in another, this is our superpower – let's use it to build a better world.

Notes

1 I. Olofinjana, 'Reverse mission: towards an African British theology', *Transformation: An International Journal of Holistic Mission Studies* 37 (1) (2019): 52–65, https://doi.org/10.1177/0265378819877902.

2 B. Adedibu, 'Origin, migration, globalisation and the missionary encounter of Britain's Black Majority Churches', *Studies in World Christianity* 19 (1) (2013): 93–113, https://doi.org/10.3366/swc.2013.0040.

3 Danté Stewart, Daily meditation: what does it mean to be Black, Christian, and American?', *Center for Action and Contemplation*, 18 May (2022), https://cac.org/daily-meditations/what-does-it-mean-to-be-black-christian-and-american-2022-05-25/, accessed 12.06.2024.

4 Church of England, 2023, 'Church Commissioners publishes full report into historic links to Transatlantic Chattel Slavery and announces new funding commitment of £100m in response to findings', *The Church of England*, 1 October, https://www.churchofengland.org/media/finance-news/church-commissioners-publishes-full-report-historic-links-transatlantic-chattel, accessed 12.06.2024.

5 Cato Pedder, 2022, 'Quakers to make reparation for slave trade and colonialism', *Quakers in Britain*, 31 May, https://www.quaker.org.uk/news-and-events/news/quakers-to-make-reparation-for-slave-trade-and-colonialism, accessed 12.06.2024.

6 The University of the West Indies, 2020, 'History, Heritage and Identity Online Symposium, November 12, 2020: Caribbean Institute for Health Research', Caribbean Institute for Health Research, https://uwi.edu/caihr/engagement/pg-history heritage.php, accessed 06.07.2023.

7 Kwame Anthony Appiah, 'The conservation of "Race"', *Black American Literature Forum* 23 (1) (1989): 37–60, https://doi.org/10.2307/2903987.

8 Oxford English Dictionary, 2023, 'Definition of racism', *Oxford English Dictionary*, Oxford: Oxford University Press.

9 D. Tutu, 1999, *No Future without Forgiveness*, New York: Image Books, p. 197.

10 C. Achebe, 2018, *Africa's Tarnished Name*, London: Penguin Modern, p. 19.

11 J. Baldwin, 1973, *No Name in the Street*, New York: Dell Books.

12 W. Brueggemann, 2001, *The Prophetic Imagination*, 2nd edn, Minneapolis, MN: Fortress Press, p. 116.

Just(ice) Love: A Public Theological Engagement on the Bible

RAJ BHARAT PATTA

At a recent house visit, one of the members of the church asked me, 'What is the gospel you are preaching to the people who don't depend on a local food bank?' In that conversation I had to quote him a biblical text: Jesus when he was questioned about eating with tax collectors and sinners said: 'Those who are well have no need of a physician, but those who are sick. Go and learn what this means. I desire mercy not sacrifice' (Matthew 9.13). This friend of mine then said, 'Isn't it your role as a preacher to see that we don't fall sick?' I then had to reply, 'It is the role and responsibility of each person to stay healthy and it is not the duty of the preacher, for preachers don't have a magic wand.'

When the world around us is increasingly hungry, with millions of people struggling for sustenance and living in severely food insecure homes, the gospel of Jesus Christ is about demonstrating love. The gospel is about sharing meals, advocating for food justice, calling on the account-ability of policy makers in addressing hunger, and becoming the bread of life for people around us. When we preach the gospel of Jesus Christ as justice from our pulpits, some of our congregation have been uncomfort-able and asking the same question: 'What is the gospel for people who do not depend on food banks?' When I further reflect on this conversa-tion, I notice a self-righteous attitude in my friend, who is exhibiting his privilege that he doesn't depend on a food bank. Second, for him the texts of the Bible have to offer assurance about 'life after death', with no sensitivity to the realities around us, particularly the realities of life before death like hunger, discrimination and injustice, which are happening in our local contexts. Third, my friend exhibits empathy towards the needs of the people who are depending on the food bank. As a churchgoer he perhaps even collects some food cans for the food bank, but he wonders whether there is a separate gospel within the texts of the Bible for people who don't depend on food banks! My friend is not the only person who has these concerns, but he represents the symptomatic nature of many in our congregations who are at dis-ease with the gospel of Jesus Christ as a justice-centred, dignity-focused and solidarity-directed message. For him, the Bible is a text which must uplift his soul, which makes him to feel good about his faith.

For me, the gospel of Jesus Christ, the God of the Bible, the God of the sacred texts, is all about love, love for one another, for God is love and God is just. A cartoon from Revd David Hayward from Canada, who draws his cartoons in the name of @nakedpastor, explains love in the context of texts; I have it hanging in my office. When people try to trick us with laws, we are called to treat them with love. In that cartoon, Jesus meets a bunch of preachers/men disciples holding Bibles in their hands and says, 'The difference between me and you is, you use scripture to determine what love means and I use love to determine what scripture means.'[1] Love therefore becomes an important public theological category in understanding the place of the Bible in the public sphere.

These conversations therefore set the tone of a discussion on the meaning and relevance of the Bible and biblical texts in our public sphere today. It also raises the question, is the Bible a church book or a public book? So in this essay I engage in a public theological conversation on the Bible. I will bring in a discussion about love from the Bible, particularly discussing the text from 1 John 4.7–12.

Over the years, we have conveniently bracketed and narrowed 'love for one another' as love for our inner circle of family and friends, making love a domestic affair and a private matter, with no engagement with the dynamics of power in our love for one another. On the other hand, we don't fall back on the language of 'justice' and 'equity' in our domestic lives, thinking these are secular words that people use out in the public sphere. This bifurcation of love as private and justice as public is not only unhelpful but also unspiritual, for as has been demonstrated in the life and witness of Jesus Christ in his mission and ministry, justice and love co-exist and co-work together. Alluding to Cornel West's expression, 'Justice is what love looks like in the public square,'[2] justice is the visible action of the invisible love, and love is the bedrock for justice.

The relationship of love and justice from 1 John 4.7–12

First things first, God is the source of love (because love is from God, v. 7b), God's self is love (for God is love, v. 8b), God is the service of love (God's love is revealed by sending God's son to the world, v. 9) and God is the strength of love (not that we loved God, but that he loved us, v. 10). In other words, any idea or thought or action of love begins with and from God, for no love exists outside of the divine. The being of God is love, the becoming of God is love and the belonging of God is love, for nothing exists outside of God's love. If it is love, then it is about the divine, and if it is divine, it will always be of love. Such a theological understanding of God as love and love as divine describes the fairness in God's creation and in God's world. God's justice springs out of God's love, ensuring fairness and equity as determinants in the reign of God. Wirzba therefore observes, 'The action of love opens people to partici-pate in the divine love that is constantly sustaining and making the world fresh and new.'[3]

Second, 'Whoever does not love does not know God, for God is love' (v. 8). Who are those who do not love and therefore do not know God, who is love? Or why is it that there are some who do not love and why are there some who are never loved? This is where we recognize and explain that due to power imbalances that exist in society on several counts such as class, gender, race, colour, caste, religion, region, language, etc., there are some people who do not love and there are some who are never loved. In other words, due to the existing imbalance of power dynamics within the society, fairness is affected, which we call injustice and which brings in a divide between some as powerful and others as powerless. Injustice is what causes some not to love, for they do not know God who is love. Structures and systems of injustice have taken deep root in our society and that allows the powerful to oppress and discriminate against the powerless, giving room to lovelessness and ultimately leading to the 'un-God(ly)', which for me means 'un-love'. Prestige, position, prejudice, privilege have crept into society as ramifications of power, causing some not to love others, for they do not know God who is love. In other words, wherever and whenever injustice thrives and life is threatened by that which is un-divine, not of God, we find there is no place for love there. If we don't let go of our privilege and closely examine how the forces of power imbalance are influencing us, we are nurturing injustices in the world around us today. The love of God and the knowledge of God chal-lenge us to disrupt the unloving nature of creatures based on power, and convict us to work for the justice of God by loving the creation without condition.

Third, God's love is revealed in God's son being sent into the world so that we might live through him, and to be the atoning sacrifice for our sins (vv. 9–10). God's love is revealed publicly by God's eruption into the world, by the demonstration of the in-breaking of love in the world, offering and affirming life for all by the act of incarnation which is solidarity with the powerless. This act of God reveals the justice char-acteristic of the divine, which risks all to be in the unjust world, giving away his life so that life is offered to all. In this process the divine in Jesus publicly takes on the criminal death of the cross in order to stand up for the cause of a just world, which the biblical writers understood as an atoning sacrifice for the injustices of the world. Just love therefore is going out into the public square to offer life for all, to be in solidarity with the weak and powerless, to stand up against the principalities and powers, speaking truth to the powers and advocating for justice, even up to the point of dying for others for the cause of the just reign of God.

The logic of empire, which manifests as violence, wants to destroy bodies by killing, scattering bodies through acts of terror, crucifying bodies by unjust means, disappearing bodies which have been tortured, and disintegrating the bio-politics of life. In contrast to this, the love of God receives and embraces material bodies into its fold. Those that are embraced by the love of God are called to receive the brokenhearted and partake in the healing of their broken bodies.

Fourth, since God loved us so much, we also ought to love one another (v. 11). Justice is spiralling, for it has after-effects. Since God has revealed God's desire for a just world, God invites each of us to strive for justice by loving one another, transcending all barriers and trespassing all boundaries. By loving one another, which is to affirm mutual self-respect and dignity in one another, we will let God live in us and allow God's love to be perfected in us. By loving one another we will all strive for a just world where God dwells and God's justice thrives. Justice is imperative for Christian discipleship. Since God loved us justly, we ought to love one another justly.

Having discussed the relationship between love and justice, let me now move on to discuss what kind of love are we talking about when we reflect on the 'greatest commandment'. There are many shades of love, and a justice-reading of our text invites us to engage with them for the cause of justice. Allow me to present two kinds of love here: first, the coloniality of love, or where love has been colonized and has been offered in colonial trappings. Second, there is a need to celebrate the decoloniality of love in the text and in our context, which is relevant for us today in our moving forward as a Church. 'In this is love, not that we loved God but that God loved us ...' (v. 10a).

Decolonizing love

Coloniality is the kind of knowledge that works on the principalities and powers of domination, by subjugating and oppressing the other. Dehumanizing and de-ecologizing[4] the creatures of the creation is how coloniality thrives. What do I mean by the coloniality of love? Love driven by the forces of power and privilege. For example, as we have read 1 John 4.7–12, how many of us have identified with the words 'we' and 'us' in the text as 'we believers', 'we Christians' and 'we church members'? And read the verse 'whoever does not love does not know God' as referring to those 'other' people who are outside of church or the Christian fold. All I am trying to say is that because we are driven by the coloniality of love, we tend to make the love of God, or for that matter God, our own possession and we then behave as if we can monopolize the love of God as our own. Exhibiting privilege and power is how coloniality works. The love of God does not work on the basis of 'we/us' and 'they/them' but it is God who first loved us, and not that we loved God. The love of God dismantles such dichotomies and distinctions. Another example is the rise of 'pseudo nationalism' among citizenry, whose motto is to 'make great' the nation again and who are implicitly saying we love our locals and we can't tolerate 'outsiders', 'migrants' 'refugees' and 'asylum seekers'. Here again we see coloniality of love at play. A further example is growing 'white supremacy' as another form of coloniality of love, which works on the principle of 'we celebrate with people who look like us, believe like us and belong where we belong; the rest are all "outsiders".' These types of coloniality of love are very dangerous for the life of a nation and for the life of our faith. A justice reading of this text should expose the coloniality of love, the narrow-mindedness of love, and should challenge us to celebrate the 'decolonial love' that is all-expansive and all-inclusive, because it is not that we loved God, but it is God who loves us.

Decolonial love is, therefore, learning to love one another and ourselves without the burdens of patriarchy, misogyny, racism, sexism, xenophobia, transphobia or homophobia. Decolonial love is about recognizing our privilege, giving up that privilege and striving for justice, equity and peace among the whole of creation. Decolonial love is about receiving and accepting one another in honesty, humility, generosity and graciousness. Decolonial love is about openness, celebrating difference, celebrating diversity and celebrating inclusion among all the creatures in the creation. Nuraan Davids, in his article 'Love in the time of Decoloniality', explains that,

Decoloniality of love [is] a form of rupturing not only of the matrices of colonial power, but also ruptures human ways that insist upon the binary ways of thinking and being. As a form of rupturing, decolonial love calls upon the individual to afford humanity to the other as a means to restore his or her own community – that is to restore what it means to be human by seeing the humanity in others. As a form of rupturing, decolonial love surrenders to an ethical conscience of what it means to be human, and as such, loves all people as a reflection of the majesty of being human.[5]

Though Davids limits this decolonial love to humanity, I want to extend the rupture to the entire creation, for decolonial love celebrates creature-liness among all of creation, for God created this creation in God's own space with the sparks of the divine present among all the creation. In our journey of faith, love has to be stripped of colonial trappings and allow us to celebrate the decolonial love which is again demonstrated by God's solidarity with the world in God's incarnation in Jesus Christ. Coloniality of love centralizes love, whereas decolonial love de-centralizes love and shares and spreads to all the corners of our society.

Love from a justice perspective? 'No one has ever seen God; if we love one another, God lives in us and his love is perfected in us' (v. 12)

Elaine Padilla, in her essay 'In the belly of the colony', explains the patterns of hatred towards migrants in the US as a symptom of her nation's *habitus* of isolation and indifference. In such a context she asks, 'Is this nation ultimately facing a precipice of de*soul*ation? Or could this also be the dark abyss out of which to ensoul itself rather than to continue erecting the towers of indignity that proudly shadow its border-history?'[6] By 'de*soul*ation' she means that the nation is *desouling* selves, and correspondingly itself, because the lives of the migrants are considered of lesser value and simply viewed as commodities. The souls of people seeking a sanctuary in a different land are stripped off from the wholistic life, and the Rwanda asylum policy[7] is a case in point for such de*soul*ing of selves today. Love, from a justice perspective, is a counter measure to de*soul*ing, which enhances the ensouling of selves, collectively towards transformation.

In western political thought, according to Giorgio Agamben, there has always been a distinction between natural life (*zoe*) and political life (*bio*), for such a distinction makes stateless citizens, like the refugees, immigrants etc., 'non-human', 'bare life', or 'state of exception', for they are either 'excluded in' or 'included out'. Alluding to Agamben, Vinayraj says,

> Life, whether it is biological or political, is nothing but biopolitical – an act of sovereignty ... For Agamben, it is impossible to get rid of this politicization of life or biopolitics of the sovereign power, and any attempt to resist it will ultimately become an entrenchment of the very power that is mobilized against it.[8]

So love is all about contesting de*soul*ation, love is an antidote to de*soul*ation of people and creation on the one hand, and on the other hand it affirms the biopolitical nature of all creatures, especially those on the margins and those people who are powerless.

Krish Kandiah, the director of Sanctuary Foundation, explains that the planned deportations to Rwanda are unjust and go against Christian heritage and humanity in at least three ways. First, he says these deportations target the wrong people, because the Rwanda plan criminalizes the trafficked and not the traffickers. Second, deportations turn asylum seekers into commodities. Third, the planned deportations contradict the current outpouring of public support and solidarity towards refugees and immigrants.[9] These pointers explain the gravity of the Rwanda deportation plan as an epitome of de*soul*ation.

Love for the 'other', particularly the 'outsiders', the 'powerless' and the 'vulnerable', is the yardstick to demonstrate the grace of God in each of our lives and communities. As churches we have been busy trying to keep up with the status quo of our church membership and have been engrossed in putting our energies into the survival of the church buildings and its properties. Feeding the hungry, giving a drink to the thirsty, welcoming the stranger, clothing the naked, caring for the sick and visiting the imprisoned, these hexagonal representative acts of love in action to vulnerable people should be the mission mandate of our churches. When our mission engagements are in such a direction, we are truly serving Christ the love. Church is all about serving in love the community outside the walls of our church building, particularly vulnerable people. No one has ever seen God; if we love one another, God lives in us, the Easter story becomes relevant and God's love is perfected in the creation.

Let love be the hermeneutic that interprets scripture, laws and life. Love should be the interpreting principle in every situation and to every person. Love for God is not expressed by hatred towards a neighbour based on any text. Scripture needs to be understood as love letters from God to faith communities in a given context, seeking relevance to the readers in demonstrating love for God and love for neighbour. Anything that discounts love does not properly understand the commandments. Are Christians known today as disciples of Christ by the new commandment of Jesus?[10] The world around us is longing for love, peace and justice. If followers of Jesus Christ in the twenty-first century don't activate the new commandment of Jesus to love one another, they not only deny their Christian discipleship but also run the risk of failing to transform the world into a 'new heaven and new earth'.

Subaltern biblical hermeneutics strives for transformation rather than understanding

How do we understand the Bible? The Bible is the Word of God. Yes, it is the Word of God in human words. Gordon Oliver explains: 'The Bible is human as well as holy and this simple fact raises lots of questions about what kind of a thing the Bible really is and how the Word of God and the words of Scripture relate to each other.'[11] This relation between the Word of God and its understanding varies from context to context. Sathianathan Clarke, in his article, 'Viewing the Bible through the eyes and ears of the subalterns in India',[12] explores the understanding of the Bible and its varied interpretations of the subalterns, those of lower status. He emphasizes that, methodologically, when it encounters post-colonialism, subalternity locates within the categories of local, domestic and particular. These serve as a basis for excavating subaltern biblical hermeneutics. Clarke then unfolds the various understandings of the Bible within subalternity, where it is understood as a native talisman, a colonial fetish and an alternative canon, for the subaltern's understanding of the text is beyond the written word, which is why he mentions the importance of the eyes and ears of subalterns in relation to the Bible. Clarke then proposes that subaltern biblical hermeneutics include seeing the Bible as recovering universal human values, and also as a resource for subversive local expressions on subjugation and subordination. The Bible for subalterns is read for 'transformation' and not for 'understanding'. It recognizes multi-scriptural, multimodal and multimedia approaches to hermeneutics. Such an understanding is a key move in making the Bible a public document.

A drum as a symbol of subaltern-based orality: a new theological locale

In interpreting subaltern religion, Clarke chooses the symbol of a 'drum', which has been used by the subalterns in expressing themselves, and transposes this rich symbol of a 'drum' into a theological world, situating it as a new locale in doing theology. In this process, Clarke explains that the underlying ethos of subaltern culture is rooted in its 'orality', for which the symbol of 'drum' becomes a hermeneutical key in organizing and interpreting 'orality'. Subaltern-based orality is expounded as sound-centred orientation that interacts with and resists the dominant expansive modes of literacy. Subalternity, in its orality, therefore aligns itself with the modes of hearing from a drum, in contrast to the dominant world as symbolized by literacy in modes of seeing and reading. Clarke describes the importance of sound by drumming and says,

> Sound can be said to have three properties that are linked with the ways in which the drum symbolizes subaltern-based orality: it unites communities by connecting 'interiority to interiority'; it situates human beings in context-dependent, present actuality, which is participatory; and it fosters collaborative and eclectic patterns of community behaviour.[13]

Therefore such subaltern-based orality, symbolized by a 'drum', becomes the new site of theologizing, where 'hearing' is prior to 'reading,' and provides a basis in moving to other forms of media like music, art, poetry, dance etc. beyond the subsuming universality of written-ness.

Moving from Theo-logy to Theo-orality: Subaltern-based orality's challenge to theology

The dominant-funded world of literacy has always projected the written word as the norm or yardstick, thereby excluding the subaltern and their orality as subordinate and irrational. Whereas, actually the oral religions of subalterns have been open and flexible, sustaining communities through their oral stories, myths, dances, songs etc. as their understanding of religious texts. It is in this context that Clarke observes that a 'drum' as a symbol of subaltern-based orality is critical of and resistant to the dogma of the Christian Bible as the sole medium and manifestation of God.[14] Drum as mediation between the divine and the human reminds us that there is mediation 'before, beyond and beside written Word', for not all God's revelations are in the medium of writing. This is an insightful contribution of subalternity to theology, based on its orality that looks beyond 'literacy' as written words and opens up 'hearing' a diversity of sounds where the voice of the divine is also present.

Indian Christian theology has always sided and theologized either with the 'western' notions of text, as in the forms of 'writing' that Clarke would call 'biblicism', or it has always colluded with the Hindu philosophical concepts based on their religious texts of literacy. Clarke observes, 'Theology has been script-and text-centred in its discourse and thus is unable to contain the mode of thought and reflection of Dalits that is oral in orientation.'[15] Therefore, subaltern-based orality provides a point of departure for theology to move beyond its cosy written texts and their script-and text-centredness towards non-textual and post-textual worlds, looking for the sounds as texts, for God's presence transcends and transgresses the written texts and textual worlds. In that sense, theo-logy has to transfigure to become theo-orality, where the divine is understood and received in varied forms of orality, liberating God's word from written-ness and the printed papers of a particular book. Theo-orality then would be sound-and-orality-centred, locating the sounds of the divine among and within the sounds of cacophonic and polyphonic voices and the noises of the mundane.

'Drum' as theological interpreter for Theo-logy/Theo-orality

Within the subaltern world and subaltern-based orality, Clarke finds 'drum' an organizing symbol that contests the standardization of 'written-ness', and he proposes it as an instrumental multi-media of orality. He also explains that 'drum' not only serves as an organizing symbol in sub-alternity but also functions as a 'theological interpretant'. In this regard Clarke says,

> I suggest that the drum is a 'well-constructed, archaeological deep, experiential interpretant of God [/the Divine]' that forces Indian Christian theology to both comprehend and utilize the collective religious experience of subaltern communities in its effort to make theological reflection more inclusive and liberative.[16]

As a symbol of the subaltern religion and worldview, 'drum' helps to affirm non-linguistic modes of theo-logizing/theo-oralizing, and also helps people to be open to multisensory forms of doing theo-logy/theo-orality. What word is for literacy, drum is for orality. 'Drum' as a theological interpretant is a subaltern offering to theo-logy/theo-orality, for as a sym-bol it deconstructs the texts to become sounds and offers a deconstructive hermeneutical tool in the art of theo-logizing/theo-oralizing. Clarke con-tends that in the collective religious life of the *Paraiyar* caste, among whom he has researched subaltern religions, drum serves three import-ant functions, which are appropriate for the Indian Christian theo-logy/theo-orality. He observes that drum serves as a medium of divine–human communication; drum links the subalternity of communities in resist-ing evil forces; and drum exemplifies and manages collective subaltern suffering.[17] The subaltern is understood through their symbols of non-literacy and non-verbal modes of expressions, which are varied, diverse and multiple among their communities. Clarke concludes his subaltern theology by proposing Christ as Drum, which is complementary to Christ as Logos.

Moving from textuality of the Spirit to spirituality of text

In the context of texting, where communication has been so naive and postmodern, one has to recognize the fluidity of the scriptural texts, because they come with lots of meaning, history and context and affirm the plurality and diversity of the revelation of God. It is high time for theories of the infallibility of the texts to be revisited and appropriated to our given signs of the digital world. Such theories withstood the tests of time only by having power ascribed to them, for it is the powerful who made the printed texts infallible and therefore nullified all other forms of the texts.

Paul in 2 Corinthians 3.6 writes, 'He has made us competent as ministers of a new covenant – not of the letter but of the Spirit; for the letter kills, but the Spirit gives life.' The emphasis is on the spirit rather on the letter, for a literal reading of any given text may not affirm its life-giving essence, but the Spirit of such texts affirms and gives life. This understanding in itself helps us to move from the textuality of the Spirit, which is represented in the form of canons of scripture, to the spirituality of the texts, which overcomes life-denying essence and proclaims life-giving meaning to the readers in any context.

Jesus is the best example in understanding the spirituality of the texts, for he overcame the temptation to stick to the literal nature of the texts and moved to affirm the spirituality of a given text in his context. For Jesus, in his Sermon on the Mount, continued to reread the law and reinterpret it for their given context, 'It is written ... but I say ...' For Jesus, the life-giving spirit of the text is more significant.

In Luke 4.1–30, we see how Jesus interweaves the textuality and spirituality of the given scriptural texts of his times. In verses 1–13 we see the tempter quoting the scriptural texts but Jesus rereading them and answering back. In verses 14–15 we see the beginning of Jesus' ministry. In verses 16–17 we see Jesus in the synagogue standing up to read the text and demonstrating the ritual of reading on the Sabbath, the reverence for the reading (he stood) and the relevance of such reading (it became his personal manifesto). In verses 21–30 we see Jesus moving into the spirituality of the texts, into his prophetic ministry, speaking about the rights of the people there and in verse 25 asking questions about the rights of widows. In verse 27 we see Jesus speaking about the rights of people with leprosy, and in verses 28–30 we see him facing the fury of the people in the synagogue. The religious leaders drove him out of the town and took him up to the hill to push him over, but Jesus 'went on his way'. Therefore, in the context of digitalization, be prepared to look for the spirituality of the texts, give heed to the oral traditions of the living experiences, look for the spirituality of cyber texts and keep recognizing the plurality of God's revelation around us and among us.

Conclusion

A public theological engagement with the Bible from the sites of Dalit subalternity and decoloniality is all about just(ice) love. The epistemology and hermeneutics of the Bible from such locales is always about love, ensuring justice to all in the community. Public theology of the Bible is celebrating the Word of God with the World of God, for it affirms the sparks of the divine all around the world that God so loved. Unfortunately, these divine sparks have been eclipsed due to the injustices around us. Therefore, decolonial love offers hope by addressing the eclipse of justice in our world today. Another offering that I have made in my reflections is that subaltern hermeneutics call for hearing the Word in the Bible as a drum beat, for in that drum beat one can hear the beats of liberation and justice. Subalternity on the one hand unsettles the '*theos*' in theology from transcendence to immanence and on the other hand unsettles the 'logos' in theology towards orality, for the hearings of theo-orality drives towards just love in, for and with the world.

The relevance of the Bible in the transnational public sphere in general and in the post-secular British public sphere in particular is that the reader or hearer of the Bible is called to transform the world, which again is an offering of subalternity. The God of the Bible has embodied love in Jesus Christ, and the Word becoming flesh is a testament to it. As I perceive it, the aim of the Bible in a 'non-biblical' world today is to inspire people to work for peace and justice for the entire creation. Tim Gee's observation in this regard is very insightful. He says,

> By one estimate there are up to five billion copies of the Bible in the world. That's five billion toolboxes for peace and liberation that exist across the planet, many of which remain unopened ... The fact that a great many of us don't [open] is no doubt a relief to those who rule today's empires. Because if enough people studied and acted on Jesus' (the word became flesh) words, then the foundations of unjust power would start looking very sandy indeed.[18]

A public theology of the Bible calls for just(ice) love which helps in opening the Bible and enacting the crux of it in work for peace and liberation today.

By the way, 'What is the gospel for those who don't depend on the local food banks?' All I have to say is love is the gospel, love coupled with justice is the gospel, love and justice demonstrated by Jesus in his incarnation is the gospel, and going out into the public sphere and doing it likewise is the gospel for our times today. The Bible is the public word for just(ice) love, and justice love is at the heart of the Bible. Public theology celebrates such affirmations.

Notes

1 David Hayward, 'Love versus the Bible digital cartoon', *Naked Pastor*, https://nakedpastor.com/products/love-versus-the-bible-1?_pos=3&_psq=love+and+bible&_ss=e&_v=1.0, accessed 12.06.2024.

2 Ashley McKinless, 2019, 'Cornel West and Robert P. George on Christian love in the public square', *America: The Jesuit Review*.

3 Norman Wirzba, 2021, *This Sacred Life: Humanity's place in a wounded world*, Cambridge: Cambridge University Press, p. 231.

4 De-ecologization is lack of sensitivity on the part of human beings to the importance of environmental issues within life policies, practices, faiths and spiritualities.

5 Nuraan Davids, 'Love in the time of decoloniality', *Alternation* 24 (1) (2019): 102–21, https://doi.org/10.29086/2519-5476/2019/sp24.2a5, pp. 117–18.

6 Elaine Padilla, 2018, 'In the belly of the colony', *Political Theology Network*.

7 On 14 June 2022, the government of the UK organized a special Boeing 767 aircraft at MoD Boscombe Down, near Salisbury, to deport asylum seekers from the UK to Rwanda as part of their new asylum policy. Thanks to the European Court of Human Rights, which at the eleventh hour gave an injunction, the flight never took off. Thanks to the church leaders who publicly called this policy 'immoral' and 'unchristian', calling on the nation to be a welcoming place for those seeking a sanctuary here.

8 Y. T. Vinayaraj, 2015, *Intercessions: Theology, liturgy and politics*, New Delhi: ISPCK, p. 24.

9 K. Kandiah, 2022, 'Scorn for Rwanda policy goes to heart of Christianity', *The Times*, 18 June, https://www.thetimes.co.uk/article/scorn-for-rwanda-policy-goes-to-heart-of-christianity-gbsldpnmo, accessed 12.06.2024.

10 Raj Bharat Patta, 2022, 'The newness of the new commandment', *Political Theology Network*.

11 Gordon Oliver, 2006, *Holy Bible, Human Bible*, London: Darton, Longman and Todd, p. xv.

12 Sathianathan Clarke, 2001, 'Viewing the Bible through the eyes and ears of subalterns in India', *Religion Online*, http://www.religion-online.org/article/viewing-the-bible-through-the-eyes-and-ears-of-subalterns-in-india/, accessed 12.06.2024.

13 S. Clarke, 1999, *Dalit and Christianity: Subaltern religion and Liberation Theology in India*, New Delhi: Oxford University Press, p. 150.

14 Clarke, *Dalit and Christianity*, p. 163.

15 Clarke, *Dalit and Christianity*, p. 158.

16 Clarke, *Dalit and Christianity*, p. 159.

17 Clarke, *Dalit and Christianity*, pp. 164–9.

18 Tim Gee, 2022, *Open for Liberation*, Winchester: Christian Alternative Books, p. 62.

13

'Less Christian, More Secular and More Religiously Plural': Twenty-first-century Census Data as Contextual Challenge and Opportunity for Christian Presence and Witness in England

PAUL WELLER

Terminological discomfort and authorial choice

This book addresses what its editors call 'ecumenical and postcolonial perspectives on "lived" mission in twenty-first-century Britain'. The Baptist theologian James McLendon Jr describes theological reflection as a process involving 'the discovery, understanding and transformation of the convictions of a convictional community, including the discovery and critical revision of their relation to one another and to whatever else there is'.[1] Informed by that approach, this chapter seeks to identify key aspects of the 'whatever else there is' that can be learned through what the decennial Census results can tell us about the religion or belief landscape of England, and to reflect on how that might inform a range of challenges and opportunities for Christian presence and witness in contemporary England.

However, I should at the outset explain why I have adopted the words 'Christian presence and witness' instead of 'mission' used in the title of this book. This is because, from both postcolonial and inter-religious perspectives, 'mission' is a word with which I have become increasingly uncomfortable and now generally avoid using. This is despite growing up in an era in which 'mission' was a word of theological preference for Christians concerned to signal an understanding of the breadth of divine creative and redemptive activity. This was in contrast to a more narrowly focused, humanly instrumentalized and targeted approach of 'evangelism' oriented only or mainly towards the conversion of individuals to Christianity.

Nevertheless, there has in recent years been a growing ecumenical awareness about the often, at the least, uncomfortable historical associations between Christian 'mission organizations' and white European colonial and imperial power. The former were established in order to extend Christianity into what can be called the 'Two Thirds World'. The latter were usually, at least in parallel (and sometimes consciously collaborative) with them, an extension of an economic, military and political project. This is notwithstanding a necessary acknowledgement of the ways in which missiological perspectives did sometimes critique culturally blind ecclesial forms and occasionally also challenged aspects of the political, economic and military structures of colonialism. But despite ongoing attempts to decolonialize the field of missiology (to which, indeed, this edited collection might contribute), while I understand that a valid distinction can be made between historical 'missions' and the broader concept and practice of 'mission' (especially so when using the Latin, *missio Dei*), by choice I personally can no longer comfortably use the English singular word 'mission'.

This is also not least because whatever meaning is intended among Christians who continue to use the word, how it is heard (and, sadly, also observed and/or experienced) by those beyond the boundaries of the Christian community is very often linked with the targeting of individuals for conversion by Christians displaying an arrogant sense of ownership of the truth. Finally, bearing in mind this book's intention to engage with a range of Christian confessional traditions, this chapter argues that a conceptualization of the Christian calling as one of presence and witness is not only more resonant with the realities of the contemporary religion or belief landscape of England. It is also more consistent with some key 'baptistic'[2] theological and ecclesiological resources that this chapter argues can, within an overall process of ecumenical development, help to better equip the Christian Church to meet the challenges and opportunities highlighted by the 2021 Census results.

In this chapter's direct reference to 'baptistic' resources I will attempt to avoid being idiosyncratic and rather will try to deploy these in ways that I think could be affirmed by a broad range of those within 'baptistic' traditions. In the final part of the chapter, however, when reflecting on what have actually been longstanding trends across the last half century or so, I will offer some more personally expressed reflections. These claim no undergirding evidence or authority other than that of my own 'lived' experience and understanding of aspects of Christian presence and witness in a world of increasing religion or belief diversity.

Religion or belief by numbers: takeaway messages and methodological issues

This chapter focuses on the 2021 Census religion or belief data and their implications for England, in part because, while the parallel results are available for Northern Ireland,[3] those for Scotland (in which the Census was delayed until 2022 by Covid) will not be available until the summer of 2024.[4] Therefore, at the time of writing, it was not possible to discuss the results for the United Kingdom of Great Britain and Northern Ireland (UK) as a whole.

It is also the case that any serious discussion of religion or belief data needs to be properly contextualized with reference to the substantive, and often substantial, differences in historical heritage and contemporary context for the relationship between religion(s), state and society found in each of the countries of what this author has elsewhere called the 'four-nations-state' of the UK.[5] Thus, the role of the Welsh language in the religion or belief landscape of Wales along with the fact that, in contrast to England, the Anglican Church in Wales is disestablished, are among the reasons why in terms of the constraints of space it is not practical to attempt an adequate discussion of the census data for Wales.[6]

There is, of course, a lot more in terms of nuance and complexity that could be said about the census data than the headline results on religion or belief alone, not least in relation to its intersectionality with data on ethnicity, gender and sexual orientation. But again, unfortunately, space precludes a full exploration of this. However, as set out in Table 1,[7] the takeaway message from the results of the 2021 Census relating to religion or belief confirms a clear statistical trend over three censuses (2001, 2011 and 2021) in which England has continued to become less Christian, more secular and more religiously plural.

Nevertheless, given that this book is centrally concerned with the 'lived' nature of religion and belief, it is important to pose properly critical questions about the relationship between complex lived realities and statistical data on what this chapter later calls 'religion by numbers'. This is not least because, while missiologists and theologians (including especially those working in social, pastoral and practical theology) have increasingly engaged in productive and fertile ways with social scientific qualitative methods and data, an informed engagement with quantitative methods and data has been less common. It is possible that this may reflect a degree of prior theological suspicion of quantitative methods and data, including because of aspects of the recording, transmission and reception of the historical enumerations taken among the peoples of Israel and Judah that are recorded in the scriptures.

Table 1

Religion	England 2001 Census		England 2011 Census		England 2021 Census	
	Numbers 2001	% 2001	Numbers 2011	% 2011	Numbers 2021	% 2021
Buddhist	139,046	0.3	238,626	0.5	262,438	0.5
Christian	35,251,244	71.7	31,479,876	59.4	26,167,895	46.3
Hindu	546,982	1.1	806,199	1.5	1,020,531	1.8
Jewish	257,671	0.5	261,282	0.5	269,303	0.5
Muslim	1,524,887	3.1	2,660,116	5.0	3,801,178	6.7
Sikh	327,343	0.7	420,196	0.8	520,093	0.9
Other religion	143,811	0.3	227,825	0.4	332,405	0.6
Total religions	38,190,984	77.7	36,094,120	68.1	32,373,843	57.3
No religion	7,171,332	14.6	13,114,232	24.7	20,715,657	36.7
Not stated	3,776,515	7.7	3,804,104	7.2	3,400,555	6.0
Total all	49,138,831	100	53,012,456	100	56,490,055	100

Resonant issues in scriptural (con)texts and contemporary census contexts

The contested relationship between religion, politics and statistics as mediated through the taking of censuses appears in a number of scriptural stories, one of which is presented in the books of 1 Chronicles 21.1–7 and 2 Samuel 24.1–25. In the differentially framed versions of the story found in these two chapters, one can see the potentially problematic issues involved in the nature of numerical data in and of itself; the articulated and other motivations for collecting it; the methods deployed to secure it; and also in the contested ways of interpreting its results. However, through a contemporary reading of the texts, some additional resonant lessons can be identified with regard to aspects of the nature and implications of data deriving from the English censuses of the twenty-first century.

Lesson 1 from the scriptural (con)text

First, even before highlighting the specific variants in the versions of the story, the very existence of such variants already underlines that what might initially otherwise be taken as a relatively straightforward matter of gathering, reporting and deploying numerical facts and figures, is actually a much more complex matter. Prior to the introduction of the modern English Census questions on religion or belief, there was extensive debate around highly contested internal and external estimates. And although census data now exists, the meanings, implications and arguments arising from that data remain subject to vigorous claims and counter-claims, especially in relation to its implications for the place of religion or belief in English public life.

Lesson 2 from the scriptural (con)text for the contemporary census context

Second, the census of Israel was not confined to numbering the whole population but also included the identification of groups within it, such as membership of the tribes of Israel and Judah. Similarly, contemporary census questions on religion or belief ask individual respondents to identify with specific religion or belief groups (while also allowing the 'write in' option of 'Other').

Lesson 3 from the scriptural (con)text for the contemporary census context

Third, in recounting how, during this data collection, the tribes of Levi and Benjamin were deliberately omitted by Joab, the Chronicles variant of the story illustrates how the reported outcome of enumerations can be significantly affected by what transpires in the gap between the design of a census and its conduct in practice. While there is no evidence of the deliberate manipulation of either process or results in the English Censuses of the twenty-first century, there are national contexts where such concerns are very real. Nevertheless, even though the 2021 Census is the third one that has asked a religion or belief question, concerns about state-sponsored enumerations of religion or belief groups have not entirely disappeared (especially among some minority religion or belief groups).

Lesson 4 from the scriptural (con)text for the contemporary census context

Fourth, in the book of Samuel version of the story it is recorded that there were 800,000 men in Israel who were capable of military service, whereas in Chronicles there were 1,100,000; and in Samuel, there were 500,000 men in Judah ready for military service, whereas in 1 Chronicles the figure of 470,000 is given. Such differentially presented outcomes can, of course, occur even without any conscious attempt to produce misleading data. Indeed, bearing in mind this chapter's focus on England alone, a not uncommon but unintentional slippage in census data presentation occurs when results pertaining to 'England and Wales' are taken as referring to England alone or vice versa.

Lesson 5 from the scriptural (con)text for the contemporary census context

Fifth, the scriptural story noted that a key motivation for undertaking the data collection was a wish for reassurance about the potential military strength of the population and its groups. In an overall context for the contemporary collection and use of religion or belief data within which social significance is often associated with numerical size, there can be a tendency (or, one might say, a temptation) for all groups to want their reported size to be maximized in order to improve their overall social positioning and to bolster their own self-confidence.

Lesson 6 from the scriptural (con)text for the contemporary census context

Sixth, and finally, in the Chronicles version of the story, alongside King David's order being reported as the proximate reason for data collection, 'behind' this it is noted that 'Satan stood up against Israel and incited David to count the people of Israel' (1 Chronicles 21.1),[8] thus identifying Satan as the ultimate motivating force. By contrast, in the 2 Samuel version, it is recounted that 'Again the anger of the LORD was kindled against Israel, and he incited David against them, saying "Go, count the people of Israel and Judah"' (2 Samuel 24.1). Here, it is the Lord who is identified as being behind everything. But in neither case does the storyteller positively evaluate what has happened.

Despite all the above, elsewhere in the Jewish scriptures other enumerations (such as those conducted of the Hebrew people both before and after their years of wilderness wanderings) are evaluated much more positively. Indeed, they even resulted in the creation of the biblical book of Numbers. In relation to the contemporary census data, this chapter is not the place to trace the twists and turns in the story about how such a question eventually came to be included,[9] except to note that there was considerable debate around whether such questions represented a potentially dangerous intrusion of the state or whether, in the context of the introduction of law and policy designed to tackle discrimination on the grounds of religion or belief, it was a necessity for implementation of that.

In either case it is not surprising that concerns have remained around the methodological challenges involved in collecting, classifying and interpreting such data. In the following sections, some of these challenges are outlined and discussed in a more social scientific way before the chapter moves to address the contextual implications for the current and future shape of Christian presence and witness in England of this problematized but (it will still be argued) nevertheless socially and religiously significant data.

The promise and perils of religion by numbers

Classification is a necessary part of the collection and dissemination of numerical data. As the Office for National Statistics (ONS) explained in a historic guide published on working with the not completely dissimilar issues involved with ethnicity data: 'A classification is used to assign data reported or measured for a particular situation into categories according to shared characteristics' and in order 'to ensure consistent description and comparison of statistics' or, in short, 'In practice, it is a set of "boxes" into which items can be put to get some kind of meaning.'[10]

Of course, while data on marital status, such as 'single (never been married), married, separated, divorced and widowed'[11] can be relatively unproblematically sorted, the ONS noted that in relation to ethnicity (and, by extension, arguably also to religion or belief), 'we are unable to base ethnic identification upon objective, quantifiable information as we would, say, for age or gender. And this means that we should rather ask people which group they see themselves as belonging to.'[12] In addition, an already less than straightforward use of pre-set options for such questions is further complicated by how respondents can understand and reply to a list of pre-selected options presented to them.

Of course, issues of this kind can, to some extent, be controlled through the kind of extensive piloting of the census questions and answers that took place around the initial introduction of the religion or belief questions. Despite this, it is important that even apparently straightforward data should be understood in a sophisticated and careful way. Otherwise, instead of it being illuminating of social realities, a simplistic use of such data can end up reinforcing the popularly expressed suspicion that 'statistics can be used to prove anything'. At the same time, while absolute and uncontested truth cannot be claimed for the data products of quantitative research, the truth contained in this data should also not be simplistically rejected.

Therefore, applying to this the wisdom of another popular saying, one should beware of throwing out the 'baby' of quantitative data with the 'bathwater' of a poor understanding and use of such data. Instead, there are three concepts – of 'reliability', 'validity' and 'representativity' – which, if deployed in a properly critical way, can ensure an appropriate evaluation and use of quantitative research data, including the religion or belief data derived from the decennial Census. 'Reliability' is concerned with the likelihood of a different person using the same method arriving at the same results. 'Validity' is concerned with whether the data collected gives a true picture of the issue being researched. 'Representativeness' is concerned with the question of how typical of a wider group and/or context is the group and/or the situation that is being studied.

'Representativeness' is, in many ways, one of the most difficult issues for quantitative research conducted on the basis of samples (however carefully selected). In relation to census religion or belief data, however, even though the question remains a voluntary one, its 94 per cent response rate means that it can reasonably confidently be taken as representative of the population of England on the census day, 21 March 2021.

Implications of 2021 Census results for Christian presence and witness in England

Taking census data seriously within theological reflection

Even bearing in mind all the limitations of census data noted above, this chapter still argues that it is possible to use such data as the basis of a valid, reliable and representative picture of what (as previously noted) James McClendon Jr calls the 'whatever else there is' of our contemporary contextual religion or belief reality that should, along with other elements, inform the overall process of theological reflection. Within this, the fact that the headline results of the 2021 Census data, when taken together with similar results from the decennial Censuses of 2001 and 2011, show a clear trajectory in which England is becoming less Christian, more secular and more religiously plural, is of substantial importance for understanding some of the key theological and ecclesiological challenges and opportunities for contemporary Christian presence and witness in England. Indeed, already in 2005, using both the first available religion or belief data from the 2001 Census, as well as drawing upon a number of key theological and ecclesiological resources from within the Baptist tradition of Christianity, I suggested that

the contemporary socio-religious reality of England and the UK might be described as 'three-dimensional' in contrast with a more 'one-dimensional' Christian inheritance or the 'two-dimensional' religious-secular modifications made to that self-understanding during the course of the nineteenth and early twentieth centuries.[13]

In other words, I argued that the kind of 'reality-matching'[14] which is arguably necessary for the doing of an appropriately and adequately grounded theology and ecclesiology includes an imperative for taking into account all three (Christian, secular and religiously plural) dimensions of England's religion or belief landscape. But also, that taking this seriously means recognizing that now is a *Time for a Change* in theological and ecclesiological theory and practice, and that in the 'baptistic' Christian traditions there are important resources that could help facilitate a creative ecumenical Christian engagement with this task.

Of course, in one sense, whether or not Christians are in a majority is itself not something that should play a *determinative* role in deciding the most appropriate form of Christian presence and witness by which to live. Indeed, one of the lessons of Christian history is that, while an appropriate 'indigenization' within a society is necessary for connecting with it in any real way, any simplistic accommodation to the social, cultural and political landscape can be at least problematic and sometimes even dangerous. But to ignore the contextual realities of the census results could also, at the very least, mean that Christianity in England might find itself in danger of being perceived as being part of (and perhaps of actually being co-opted into), a retroactive internal religio-colonial project that tries to defend its historically powerful and privileged position against the increasingly complex reality of a 'three-dimensional' socio-religious reality.

Nostalgia for Christendom and moving beyond privilege

Illustrative of this danger and reflective of what I have elsewhere described as the 'complex aspects of the relationship between religion, belonging, loss and nostalgia in the context of a changing religion and belief landscape',[15] the ease with which echoes of the loss of empire can become elided with the loss of Christendom was poignantly illustrated by an Anglican vicar's interview in a 2010–2013 research project on the nature and extent of religion or belief discrimination. In this, the vicar concerned described the changed position of Christianity as being 'almost like losing the empire all over again, it's just that it's the empire of your own country'.[16] Such a revealing elision, in the context of the ever more 'three-dimensional' religion or belief landscape of England, should arguably make it increasingly difficult to support the continuation of what Stuart Murray calls the 'vestiges of Christendom',[17] an important part of which in England includes the continued establishment of the Church of

England, which must surely be one of the things that the results of the 2001 Census calls into question.

This is, as I have also elsewhere acknowledged, despite the often open and generous stances taken by that Church and many of its leaders and theologians in relation to the religion or belief diversity of contemporary English society.[18] This is because, in the final analysis, the difficulties that arise from the continuation of an established form of Christian presence and witness in a 'three-dimensional' society are ultimately ones of structural privilege. The privilege means that, however inclusive might be the intentions of those within that system, as a number of important figures within the Church of England itself have themselves recognized,[19] in the end its establishment embodies a fundamental lack of honesty. However, similar issues extend to and impact many other denominational forms of Christian presence and witness which, in different ways, also rely upon the social, political, legal and constitutional institutionalization of privileged positions and roles conferred by the Constantinian inheritance of Christendom.

As the former Archbishop of Canterbury, Michael Ramsey, used to remind those who questioned the Church of England's establishment, 'Disestablishment is itself a negative formula. It says what should be discarded. It would be better to ask *quo tendimus?*'[20] Indeed, it is because of this that in my 2005 book *Time for a Change* I argued that resources from the Baptist Christian tradition could offer positive impulses to an ecumenical development in which Christians and the Churches could become better placed to be able to make an appropriate contribution to the necessary task (as suggested by that book's subtitle) of *Reconfiguring religion, state and society* in ways more reflective of its 'three-dimensional' reality.

'Baptistic' theological, anthropological and ecclesiological resources

Unfortunately, it is not possible within this chapter's word constraints to repeat or even to summarize the detailed arguments in support of the above (or to acknowledge some of the counter-arguments), but those who may be interested to explore these in further detail are referred to that book as well as to other relevant publications by the present author.[21] However, for some sense of what these resources might entail for the theology and ecclesiology of Christian presence and witness in England today, the approach taken by the 1606 Gainsborough Covenant might offer some insight.

This was the founding covenant of a Christian 'Separatist' group established by Thomas Helwys and John Smyth which (through subsequent exile in the Netherlands) went on to become the first explicitly

Baptist congregation. As reported by William Bradford, their covenant explained that they had 'joined themselves (by a covenant of the Lord) into a Church estate, in the fellowship of the Gospel to walk in all his ways, made known, or to be made known unto them, according to their best endeavours, whatsoever it should cost them, the Lord assisting.'[22]

This kind of ecclesiological vision was rooted in an understanding of the freedom of religion and belief as a foundational theological value that was classically and succinctly expressed by Thomas Helwys' famous 1612 advocacy of religion and belief freedom. This declared, 'Let them be heretics, Turks, Jews, or whatsoever, it appertains not to the earthly power to punish them in the least measure.'[23] Such an inclusive commitment to religious freedom can in principle enable ecclesiology to be capable of affirming the religion or belief freedom of the 'other' as having an individual and corporate theological and social legitimacy. At the same time it also affirms the possibility that through Christian witness, in a freely chosen way, people of all religion or belief backgrounds can become disciples of Jesus and join the community of the Church.

Such an understanding of Christian presence and witness is why, in his book *The Open Church*, the German Reformed theologian Jürgen Moltmann was able to argue that the 'Free Church' and congregational pattern of Christian presence and witness was the way forward for the Church instead of inherited models rooted in a Christendom understanding:

> Whatever forms the free churches in England, America, and then, since the beginning of the nineteenth century also in Germany have developed (there are, of course, dangers, mistakes and wrong developments enough here too), the future of the church of Christ lies in principle on this wing of the Reformation because the widely unknown and uninhabited territory of the congregation is found here.[24]

Despite, as noted by Moltmann, the tendency towards a biblical fundamentalism and a 'closed' form of congregationalism of a kind that can be found among some contemporary Baptists, the historical mainstream of the Baptist Christian tradition has been more concerned to articulate freely expressed *confessions* of faith as developed in interaction between the fellowship of believers and Christian scriptural tradition. The implications of this for a more dialogical form of Christian presence and witness contrast with more declamatory *definitions* of faith. In the context of the original emergence of the social and political reality of Constantinian Christendom, *definitions* of faith became socially, legally and politically instrumentalized to ensure the 'unity' of the Church, of Christendom, and its privileges.[25] In relation to this, McClendon Jr asked the intriguing and challenging theological and ethical question:

Is it not worth considering how different might have been the history of Christianity if, after the Constantinian accession, the Christian leaders had met at Nicaea, not to anathematise others' inadequate theological metaphysics, but to develop a strategy by which the Church might remain the Church in the light of the fateful political shift – to secure Christian social ethics before refining Christian dogma?[26]

A contemporary acceptance of McClendon's challenge will entail what might be called a historical 'Christology of gatekeeping' being replaced by 'Christology of invitation'[27] within which the confession of Jesus and the telling of the story about him is likely to prove more capable of enabling an encounter with his life, teaching and work than can definitions about him. At the same time, such an approach maintains the centrality of Jesus as the key and distinctive point of reference in the grammar of Christian presence and as the substance of Christian witness in terms of words about him and actions patterned upon him.

However, in moving away from a Christendom mode of Christian presence and witness it is also likely that, because of the damage done by colonialism, we may need (as advocated by the Baptist theologian, Nigel Wright) to 'disavow' Constantine.[28] Even more challengingly, we are likely to need to divest ourselves of at least some of the historical and cultural inheritances which, in the context of a Constantinian Christendom, have 'magnetically' clustered around the name of Jesus.[29]

Liberating Jesus

The portrayal of Jesus in connection with Christian mission activity originating from the western world has often been that of a very particular kind of blonde-haired, blue-eyed version of European-ness, even though, since Jesus was of Jewish genetic stock in a Mediterranean context, it would be highly unlikely that he would be white skinned, much less blonde-haired or blue-eyed. Today, the ramifications of this for the perception of Christian presence and witness among people of other than European descent are widely recognized. However, there are also other, perhaps less obvious, ways in which the portrayal of Jesus can become a barrier to Christian presence and witness.

Several decades ago, the former Anglican priest Alan Watts threw out what was then – and likely still will be for many Christians today – the disturbing challenge that 'We are spiritually paralysed by the fetish of Jesus.'[30] In more reflective mode, but still ending in a challenging way, Watts went on explain that by this he meant of Jesus that, 'His literary image in the Gospels has, through centuries of homage, become far more of an idol than anything graven in wood or stone so that today the most genuinely reverent act of worship is to destroy that image.' In going still further with what such a challenge might imply, Watts referred to the example of the Zen Buddhist tradition that said, 'Wash out your mouth every time you say "Buddha"!' on the basis that even the concept of the Buddha can get in the way of the goal of Buddhism, which is the realization of the Buddha-nature. Building on this example, Watts even more sharply and radically made the, no doubt for many, shocking claim that 'The new life for Christianity begins just as soon as someone can get up in church and say, "Wash out your mouth every time you say 'Jesus'" !'

In relation to this, it is likely that many Christians (including not least those who might bear witness to having found in Jesus an empowering way of liberation from the destructive powers of this world) will find such a way of expressing this challenge to be at the least emotionally difficult. However, it is also at least arguable that taking such a challenge seriously may help to liberate the Church from the temptation of thinking and feeling that Jesus is the property of Christians. Indeed, to treat Jesus as such property would, ironically, in practice deny precisely what the classical Christological and credal formulations were originally concerned to point to: namely, that Jesus is not a 'Christian deity' but is rather, in the words of the title of one of John Robinson's books, *The Human Face of God*.[31]

While the traditional credal formulations of Christian theology have always affirmed at least the presence (and usually the special and decisive presence) of divine in Jesus, the theological significance of this is not at all the same as saying 'Jesus is God'. This expression comes very close to what might, in terms of spirituality, be described as 'Jesuology' or, in classical doctrinal terms, as 'Christomonism'. As the Baptist theologian Brian Haymes put it:

> for all there is a crucial relationship between God and Jesus, there is more to God than Jesus Christ. In speaking of Jesus we believe we are making a statement about God and so we have resisted turning Jesus into a personal experience. It is in no way dishonouring to say that statements about Jesus Christ do not exhaust the meaning of God.[32]

Liberating 'God'

To set confession of, and witness to, the person of Jesus within the context of the 'bigger' Mystery at the heart of life to which the Christian and other religious traditions point and testify could, if positively explored and embraced, open up for Christian presence and witness a dialogical process of inter-cultural, inter-religious and inter-convictional discernment. Half a century ago John Robinson called, in the title of his famous book, for Christians to be *Honest to God*, and an interview with him in *The Observer* newspaper (1963) was published under the title 'Our Image of God Must Go'. Alongside the need to liberate Jesus from colonial control and religious domestication, it is arguable that there still remains a need to liberate 'God' from the theological imprisonment into which Christians have all too often confined their vision of the divine. Indeed, this is also a reminder that for more than half a century before the religion or belief results of the 2001 Census in England were available, the contextual trends which that data embodies were already well under way.

Personal expressions of overcoming fearfulness and rediscovering 'Good News'

In moving towards the close of a chapter that has thus far built on more academically articulated arguments of an historical, sociological, statistical, theological and ecclesiological kind, I conclude in a more personal way by sharing two poems that I wrote some decades ago, but when the trends and trajectories of the 2001 Census data on religion or belief were already well under way. The first of these was an attempt to challenge both myself and other Christians in relation to our all too limited and impoverished sense of the divine.

God in a Box (1986)

'The Tao that can be expressed is not the eternal Tao.
The name that can be defined is not the unchanging name.'
The Tao Te Ching

What is this god in a box
Put away in our cupboards
And pulled out for tricks?
To excuse our excuses
And our failures to decide,
Our Daddy in the sky
And answerer of why.

What is this god in a box
Bound by covers of leather

And pages of ink?
The god of our yesterdays
And deliverer from reason,
The freezing of living
Suspended in time.

What is this god in a box
Behind doors that are bolted
And steeples and spires?
That's possessed by its owners
Who sell tickets for access
And then fight for his cause
To keep him alive?

What is this god in a box
But a puppet on a spring
That's locked within a cell?
But with god in a box
It is we who are prisoners
And we won't find the key
Till we set God free.

In the second, even earlier poem, I gave expression to the longing to be
liberated from the fearfulness within which Christians have all too often
imprisoned ourselves.

An Easter Prayer (1978)

Lord, they say you came when the doors were closed:
Jesus, we are frightened too.
We are huddled together in our buildings,
And even in our hiding-places we hide.
We are hurt little children of shattered dreams.
Come, Lord Jesus,
Ignore our bolted doors,
Melt our masks,
Stand in our midst,
And heal us.

Lord, we are weary:
Our legs are lead and our voices muffled.

Pied Piper Jesus, play your flute
And lead us in your dance.
Touch our lips,
Take our tongues,
And teach us how to sing again.

Lord, they say you burst out of the tomb:
Let us not watch like we do on a TV screen.
Come, risen Lord Jesus, and bring your Spring-time joy
To fill the dark, dank dungeons of our lives
With your morning radiance.
Come, Lord Jesus, come.

Attempting to understand and to live by the forms of Christian presence and witness as intellectually argued for and personally expressed in this chapter could hopefully mean that the challenges arising from an increasingly 'three-dimensional' religion or belief society will increasingly be experienced not as a *set of problems to be solved* but, rather, as a *liberative opportunity to be explored*. This exploration could, in turn, lead to a deeper and wider appreciation of the unbounded and limitless reality of the love which Christians affirm is at the heart of the universe – which cannot be possessed by individuals but is also the precondition for their existence; the grounding of their interaction and the criterion by which all things are judged. Within this process of theological liberation, our Christology might also be able to undergo a process of post-Constantinian and postcolonial liberation from the promotion of definitive interpretations of Jesus' person and significance that can have the effect of closing him off from people of another religion or belief.

In these ways, instead of being imprisoned in a defensive spirit of fearfulness, our embrace of such new forms for Christian presence and witness in England could facilitate the (re)birth of the kind of vital spirit that animated what was proclaimed by the original Christians as 'Good News'. This could be in ways that might once again become capable of being widely *received* as 'Good News', including among those who have been historically excluded from, and/or alienated by, inherited Constantinian forms of Christian presence and witness.

Notes

1 J. McClendon Jr, 'What is a Baptist Theology?', *American Baptist Quarterly* 1 (1) (1982): 16–39, 20.

2 'Baptistic' is a term that has been used to refer to aspects of the historic Baptist Christian vision that is shared by other Christian Churches and traditions that

have a similar ecclesiology, but which are not formally called Baptist; for example, the Mennonites and some other congregationally based traditions.

3 See NISRA, 2021, '2021 Census', *Northern Ireland Statistics and Research Agency*, https://www.nisra.gov.uk/statistics/census/2021-census, accessed 12.06.2024.

4 See Scotland's Census, 2024, 'Census outputs schedule', *Scotland's Census*, https://www.scotlandscensus.gov.uk/about/2022-census/census-outputs-schedule/, accessed 12.06.2024.

5 P. Weller, 2005, *Time for a Change: Reconfiguring religion, state and society*, London: T & T Clark, p. 73.

6 The author recommends Kevin Ellis, 2023, 'See, Judge, Act. Wrestling with the effects of colonialism as an English priest in Wales' in Anthony Reddie and Carol Troupe (eds), *Deconstructing Whiteness, Empire and Mission*, London: SCM Press, pp. 208–21.

7 For the 2001, 2011 and 2021 data, see the Office for National Statistics (ONS) website: www.ons.gov.uk. Crown copyright material is reproduced with the permission of the Controller of HMSO.

8 Quotations from the scriptures both here and in what follows are taken from the *New Oxford Annotated Bible, New Revised Standard Version with the Apocrypha: An Ecumenical Study Bible*, 2018, fifth edition, fully revised and expanded, New York: Oxford University Press.

9 See P. Weller and A. Andrews, 'Counting religion: religion, statistics and the 2001 Census', *World Faiths Encounter* (21) (1998): 23–34; P. Weller, 'Identity, politics and the future(s) of religion in the UK: the case of religion question in the 2001 Decennial Census', *Journal of Contemporary Religion*, 19 (1) (2004): 3–21.

10 ONS (Office for National Statistics), 2003, *Ethnic Group Statistics: A guide for the collection and classification of data*, London: HMSO, p. 8.

11 ONS, *Ethnic Group Statistics*, p. 8.

12 ONS, *Ethnic Group Statistics*, p. 9.

13 Weller, *Time for a Change*, p. 73.

14 Weller, *Time for a Change*, p. 185.

15 P. Weller, Kingsley Purdam, Nazila Ghanea and Sariya Cheruvallil-Contractor, 2013, *Religion or Belief, Discrimination and Equality: Britain in global contexts*, London: Bloomsbury, p. 114.

16 Weller, Purdam, Gahnea and Cheruvallil-Contractor, *Religion or Belief*, p. 114.

17 S. Murray, 2004, *Post-Christendom: Church and mission in a strange new world*, Carlisle: Paternoster Press, pp. 188–200.

18 See P. Weller, 1986, 'The theology and practice of inter religious dialogue: a Baptist contribution to ecumenical debate in England', unpublished MPhil in Social and Pastoral Theology, Manchester: University of Manchester.

19 P. Cornwall, 1983, *Church and Nation*, Oxford: Basil Blackwell; C. Buchanan, 1994, *Cut the Connection: Disestablishment and the Church of England*, London: Darton, Longman and Todd; K. Leech (ed.), 2001, *Setting the Church of England Free: The case for disestablishment*, Croydon: The Jubilee Group; Jonathan Chaplin, 2022, *Beyond Establishment: Resetting church–state relations in England*, London: SCM Press.

20 M. Ramsey, 1974, *Canterbury Pilgrim*, London: SPCK, p. 176.

21 Weller, *Time for a Change*; P. Weller, 'Theological ethics and interreligious relations: a Baptist Christian Perspective', *Internationale Kirchliche Zeitschrift/Bern Interreligious Oecumenical Studies* 1 (2014): 119–40; P. Weller, 'Balancing within three dimensions: Christianity. secularity and religious plurality in social policy and

theology', *Internationale Kirchliche Zeitschrift/Bern Interreligious Oecumenical Studies*, 3 (2016); P. Weller, 'Changing socio-religious realities, practical negotiation of transitions in the governance of religion or belief, state and society', *Internationale Kirchliche Zeitschrift/Bern Oecumenical Studies* 30 (2) (2020: 145–62; P. Weller, 'Historical sources and contemporary resources of minority Christian Churches: a Baptist contribution', *Internationale Kirchliche Zeitschrift* 111 (3–4) (2021): 140–57.

22 W. Bradford, 1912, *History of Plymouth Plantation, 1620–1647*, C. Ford Worthington (ed.), two volumes, Boston, MA: Houghton Mifflin Company for the Massachusetts Historical Society, p. 20.

23 R. Groves (ed.), 1998, *Thomas Helwys: A Short Declaration of the Mystery of Iniquity*, Macon, GA: Mercer University Press, p. 69.

24 J. Moltmann, 1978, *The Open Church: Invitation to a Messianic Lifestyle*, London: SCM Press, p. 197.

25 A. Kee, 1982, *Constantine Versus Christ: The Triumph of Ideology*, London: SCM Press.

26 McClendon Jr, 'What is a Baptist Theology?', p. 39.

27 P. Weller, 2006, *God, Jesus and Dialogue: The Beach Lectures for 2005*, Bracknell: Centre for the Study of Religious and Cultural Diversity Occasional Papers, No. 3, Newbold College.

28 N. Wright, 2000, *Disavowing Constantine: Mission, church and the social order in the theologies of John Howard Yoder and Jürgen Moltmann*, Carlisle: Paternoster Press.

29 P. Weller, 2023, 'Coming full circle: Christianity, empire, whiteness, the global majority and the struggles of migrants and refugees in the UK', in Anthony Reddie and Carol Troupe (eds), *Deconstructing Whiteness, Empire and Mission*, London: SCM Press, pp. 173–92.

30 A. Watts, 1976, '"Wash out your mouth"' in Robert Sohl and Audrey Carr (eds), *The Gospel According to Zen: Beyond the Death of God*, London: Mentor New American Library, pp. 16–17.

31 J. Robinson, 1972, *The Human Face of God*, London: SCM Press.

32 B. Haymes, 1985, 'Covenant and the Church's mission' in P. Fiddes, R. Hayden, R. Kidd and K. Clements (eds), *Bound to Love: The covenant basis of Baptist life and mission*, London: The Baptist Union, pp. 63–75.

14

Reimagining Mission from the Margins: Reclaiming Dignity, Agency and Power Together

NIALL COOPER

Introduction

In the UK there are strong and deep-seated public attitudes that stigmatize and blame individuals for their own poverty. Over decades, these attitudes have been embedded in the welfare system and internalized by many people living in poverty themselves.

Sadly, the Churches are not immune from these attitudes, from victim-blaming, treating poverty as a problem to be addressed through individual behaviour change, or in more theological language 'saving' people from their self-inflicted poverty.

This is the context in which poverty – and even many attempts to tackle it – rob people of their dignity, agency or power over their lives. What would it mean to reimagine mission from the perspective of people and communities 'on the margins'? What would it mean to prioritize the task of reclaiming dignity, agency and power together? Or, in the words of Pope Francis, to become 'a true church of or for the poor'?

Do the main UK Christian denominations adhere to the gospel priority to work with, and alongside, the poorest and most marginalized people in society? Poverty and marginalization are a reality in the UK for millions of households, and this reality is worsening. Where is the Church and where should it be?

The lived experience of poverty and marginalization

Poverty is not entertainment, it's not noble or romantic.
Poverty is ... heavy.
It's heavy hearts and heavy legs.
It's sore skin and hollow eyes.
It's upset and downhearted.

It's hunger. Malnourishment. It's always thinking about the next meal.
Poverty is bailiffs, it's food banks, it's queues and lists, it's never being
told what you're entitled to but always being told.
Poverty is being shown up then put down.[1]

The opening lines of Tony Walsh's poem 'Poverty', written over a week-
end workshop with a group of people who shared and reflected on their
own personal experiences of poverty, reveals something of the indignity
of living in poverty in the midst of a supposedly affluent society.

Poverty and marginalization are a reality in the UK for millions of
households. In rural and urban spaces, people without enough food to
eat or money to live on experience social exclusion and negative perception and this reality is worsening. People with lived experience of poverty
are 'marginalized from effective participation in mainstream economic,
social and political life'.[2]

Poverty is not only deprivation of economic or material resources but,
according to the United Nations, it is also fundamentally a violation of
human dignity.[3] This is a scandal – dehumanizing people who experience
economic (or other) marginalization and poverty. False and damaging
assumptions about their value, worth and purpose are all too common,
even in the Church. This is the context in which poverty – and even many
attempts to tackle it – rob people of their dignity, agency or power over
their lives.

It's about us and them: Living at the margins

Within the UK one of the most profound factors affecting the experience
of poverty are the deeply negative – and damaging – social attitudes to
poverty. The way in which deeply ingrained habits, language, culture and
social attitudes conspire to 'other' people in poverty, to stereotype, stigmatize, blame and shame people in ways which mean that even people 'in
poverty' reject the term, or use it of others in an equally negative manner.
Professor Ruth Lister describes this in terms of the 'othering' of people
living in poverty.[4]

There is a popular argument that if people are poor, it is because
of their own poor 'state of mind', poor attitude to work and poor life
decisions. The implication is, by contrast, that middle-class people have
earned their position because of their own hard work and merit. As Iain
Duncan Smith, founder of the Centre for Social Justice, has argued: '[T]he
inner city wasn't a place; it was a state of mind – there is a mentality of
entrapment, where aspiration and hope are for other people, who live in
another place.'[5]

Over many decades, these attitudes have been embedded not just in the welfare system but in the way many professional agencies exercise moral judgements and highly intrusive methods of controlling the behaviour of people living in poverty. These attitudes have also been internalized by people in poverty themselves, to the extent that they describe a sense of shame, or in the words of Wayne Green, who spoke at our first National Poverty Hearing in 1996: 'What is poverty? Poverty is a battle of invisibility, a lack of resources, exclusion, powerlessness ... being blamed for society's problems.'[6]

To a greater or lesser extent, the impact of this is to isolate people in poverty, to create a culture of shame in which it is important to 'hide' one's poverty from others, or worse, a culture of blame, in which people at some level think it is 'their fault'. Both make it much harder to bring people together, or for people to see that they are not alone: That others are in the same boat, and that the 'causes' of their poverty may not lie in themselves but somewhere else.

At a more personal level, the experiences of people struggling with poverty are profoundly shaped by their social surroundings. This may be the sense of isolation created by living in poverty in a community which tells itself that 'everyone is wealthy and successful' (even though the statistics tell us that even in the most affluent areas this is not the case). Or it may be the sense that 'this is just how things are' if you are living in poverty in a community where pretty much everyone you know is struggling to put food on the table on a regular basis.

'Chavs' and others we like to look down on

This is where the experience of poverty and living 'at the margins' come together and intersect with other experiences of living at the margins. Being 'at the margins' involves a sense that 'society isn't for people like me'. The idea that 'society is organized by and for' other people can come in many forms – people with money, power, privilege, a certain education or accent, people who can afford their own homes, cars, internet access. This in turn intersects with experiences of marginalization on the basis of race, gender, age, disability, religion (while we may feel increasingly 'marginal' as Christians in a secular space, we cannot deny the fact that Christianity continues to hold a privileged position vis-à-vis people of other faiths in the UK) – and not least with ideas of social class.

TV series such as *Benefits Street* and 'poverty porn' television more generally have maliciously played on popular myths of the laziness of working-class people and communities. Similarly, mainstream representations of blackness have associated black people with crime, violence, gangs and hyper-sexuality.[7] Working-class and BME people have to bear such stereotypes as they navigate their lives.[8]

Class is deeply embedded in British society, in ways that are sometimes hard to see; but it is in many ways 'the elephant in the room' when it comes to discussions about poverty and marginalization. The sense that society is organized around the needs, wants, choices and aspirations of the 'middle class' is one of the most powerful norms within contemporary British society – to the extent that in many areas of life it would simply be classed as 'the norm'. Class-based prejudice against non-middle-class culture, people and places is longstanding – and in many cases barely disguised – but equally, rarely discussed (or challenged).

The Churches themselves are certainly not immune from class prejudice, both in traditions of 'church' versus 'chapel' and in the ways in which nonconformity has acted as a 'social escalator' for the respectable, chaste, teetotal and well-mannered to set themselves aside from (and above) the lumpen proletariat from whom they have escaped.

Getting by: Dignity, agency and human worth

At a fundamental level, poverty and marginalization are also about questions of 'human worth'. If you spend any amount of time talking with or listening to conversations among people in poverty, it's striking how often the discussion centres on stories of indignity, or being belittled, judged and left humiliated or powerless (although sometimes well treated). Often you are at the mercy of other people or institutions that don't appear to understand, or care for your well-being – council officers, benefit assessors, immigration tribunals, courts, GPs, teachers, social workers. Many of the people and institutions, in fact, that would say they have the interests of people at heart …

But listen hard enough and there is frequently another story to hear: that, in spite of everything, people lead dignified lives, find ways of 'getting by', based as much as anything on their own creativity and resourcefulness. Their ability to make their limited money stretch to the end of the week by 'robbing Peter to pay Paul'; knowing where to find the best bargain (or simply by choosing what to go without); their own informal networks of family and friends; and unwritten codes and rules as to what kind of behaviour is and isn't acceptable within working-class (and other) communities. For many, these are deep moral codes that may differ from middle-class norms, but which have no less force and validity (or indeed, congruence with Christian faith and life).

Mission to, not mission with

Sadly, the Churches are not immune from othering, victim-blaming and treating poverty as a problem to be addressed through individual behaviour change, or in more theological language 'saving' people from their self-inflicted poverty. The idea that mission strategies – let alone new theological insights – could be generated by people and communities who are themselves on the margins remains anathema to many.

In the Church, as in the country, poverty is normally perceived from the standpoint of those who are not poor. As Martin Charlesworth and Natalie Williams have powerfully documented in *A Church for the Poor*:

> A YouGov survey, conducted in 2014, found that 62 percent of people who regularly attend church identify as middle class, while only 38 percent identify as working class. More surprisingly, Talking Jesus research, conducted in 2015, found that 81 percent of practising Christians in Britain today have a university degree. This compares to around 27 percent in the population as a whole. So, the demographics in our churches do not reflect the demographics in our communities. We are missing a large section of society.[9]

This is the context in which it becomes easy for 'the Church' to become associated with a middle-class non-poor perspective, where the overriding assumption is that 'the poor' are 'outside' the Church, and with this can easily come pejorative or patronizing assumptions that 'the poor' are a helpless, hapless, homogenous group in need of 'our' help. Beyond this, 'poor communities' can easily be characterized as Godless, hopeless places of failure that are either 'beyond redemption' or in need of 'saving'.

Michael Hirst has investigated how far the Methodist Church's priority for the poor intersects with the actual geography of its local presence, in terms of where churches, ministers and its lay leadership actually live. Matching the middle-class drift of the churches more generally, Hirst's key finding is that Methodist ministers, supernumeraries and lay people who guide policy and practice at the national level lived predominantly in the least deprived neighbourhoods. The shift out of poorer neighbourhoods actually became more marked in the ten-year period between 2001 and 2011.[10]

This finding was mirrored in a survey for the Church of England's Church Buildings Council (CBC), which found that between 2004 and 2018, churches in the most deprived parishes were much more likely to close – 'the very places which may be missional priorities'. Commenting on the report, Bishop Philip North said:

urban areas have suffered from 10 years of austerity, with countless services withdrawn and places of assembly closed, and it is dispiriting that the Church appears to have been part of this pattern of slow abandonment.[11]

In March 2023 Church Action on Poverty published the findings of its own three-year Church on the Margins research programme. This involved in-depth statistical research into patterns of church closures across five Christian denominations (Church of England, Roman Catholic, Methodist, Baptist and United Reformed Churches) within Greater Manchester over the last ten years, mapped against the indices of deprivation.

The key finding was that significantly more churches have closed in low-income areas than in more affluent areas in Greater Manchester. Most church closures within the Church of England, Catholic, Methodist and Baptist denominations were in the most deprived areas. Only the United Reformed Church had more closures in affluent areas than in low-income areas. Reasons for closures included: declining attendance at church services; buildings falling into disrepair, coupled with churches being unable to afford their upkeep; and fewer priests or ministers to serve the churches. This does not explain why many more churches have closed in 'deprived' areas compared to more affluent areas.

The Church's theological life and imagination has something else to say, which should and could offer vision. There need to be reinvigorated understandings of the intrinsic value of all people, of their stories as alive with good, meaning and purpose – and of their significance in the world regardless of economic impact.

The question and challenge presented by Pope Francis is this: do we really believe that God can be found at the margins; do we really believe in a countercultural church of and for the poor; are we prepared to let go of our own power?

Foundational principles for reimagining mission

Before seeking to explore what mission, or indeed a 'church on the margins' might look like in practice, it is important first to explore three core values which have consistently emerged from Church Action on Poverty's work with people and communities who have been struggling against poverty over many years. These values should underpin any meaningful long-term engagement with people and communities at the margins.

Human dignity

As Duncan Forrester has written, 'Human beings are entitled to be treated with respect because they are of equal worth, independently of their ability, contribution, success, work or desert. That is the bottom line.'[12]

For Christians, the centrality of human dignity is based on the foundational theological principle that all human beings are created in the image and likeness of God. In *On Human Worth*, Forrester explores this theme in some detail:

> All human beings are created in the image of God, they all share equally in this crucial, definitive characteristic. There is no question of some being more and others less involved in the *imago Dei* as the created order is concerned. The *imago Dei* speaks both of the importance of equal relationships and of the need to give equal respect, treatment and indeed reverence to all, for all bear the image even if now only in partial and broken form. The image of God is thus a way of affirming and interpreting human dignity.[13]

This approach to placing human dignity – and human rights – at the centre of a Christian response to poverty is also reflected in Pope Francis' recent encyclical, *Fratelli Tutti*. As Maria Power has reflected, this

> offers a new vision of society in which human dignity and the human rights of all are respected ... He has always wanted to make it clear that his papacy is one of action – placing the needs of the poor, marginalised and disenfranchised at the centre of his ministry.[14]

God's 'preferential option for the poor' is not some idea concocted by liberation theologians in Latin America in the 1970s, but a core element of Jesus' life and ministry.

Agency

I have a voice
abused and berated downcast
shunned by government and society
unloved and forgotten
I have a voice
I use my voice

loud and clear
shout and scream
for all to hear
(Penny Walters, extract)[15]

To be truly human means not only being invested with dignity but also with agency. By agency, we mean here 'the capacity of individuals to act and to make their own free choices'. We all value the opportunity to make choices for ourselves, to have our skills, talents and ideas recognized, to play an active part in our own churches and communities, to 'have a voice'.

However, in the UK at least, there is a commonly held view that people in poverty simply lack any capacity to have agency. There is a deep-seated prejudice, closely associated with attitudes to class, that people in poverty lack the intelligence, motivation or wisdom to contribute anything positive to their own lives, let alone to wider society.

In his 2001 book *On Human Worth*, Duncan Forrester traces some of these ideas back to 'a once-powerful trend in the British Fabian and idealist tradition which held, sometimes chillingly, that educated, well-intentioned people were adequately equipped to decide what was good for others without the need to consult them.'[16]

Darren McGarvey, writing on his own experience of growing up in poverty in Glasgow in his award-winning book *Poverty Safari*, describes the impact that being ignored and dismissed over years has on people:

It's an understatement to say that many have become angry, disillusioned or apathetic after years of feeling ignored, dismissed and bullied by agencies and institutions speaking in the mechanical jargon of re-generation. There's a feeling in sections of these communities, among those who want to actively participate, that things are not done with the community, but to it.[17]

However, the question as to who has 'the agency and ability to tackle poverty' can be a tricky one to answer. People on the political right too easily seek to blame people for their own poverty, without understanding the wider forces that come into play on people's lives to restrict their agency to act. People on the left can focus so much on structural forces that create poverty and inequality that they risk denying people any agency to change anything.

Darren McGarvey goes on to challenge the way in which, even among well-intentioned people, 'the problem of poverty' is discussed in ways that deny people themselves any ability to bring about change,

Every problem is discussed like it's beyond the expertise of the average person. The cumulative effect being that responsibility for poverty and its attendant challenges is almost always externalised; ascribed to an unseen force or structure, a system or some vaguely defined elite. A systemic analysis which focuses on external factors unwisely forgoes the opportunity to explore the role we as individuals, families and communities can play in shaping the circumstances that define our lives.[18]

In Church Action on Poverty's experience, people who struggle against poverty on a daily basis have not only far greater insight into the challenges they face, but a really deep understanding of what needs to change, and some of the best ideas for doing so. Drawing on his own experience again, McGarvey affirms the resilience and determination of people to bring about change, even in the face of their own poverty:

It's one of the paradoxes of poverty: the harder things get, the more resilient some people become. Cultures of resistance are forged on the anvil of social deprivation and for every person who withers in poverty's wake, another grows more resolute and determined. Social deprivation can tear communities apart, but it can also renew them because it forces them to cooperate, innovate and evolve to find the solutions to their common problems.[19]

In my experience, there is nothing more transformative than enabling a group of people to bond together through sharing their own experiences and 'truths' about poverty, and to discover that these are not 'personal' problems but shared experiences – and then to generate ideas and take action to address them together. This process of making people's voices heard is at the heart of enabling people to reclaim a sense of agency, not just over their own lives, but to challenge and change the wider decisions, institutions and attitudes which so often constrain or negatively impact on them.

Power

Power properly understood is nothing but the ability to achieve a purpose. It is the strength required to bring about social, political, and economic change. (Martin Luther King)[20]

I frequently find that people in church circles often have a problem with the idea of power. It makes us uneasy. But I'm reliably told that there are more references to power in the Bible than to prayer. According to Robert Linthicum in his book *Transforming Power*,

[P]ower is always present in all human situations, because power is nothing more than the ability, capacity and willingness of a person, a group of people or an institution (whether it is a church or a nation) to act. The ability, capacity and willingness to act is, in itself, neither good nor bad. What makes power constructive or destructive is how it is used and for what purpose it is used (that is, whether it is designed to control and dominate people or to enable people to be in charge of their own destinies).[21]

For some reason, Christians like to focus more on loving our neighbours than on claiming or challenging power. But Martin Luther King challenges us to think differently:

Power without love is reckless and abusive, and love without power is sentimental and anaemic. Power at its best is love implementing the demands of justice, and justice at its best is power correcting everything that stands against love.[22]

In 2006 the independent 'Power Inquiry' came to the conclusion that power is one source of critical inequality in Britain. People on a low income are often engaged in a constant, and usually unequal, struggle to assert their rights and decisions against the institutions they rely upon for their limited well-being – whether that be employers, the Department for Work and Pensions, the police or the National Health Service. A rising sense of powerlessness rather than self-determination has been the lot of those individuals, families and communities hit hardest by post-industrialization.

Its explanation? The social, cultural and political organizations that gave the industrial working-class majority political power and shaped their political aspirations have little or no purchase among newly marginalized groups, and as yet no new organizations have filled the political vacuum. Thus a wide section of society enjoys only a very limited and fragmented dialogue with those in power.

For anyone familiar with the five marks of mission that have been adopted both by the Anglican Communion and the World Alliance of Reformed Churches, transforming unjust structures is core to the mission of the Church. Yet if we are serious about transforming unjust structures, then we have to be willing not just to speak truth to power, but to enable people to do so for themselves.

What would it take to become not just a community of faith, witness and solidarity, but a movement of change agents? A community which seeks to embody the change we want to bring about?

[O]ur deepest fear is not that we are inadequate. Our deepest fear is that we are powerful beyond measure. It is our light, not our darkness, that most frightens us. We ask ourselves, Who am I to be brilliant, gorgeous, talented, fabulous? Actually, who are you not to be? You are a child of God. Your playing small does not serve the world. There's nothing enlightened about shrinking so that other people won't feel insecure around you. We are all meant to shine, as children do. We were born to make manifest the glory of God that is within us. It's not just in some of us; it's in everyone.[23]

Making change happen must always start at street level, at local level, as a result of small groups of people coming together to reclaim their own dignity, agency and power. Church Action on Poverty's vision for building a social movement is rooted in this approach – finding ways to enable groups of people to come together in ways which are transformative for themselves personally, for their friends, neighbours and wider community, and ultimately transformative of society as a whole.

Reimagining mission from the margins

So what might it mean for the Churches to put these principles into practice? How might we reimagine mission from the margins, not to the margins? How might we conceive of a true Church of and for people and communities struggling against poverty? What would it take for the Church to work alongside people to reclaim dignity, agency and power together? Indeed, what might a church on the margins be?

The good news is that this is not, in fact, a new task. As Aidan Donaldson has argued, this was an intrinsic element of Jesus' own mission and ministry:

The sense of fear, isolation, loneliness and rejection experienced by people living in the margins was no doubt experienced by many of those whom Jesus encountered. Throughout the Gospels we are told not only that there were numerous groups of people who were marginalised by society and whose human dignity was not recognised – including lepers, women, sinners and the poor – but also that Jesus actively sought out these people and brought them back into the community. What is remarkable, indeed revolutionary, about the way Jesus approached those who were social outcasts is that he preferentially reached out to them.[24]

Indeed, as Anna Ruddick argues, God is frequently to be found on the margins, and in many ways turns upside-down our conventional thinking about the importance of 'the margins' and 'the centre':

> Our tradition reminds us that God kind of likes the margins. God isn't a very 'centre of power' type God. God is a 'create a world and entrust it to humanity, choose a people and follow them through their mistakes, prefer prophets over kings, choose a teenage virgin from Nazareth and become human, hang out with social outcasts and annoy the establishment, refuse to become their Che Guevara and instead wash people's feet, die on a cross' type of God. So God seems to be a marginal God, and God's not the only one for whom marginal space is generative.[25]

This is the same story that emerged from in-depth conversations with groups of people 'on the margins' from a range of churches in low-income communities, which was a core element of Church Action on Poverty's Church on the Margins research programme.[26] At times moving, at times frustrating, the voices and stories shared were powerful and insightful. Faith and action were married in all the conversations, with markers of identity being attached to presence, welcome, hospitality and persistence. The joy of gathering in groups is hard to capture.

> I think we've just thought this is where we live. We want to see the gospel flourish here, and this is where our kids are growing up. So, we want it to be a good place for them. And a lot of people speak badly of Partington. They just do. Why would you want to go there? It's an awful place, but we really love the community here and we'd never want to speak badly of the community. Yes. I think it's just 'make a difference' where you are. Just try to live the gospel where you are, and that's it really, have a go. (Partington group participant)

In various ways scripture dripped into the conversations. Most particularly as a reason for engagement and also as something people could draw on, engage in, reflect and 'preach' from themselves. The significance of spiritual resources and the ways people had encountered church in the first place was also a lively conversation. Inclusion in leading, preparing and shaping the worshipping experience of communities was a feature, and the incorporation of local leaders into the life of the congregation was important. This particularly revolved around Sunday worship, but also involvement in deacons' groups, running activities and participating in determining the direction of groups.

Power, empowerment and helplessness in the light of denominational structures and expectations emerged, from being excluded from leadership but used extractively for skills, or being involved in new ways and discovering new possibilities. We heard repeatedly of the dignity of people empowered to lead and serve in clear ways in and beyond a Sunday. Dignity, personhood and the sense of 'family' created around themes of acceptance and participation – being treated normally and encouraged to 'be' oneself – emerged repeatedly. A sense of the family of church was expressed. The 'relationships not blood' conversation was gripping.

The sense of creating and crafting real church beyond the walls of the church, a Sunday morning, or a drive-in church repeatedly came up. To develop theologically what it means to be 'church', and understanding this in a broad sense, seemed imperative.

> It doesn't matter what race you are, how rich you are, or who you are. … everybody is loved. People don't understand that, when you talk about love, they think that's soppy. No, it's not soppy, Christ loved everybody, Christ never kicked anybody out. He never refused anybody. It doesn't matter who you are or what you are … in Christ's eyes we're all the same. Everybody in God's eyes is welcome. (Brunswick group participant)

There was something quite special about talking, listening and being heard that may well be the most powerful outcome: better questions, better ears, deeper love as a model possible of replication.

The positivity of such stories was balanced by other experiences that illustrated why people on the margins also experience church as difficult. Often people leading denominational initiatives can actually be distant from people with lived experience of marginality.

In many places, groups have had their stories used extractively, or with the hero figure emerging as the professional leader rather than the people themselves. Although the groups discussed wider intersectional things – disability, literacy, class, language, over and over again tensions emerged that implied that the welcome, inclusion and belonging create a challenge within churches themselves. There was also a sense that types of leadership developed within the community were very real, but not necessarily recognized or authorized in relation to the local church. There was, though, a real desire for church to be truly reflective of the local people.

A challenge to the Churches

The question remains: what does it mean to be a church on the margin?

Ideas of church as overly rigid, static, Sunday-bound and inflexible need challenging. There is a need to shift perceptions from identifying places as 'on the margins' to places and neighbourhoods of hope. There is a need to privilege the voice(s) of those with lived experience, acknowledging and celebrating who they are and the gift they are to the church and the community. Resources are both needed and need to be released. People are the primary resource in a place, but are often not empowered, seen as equal participants or offered genuine leadership. Developing mutuality and solidarity are key – that affirmation of your story in the story of others. Difference is to be affirmed and stories told, perspectives shared in ways that resonate but do not conform to rigid structures.

There is a pressing need to celebrate contributions, disruptions and interruptions as gift, including affirming the dignity and agency of all people. This includes realizing that people have inherent dignity; it is not a gift given by outsiders, it exists already in people and places on the margins. So are denominations prepared to reverse their retreat from low-income areas? Are they willing to truly adhere to the gospel priority to stand with and alongside people and communities on the margins? This in turn raises questions about how Churches are structured and allocate resources. But do the Churches really believe that people on the margins are capable of exercising agency and sharing their own truths in the context of faith? Over 30 years ago Laurie Green issued a clarion call to reclaim theology from its entrapment in the hands of a priestly elite:

> [Theology] must never again be left in the hands of a scholarly or priestly elite but must be reclaimed as an essential component of every Christian's kitbag ... As Ian Fraser has it in his little book, we must set about 'Reinventing Theology as the People's Work'.[27]

The Churches are all too often accused of being White, middle-class spaces. In order to reach more people, Churches need to reflect the diversity of the UK, including working-class people, communities facing racial injustice, people with disabilities, LBGTQ+ and many more. Over ten years ago the Church of Scotland's model of 'Priority Areas' gave precedence to churches in communities where deprivation falls within the 5 per cent most deprived according to the Scottish Indices of Multiple Deprivation (SIMD).[28]

Congregations in these areas have access to a wide range of programmes run by the Church of Scotland Priority Areas team. Such programmes aim to identify the causes and tackle the effects of poverty; they are designed to support local people who are working to alleviate poverty, deprivation and isolation in the community. The aim is for churches in Priority Areas to be indivisible from their communities; to recognize local people as gifted, creative, resilient leaders; to reach out and stand with people in difficult situations; to live the gospel in all ways possible; to establish a family of church communities and embrace a wide range of theology. To be intolerant of, and prophetic about, injustice.

In a similar vein, in 2020 the Methodist Church launched its own 'Church at the Margins' programme, which is committing over £6 million over five years into missional activities led by people and churches on the margins.

A distinct, crucial and inextricably connected part of the Methodist Churches' vision for 'New Places For New People' is a commitment to be church at and from the economic margins. The potential for transformation, new life and new leaders exists in all marginalized communities. The Church must learn from and be led by our indigenous leaders, who already have deep knowledge and wisdom about their communities. From that leadership, people across socio-economic classes can imagine new ways of being church and community together.

The Church at the Margins strategic area of God For All is focused on equipping the Methodist Church to steward the majority of planting and pioneering resources with a faithful and preferential bias for people and communities experiencing marginalization. It aims to:

- Start a movement of new Christian communities led by those at the margins.
- Work alongside people experiencing poverty to deepen community engagement.
- Build on the biblical connection between evangelism and social justice.[29]

These are positive signs that elements of the Church are starting to wake up to the challenge, but there is still a long way to go before the margins are truly centred in the life of the Church.

The Good News of the gospel of Jesus of Nazareth is that God is – and always has been – a God of the margins. God is on the side of those whom society would count as worthless. As a Church, our mission is to recognize the value in every human being, the creativity in every human being, the love and the capacity to be loved in every human being. To recognize that God is already present and active in places that society considers to be marginal, economically useless, 'hard to reach' or hopeless is truly radical. Churches, at their best, are thriving hubs at the heart of their communities – open and inclusive to all believers and everyone else. Churches at their best connect with and support the local area through local collaborations, shared spaces and resources, and genuine community. By reinvesting in poorer areas instead of retreating, Churches can help whole communities to thrive and build better futures.

This demands that we engage in 'deep listening' to each person's story, build friendships and take action together. It demands that we ask difficult questions of people and institutions that are responsible for acting unjustly, and be bold in creating space for people to make change happen. To transform the unjust structures of society demands that we accept that the Church itself needs to be transformed in and through the process. But above all, it demands that we stand back from the urge to 'be the solution' in order to take seriously the fact that it is those who have personal experience of poverty and marginalization who have the deepest insights into what needs to change. As the saying goes, 'Nothing about us without us is for us.'

Notes

1 T. Walsh, 2022, 'Poverty Is many things', in N. Cooper, C. Howson and L. Purcell, *Dignity, Agency, Power*, Glasgow: Wild Goose Publications, pp. 67–8.

2 J. Atherton, 2000, *Public Theology for Changing Times*, London: SPCK, p. 44.

3 'All human beings are born free and equal in dignity and rights.' Article 1, *United Nations Declaration of Human Rights*, https://www.un.org/en/about-us/universal-declaration-of-human-rights, accessed 27.06.2023.

4 R. Lister, 2004, *Poverty*, Cambridge: Polity Press, pp. 100–3.

5 I. Duncan-Smith, 2007, *Breakthrough Britain: Ending the costs of social breakdown*, London: Centre for Social Justice, pp. 4–5.

6 N. Cooper, C. Howson and L. Purcell, 2022, *Dignity, Agency, Power*, Glasgow: Wild Goose Publications, p. 146.

7 Akala, 2019, *Natives: Race and Class in the Ruins of Empire*, London: John Murray Press, pp. 89–122.

8 D. Snoussi and L. Mompelat, 2019, *We Are Ghosts – Race, Class and Institutional Prejudice*, London: Runnymede Trust, pp. 12–14.

9 M. Charlesworth and N. Williams, 2017, *A Church for the Poor*, Eastbourne: David Cook, p. 69.

10 M. Hirst, 'Poverty, place and presence: positioning Methodism in England, 2001 to 2011', *Theology and Ministry* 4 (2016), pp. 1–25.

11 M. Davies, 2020, 'Huge cuts to church building stock "Missional priority" churches among those most likely to close', *Church Times*, 14 February.

12 D. Forrester, 2001, *On Human Worth*, London: SCM Press, p. 30.

13 Forrester, *On Human Worth*, pp. 83–4.

14 M. Power, 2020, '*Fratelli Tutti*: Pope Francis delivers new teaching aimed at healing divisions in the face of coronavirus', *The Conversation*, 5 October, https://theconversation.com/fratelli-tutti-pope-francis-delivers-new-teaching-aimed-at-healing-divisions-in-the-face-of-coronavirus-147487, accessed 29.06.2023.

15 P. Walters, 2022, 'I have a voice', in Cooper, Howson and Purcell, *Dignity, Agency, Power*, p. 137.

16 Forrester, *On Human Worth*, p. 18.

17 D. McGarvey, 2018, *Poverty Safari*, London: Picador, p. 76.

18 McGarvey, *Poverty Safari*, p. 111.

19 McGarvey, *Poverty Safari*, p. 139.

20 M. Luther King Jr, 1967, '*Where Do We Go From Here?*' *Annual Report Delivered at the 11th Convention of the Southern Christian Leadership Conference,*

16 August, Atlanta, GA, http://www-personal.umich.edu/~gmarkus/MLK_Where DoWeGo.pdf, accessed 29.06.2023.

21 R. Lithicum, 2003, *Transforming Power*, Downers Grove, IL: InterVarsity Press, p. 12.

22 Luther King, *'Where Do We Go From Here'*.

23 M. Williamson, 1992, *A Return to Love: Reflections on the principles of a course in miracles*, New York: Harper Collins, p. 165.

24 A. Donaldson, 2010, *Encountering God in the Margins*, Dublin: Veritas Publications, p. 109.

25 A. Roddick, 2020, 'A marginal God' in United Reformed Church, *In the Thick of It: Stories, experiences and reflections on God's kingdom in the margins*, London: United Reformed Church, p. 10.

26 D. Brower Latz, C. Murphy Elliott and S. Purcell, 2023, *Church on the Margins, What does it mean to be a church on the margins?* Manchester: Church Action on Poverty.

27 L. Green, 1987, *Power to the Powerless: Theology Brought to Life*, Basingstoke: Marshall Pickering, p. 10.

28 The Priority Areas committee use data on income, education, employment, health, crime, housing and access to services/amenities to identify the 5% of parishes with the highest levels of deprivation. See The Church of Scotland, 'Priority Areas', *Church of Scotland*, https://www.churchofscotland.org.uk/connect/priority-areas, accessed 30.06.2023.

29 Methodist Church, 2020, *God For All: The Connexional Strategy for Evangelism and Growth*, London: Methodist Church, p. 18.

15

Communities of Resistance, Migrant Rights and the Climate Crisis: Ambalavaner Sivanandan's Prophetic Challenge to 'Lived' Mission

ANUPAMA RANAWANA

Because it is only we, the heartbroken, who can truly battle and long for a world where no one ever feels like this again.[1]

There is a lived experience to any piece of written work. Two things have affected the shape and focus of this chapter. The first is that in the summer of 2023 the government of the United Kingdom passed an act of law called the Illegal Migration Bill. This bill removes protections for vulnerable people and disrupts existing case resolution principles. Legal opposition to this, as well as charities such as the Joint Council for the Welfare of Immigrants, have noted that the bill is an effective ban on asylum and completely undermines the principle of refugee protection. It strips survivors of trafficking, pregnant people and children of essential protections and support, vastly expands the detention estate and makes thousands more people undocumented and vulnerable to 'Compliant Environment' policies.[2] It also completely removes any access to justice routes for refugees and migrants who need it the most.[3] The bill in itself is alarming but holds further concern when we consider how the exacerbation of the climate crisis also increases the number of climate refugees. A UNHCR report estimates that this number has grown to 21.5 million since 2010.[4] With government and industrial actors in the Global North reluctant to commit to reparations and loss and damage financing, individuals facing significant climate events will seek to build lives elsewhere. At COP 27, a historic 'loss and damage' deal was finally agreed upon to create a mechanism whereby economically disenfranchised countries, those often facing the most significant impact of climate change, could receive monetary assistance to cope with the impacts of extreme weather events. In particular, this underlines the fact that countries with higher concentrations of poverty are further destabilized because of the impacts of extreme climate events. This deal was significant in several ways. A culmination of decades of campaigning by various activists and organizations of and from the Global South, the loss and damage deal represented a kind of justice that formalized in policy a recognition that certain countries were more vulnerable to the effects of extreme weather events than others. It was also significant, however, in what it omitted.

Loss and damage compensation does not include liability or compensation for the over-exploitation of natural resources during and after colonization, which in turn caused adverse climate impacts. It only includes provision for unavoidable climate impacts in the present such as crop failure, rising sea levels and desertification. This strikes a jarring note when we consider that, in 2022, the Intergovernmental Panel on Climate Change (IPCC) finally recognized the link between climate change and colonialism. In section B.2, the report notes that colonialism exacerbated the effects of climate change. In particular, historic and ongoing forms of colonialism have helped to increase the vulnerability of specific people and places to the effects of climate change. An excerpt from the section runs thus:

> Vulnerability of ecosystems and people to climate change differs substantially among and within regions (very high confidence), driven by patterns of intersecting socioeconomic development, unsustainable ocean and land use, inequity, marginalization, historical and ongoing patterns of inequity such as colonialism, and governance.

We can, and must, argue that in passing the Illegal Migration Bill, the government of the United Kingdom effectively 'doubles down' on the colonial logics that created the climate crisis by forcing a racialized border system on the black and brown bodies that seek asylum.[5] As Lopes Heimer and Rosa Dos Ventos have discussed in their study of Latin American female migrants in England, there is an explicit nature to how the logics of colonialism, as embedded in border legislation, reproduce hierarchies of who is seen as human, and in doing so further entrenches the necropolitics of border violence.[6] This is especially revealed in the way that climate migrants, and indeed migrants of any kind, are classed as threats to security and social cohesion because they do not typify those who are thought of as 'ideal' migrants. Climate refugees are seen as threats to the geopolitical order.[7] Harsha Walia, for example, argues that even the classifications of 'migrant' and 'refugee' are not in themselves unified social groups; instead they symbolize state-regulation of the relation between the 'local' populations and those seeking sanctuary.[8]

'One refugee may summon pity, but large groups are painted as a threat.'[9]

Both the reluctance to carry out commitments to loss and damage and the motivations for the United Kingdom's hostile environment are part of the same racialized, colonial logic. Historically, mission and missionary work itself was also connected to this self-same logic, which in our understanding categorized black and brown bodies as in need of civilizing mission.[10]

The second factor is that in the few weeks in which I wrote this chapter, I was also preparing to speak at a public forum on hope, and the ways in which faith-filled living offers hope. I found myself deeply uncomfortable with the idea of having to formulate a response on what hope was, is and could be. This was not because of some kind of sunken hopelessness, but because it felt impossible to think of hope without troubling the category itself. This is because hope is not only some kind of eschatological, theological promise; it is also a political category. In many communities and global situations, such as that of refugees and asylum seekers, hope is something that is only meant for a select group. Hope motivates an asylum seeker to take on a dangerous journey on a boat, but at the end of their journey is either a watery demise, or detention and deportation.

Hope is often taken away through deliberate silencing, and hope is also a myth sold to us in the global economic system. The hope of Christ is a central part of missional dialogue that can often feel dissonant in lived experience, where hope as something concretely liberative or redemptive is only meant for a select few. There is a coloniality to the logic of hope. Much of this dissonance and discomfiture is connected to the particular cultural hegemony in which we, as persons of faith, are attempting to engage in mission. How can we speak of mission and a missionary understanding when hope is often deliberately taken away or weaponized? A revolution, arguably, is necessary.

It is argued that to revolutionize a culture, the first step we must take is to carry out a radical assessment of it.[11] The particular task assigned to those of us writing contributions to this edited collection is to think in terms of epistemic disobedience, in order to approach the 'lived' aspect of mission and how mission and missiology can be reframed or, perhaps, unlearned.[12] In essence, then, the task is one of revolutionizing the culture and practice of mission and, in doing so, taking on a radical assessment of it. We can therefore say that the task is not only to challenge the violence of the present, but also to try to understand it.[13] This, too, is like thinking about hope. It is a complicated task when the reality of the present, as well as of the past, is that of multiple forms of violence that intersect and manifest in power relations. Critical inquiry and praxis in our lived experience suggest that intersecting power relations equate to a present violence that is a saturated site of such relations.[14]

Let us consider as an example the climate crisis, which cannot be analysed through any single lens. Understanding the *why* and the *how* of how we got to *here* requires an engagement with racial capitalism, imperialism, white cultural and economic superiority, gender injustice, the intensification of militarization, and the funding structures of the global financial systems, to name only a few. There is a need to understand the entire ecosystem of meanings, values, ideas and institutions that maintain these intersecting violences. What I would like to propose in this chapter, as others also have, is that the task of a lived mission for persons of faith is to take up the call to do this radical assessment and thus revolutionize culture.[15] How can we think less in terms of mission but more in terms of mobilizing communities in order to radically transform hegemonic culture?

When I consider the social movements I have been a part of, as well as much of the ongoing mobilizations that bring together anti-racism, pro-refugee and environmental justice work, I can see a clear framework for doing so in the cultural theorist Ambavalaner Sivanandan's understanding of 'communities of resistance'. Importantly, in Sivanandan's thinking this resistance, this 'coalitional solidarity', to use Jonathan Tran's phrase, comes from a holistic struggle that breaks down island and ethnic affiliation.[16] Sivanandan's analysis very specifically does not dwell on black and brown bodies as victims or subjects of oppression. Rather, he details the history and present of opposition and resistance that occurred at very local levels. It is framed and created with the agency of the communities affected. So to be epistemologically disobedient we have to organize, but we cannot organize as we *presently* are. To illustrate why such a framing is important, I draw from the empirical case of refugees and migrants in the United Kingdom, and how this links to the larger and interconnected struggle for environmental justice. I write this chapter holding together two positions, that of a theologian and also that of a migrant in the United Kingdom.

Communities of resistance: a framework for lived mission

Ambavalaner Sivanandan worked to understand the sociopolitical culture in which he, an immigrant to the United Kingdom, lived. His analysis concerned power, racism and how communities that were denied agency were finding ways to organize. Importantly, he documented the self-activity and mobilizing of immigrants for dignity and against injustice. He noted, in particular, the political economy of racism, which kills and excludes and which informed a generation of social workers, schoolteachers, university workers and so on. In doing this as far back as the early 1980s, Sivanandan was making the link between refugees and migrants as the new scapegoats of the state; he saw the racism of Fortress Europe as playing out against refugees, working-class Eastern Europeans and Muslims as it had done to their ancestors in the colonial matrix.[17] In the 1981 Scarman Report, Sivanandan outlines an analysis of the state that defines institutional racism as something which 'covertly or overtly, resides in the policies, procedures, operations and culture of public or private institutions – reinforcing individual prejudices and being reinforced by them in turn'.[18]

With such a focus in mind, Sivanandan had also begun to chart what he could do through his intellectual life by making the links between race and class. In particular he saw the ways in which the consciousness of racism and colonialism had bound immigrants from across the British empire and forged them into a new working class in a declining imperialism.[19] Thus, Sivanandan's vision of the working class is thus a multiracial one.

'Your problem, you see, is mine – in more ways than one.'[20]

It is in thinking along these lines that Sivanandan focuses his mobilizations on the idea of political blackness. Political blackness is essentially a radical consciousness that emerged in the 1960s in the UK as a reaction to the racism being experienced by Commonwealth communities.[21] When Sivanandan seeks to understand and define this, he discusses 'Black Power' which is envisioned as a political metaphor focused on transforming the condition of powerlessness, and which must be understood as a call to arms. He links the Black Power movements of the United Kingdom and the United States to the various movements in the Third World that sought to end white hegemony.[22] In short, we can define this as a political identity appropriated by Black and Asian activists, thus transforming and reclaiming what was once a pejorative and disparaging term used to denigrate people of African descent, 'with a new ideological meaning out of which were fashioned "communities of resistance"'.[23] In recent years, this understanding of political blackness has fallen away in anti-racist organizing, partly because it has become somewhat divisive and also because of increasing cleavages caused by trust issues that have appeared in cross-racial organizing. As Tariq Modood argues, in terms of reclaiming a pluralistic vision of anti-racist organizing, a 'solidaristic monism' can be somewhat corrupting. It can also deny the specific issues faced in different communities, as well as denying inter-community prejudices such as, for example, the distinct levels of anti-blackness in the Asian diaspora.[24] However, while acknowledging this, I agree with John Narayan that, in thinking how to move forward in terms of mobilization, we must not lose the distinct anti-imperialism and anti-racist solidarity that drives political blackness.[25] This is especially required in terms of thinking of the racialized borders that meet climate refugees, and in the face of a growing and well-organized far right movement that exists not only in the popular sphere but also within state regulations. For this reason, I prefer to work with the idea of 'communities of resistance', seeing this as a more coalitional way in which to think of multilayered mobilization. This phrasing retains the essence of political blackness but acknowledges pluriversality.[26]

In examining the lived experience of communities of colour in the Britain of the 60s and 70s, Sivanandan notes how important it was for Asian, Caribbean and African communities, who all lived on the periphery of British society, to organize together. In fact, he notes that they were compelled to organize together through platforms of community and culture and, importantly, the development of a radical political consciousness.[27]

Such organizing could also provide a robust way forward for the practical forms that a missiology that is disobedient and committed to anti-racism and anti-imperialism might take, especially if it considers practically emulating these forms of grassroots organizing. In fact, what Sivanandan found was that mobilization occurred through cultural platforms such as turning social centres, dance halls, youth centres and bookshops into key nodal points of a political network and working to organize localities into communities of resistance against institutional and popular racism. For example, as Sivanandan documents, it was not only the use of social centres to teach skills to young persons, but also the setting up of Sawh's Free University for Black Studies and producing weekly and monthly newspapers housed at bookshops.[28] Excitingly, some of these forms of organizing continue in the present day. For example, in 2020 the scholar Melz Owusu raised £60,000 in order to set up, again, a Free Black University, with the key goal of the redistribution of knowledge, and to teach historical and philosophical approaches to black liberation.[29] Owusu also saw this as a form of reparative justice, asking well-known universities to redistribute funds to the Free Black University as part of their recognition of how many universities in the United Kingdom have benefited from colonialism and the Atlantic Slave Trade.[30] Another visible example of this in action is the Racial Justice Network (RJN) in Leeds, which is a network of individuals and communities working across broad platforms in education and the arts in order to address the legacies of colonialism, particularly in terms of racialized borders. A key movement of the

RJN has been how communities can build resilience through storytelling, which in itself fosters collectivism.[31]

Sophia Siddiqui notes that part of the development of this concept in Sivandan's analysis was the fact that these mobilizations were not necessarily happening through the Labour party or through trade union mechanisms.[32] This, for Sivanandan, was what made such community resistance powerful: the combination of the breaking down of ethnic silos and the very local and community-level mobilization.[33] It is this that motivated him to argue for the need to organize to centre on the common denominators of oppressive exploitation and through this to suggest how we can move forward in terms of a common struggle.[34]

This is of immense importance, because for Sivanandan the concept of a common struggle – that is, communities being in resistance together – also rejects the disconnection between race politics and anticapitalism and the increasing racialization of class politics. As Arun Kundnani notes, for Sivanandan racism was not only a historical legacy of slavery and colonialism but had been regenerated by contemporary capitalism and imperialism in new forms. The analysis of racism, for Sivanandan, must therefore begin with the nature of capitalism in the present era, its international division of labour and the associated forms of global domination.[35] Sivanandan's thinking has been important for my own work, where I stress the importance of understanding how these forms of global domination and division are intimately linked to the climate crisis and the work to seek environmental justice.[36] As briefly alluded to above, Sivanandan's understanding of such communities of resistance comes from his careful documentation of how communities organized and resisted, rather than staying in their 'victimhood'. It is a recognition of themselves as equal participants.

Meaning and mission for climate refugees

What does the work of mission and the idea of missiology look like if considered through the concept of 'communities of resistance'? In the first instance, as I have already mentioned, this requires not just transform-ing the idea of mission but refusing it entirely. In the political and social context in which we find ourselves, the public work of radical Christians must be completely focused on the transformation and revolutionizing of society. We can look back to the liberation theologies of the 60s and the 70s, as well as to cultural theorists like Sivanandan who argued for work that was constantly antagonistic to the status quo.[37] In this sense, refusing mission is to reclaim the anti-imperialism and anticolonialism of such thinking, which was always both thinking and mobilization. Such mobilization, in particular, seeks to memorialize and analyse the subjective experiences of those who have suffered from colonial and imperial domination, whether it be economic, social, political, cultural or institutional. Anticolonialism is at once a set of events, a historical process and several social movements and, especially in terms of how Sivanandan sees communities resisting, it employed diverse methods.[38] This is a focus on bringing together subjective experience and the ideas that come from such experience in order to analyse the nature of domination and then use this to outline the political strategies necessary for confronting domination and moving towards liberation.[39]

What does this look like in practice? In the first instance, it will require advocating for the greater inclusion in everyday church practices such as prayer and liturgy of moves to develop and maintain a radical political consciousness. This requires in the main rethinking the role and idea of the parish or church community. Churches, as social centres, are already excellent spaces from which to engage in public pedagogy and can also be community spaces in which we may begin to radically organize. In the same way as training skills and classes on liberation were operated out of bookstores and youth hostels, why cannot the same occur in local parishes? Church communities may also consider allying themelves with such efforts as the Racial Justice Network mentioned above, or seeking out such networks and collaborating with them on anti-racist efforts. Special liturgies can also be written that are not only focused on, for example, 'prayers for the climate', or 'laments for climate refugees', but written specifically to teach and mobilize congregations towards becoming active communities of resistance. Perhaps a challenge I may propose to the reader, if you are still with me at this stage, is to consider a liturgy written for the Lenten season which focuses in particular on repentance. How might such a liturgy be rewritten if its focus was not repentance but a recognition of the situation of climate refugees and a commitment to the work that must be done to transform this status quo? There are already efforts to write special liturgies for creation and creation care, but these could also have the intersection of racial justice within them. There could also be efforts to use specific calendar events such as Easter and Christmas and to refocus the biblical readings for these events towards building a radical consciousness. For example, Christian Aid, an organization for which I consult, has a Christmas Just Scripture session focused on reading the Nativity story not in terms of the miraculous event of the birth, but in terms of making the story of the Holy Family's political exile central.

It must be underlined here that the 'lead' on such efforts cannot primarily be taken by the church community but must be guided and framed by, in this instance, climate refugees who will be recognized and understood as full participants in these efforts. If we recall once more what

Sivanandan documented, it was the ways in which the communities that were experiencing racist oppression refused such victimhood and began to organize. Efforts at organizing are already evident in such communities, with many taking an active part in groups such as Migrants Organise. Church communities can seek out such networks and bring them in to lead and teach on the ways in which churches can shift towards forms of direct action. Many climate refugees are cared for by church communities in terms of charitable provision, but by thinking in terms of communities of resistance, I am advocating for care that is provided in terms of centring justice rather than charity. To echo Sivanandan, we must make a radical assessment of the cultures of our churches, and resituate them in order to be revolutionary.

Notes

1 G. Bhattacharyya, 2023, *We, the Heartbroken*, London: Hajar Press.

2 E. Fotheringham and Caitlin Boswell, '"Unequal impacts": how UK immigration law and policy affected migrants' experiences of the Covid-19 pandemic', *Joint Council for the Welfare of Immigrants*, May 2022.

3 S. York, 2022, 'The UK Immigration Control responses to asylum: exclusion, disbelief, stigma and neglect', in *The Impact of UK Immigration Law: Declining standards of public administration, legal probity and democratic accountability* Cham: Springer International Publishing, pp. 57–100.

4 M. Garlick and I. Michal, 2022, 'Human mobility, rights and international protection: responding to the climate crisis', *Forced Migration Review*, 69 (2022): 58–61; Guy J. Abel, Michael Brottrager, Jesus Crespo Cuaresma and Raya Muttarak, 'Climate, conflict and forced migration', *Global Environmental Change* 54 (2019): 239–49; A. Bilak and Walter Kälin, 'Climate crisis and displacement – from commitment to action', *Forced Migration Review* 69 (2022).

5 The glaring difference between the treatment of white Ukrainian migrants and black and brown migrants from various locations has been a clear and recent example. See Phillip Howard, Bryan Yan Chen Johnson and Kevin Ah-Sen, 2022, 'Ukraine refugee crisis exposes racism and contradictions in the definition of human', *The Conversation* (blog), 21 March, https://theconversation.com/ukraine-refugee-crisis-exposes-racism-and-contradictions-in-the-definition-of-human-179150, accessed 14.06.2024.

6 Lopes Heimer, Rosa dos Ventos, 'Bodies as territories of exception: the coloniality and gendered necropolitics of state and intimate border violence against migrant women in England', *Ethnic and Racial Studies* 46 (7) (2023): 1378–406. All the articles cited in these notes were accessed on 14.06.2024 via doi.org.

7 Maya Goodfellow, 2020, *Hostile environment: How immigrants became scapegoats*, London: Verso Books. It is also good to note that this attitude is not exclusive to the United Kingdom. As Keston Perry, in his study of climate refugees from the Caribbean has documented, in the United States, under the Obama administration, climate refugees were classed as a serious threat to national security. In 2016, after Hurricane Matthew, climate refugees from Haiti were repeatedly denied protection and legal recognition. Keston K. Perry, '(Un)just transitions and black

dispossession: the disposability of Caribbean "refugees" and the political economy of climate justice', *Politics* 43 (2) (2023): 169–85.

8 Harsha Walia, 2021, *Border and Rule: Global migration, capitalism, and the rise of racist nationalism*, Chicago, IL: Haymarket Books.

9 Walia, *Border and Rule*, p. 14.

10 Alice L. Conklin, 2000, *A Mission to Civilize: The Republican idea of empire in France and West Africa, 1895–1930*, Stanford, CA: Stanford University Press; Firoze Manji and Carl O'Coill, 'The Missionary Position: NGOs and development in Africa', *International Affairs* 78 (3) (2002): 567–84; Priyamvada Gopal, 2019, *Insurgent Empire: Anticolonial resistance and British dissent*, London; New York: Verso Books; Peter Cruchley, 'Silent no longer: the roots of racism in mission', *The Ecumenical Review* 72 (1) (2020), pp. 98–107; Andrew Ratanya Mukaria, 2020, *A Synopsis of Racism in the African Christian Mission of 19th and 20th Centuries*: Hilary M. Carey, 2011, *God's Empire: religion and colonialism in the British world, c. 1801–1908*, Cambridge: Cambridge University Press; Patricia Grimshaw and Elizabeth Nelson, 'Empire, "The civilising mission" and indigenous Christian women in colonial Victoria', *Australian Feminist Studies* 16 (36) (2001): 295–309; Enrique Dussel, 1981, *A History of the Church in Latin America: Colonialism to liberation (1492–1979)*, New York: Eerdmans; Norman Etherington (ed.), 2005, *Missions and Empire*, Oxford: Oxford University Press.

11 A. Sivanandan, 2019, *Communities of Resistance: Writings on Black Struggles for Socialism*, London: Verso; A. Sivanandan, 'From resistance to rebellion: Asian and Afro-Caribbean struggles in Britain', *Race & Class* 23 (2–3) (1981): 111–52; Aijaz Ahmad, 2008, *In Theory: Nations, classes, literatures*, Radical Thinkers 25, London; New York: Verso.

12 Walter D. Mignolo, 'Epistemic disobedience, independent thought and de-colonial freedom', *Theory, Culture & Society* 26 (7–8) (2009): 159–81; Aimé Césaire, 2008, *Discours sur le colonialisme*, Nachdr. Paris: Présence Africaine; Walter D. Mignolo, 'I am where i think: epistemology and the colonial difference', *Journal of Latin American Cultural Studies* 8 (2) (1999): 235–45.

13 Rohit Dasgupta, 2018, 'Ambalavaner Sivanandan and Black Politics in Britain', *Theory, Culture and Society*, 24 January, https://www.theoryculturesociety.org/blog/rohit-dasgupta-ambalavaner-sivanandan-black-politics-britain, accessed 14.06.2024.

14 Patricia Hill Collins, 'On violence, intersectionality and transversal politics', *Ethnic and Racial Studies* 40 (9) (2017): 1460–73.

15 Anthony Reddie and Carol Troupe (eds), 2023, *Deconstructing Whiteness, Empire and Mission*, London: SCM Press.

16 Jonathan Tran, 2022, *Asian Americans and the Spirit of Racial Capitalism*, New York: Oxford University Press.

17 B. Shanthakumar, 2018, 'At the interstices of race, class and imperialism: A. Sivanandan (1923–2018)', *Socialist Project*, February, https://socialistproject.ca/2018/02/interstices-race-class-imperialism-sivanandan/, accessed 14.06.2024.

18 A. Sivanandan, 1981, 'What is institutional racism?', Institute of Race Relations.

19 Sivanandan, *Communities of Resistance*; A. Sivanandan, 1983, *A Different Hunger: Writings on Black Resistance*, London: Pluto Press.

20 A. Sivanandan, 'Black Power: the politics of existence', *Politics & Society* 1 (2) (1971): 225–33.

21 John Narayan, 2019, 'British Black Power: the anti-imperialism of political

blackness and the problem of nativist socialism', *The Sociological Review* 67 (5) (2019): 945–67.

22 Sivanandan, 'Black Power'.

23 Satnam Virdee, 2014, *Racism, Class and the Racialized Outsider*, Basingstoke: Palgrave Macmillan, p. 100; and also Kalbir Shukra, 1997, 'From Black Power to Black Perspectives: the reconstruction of a black political identity' in Ba-Nikongo Nikongo (ed.), *Leading Issues in African-American Studies*, Durham, NC: Carolina Academic, pp. 587–602.

24 Tariq Modood, 1999, 'The rise and fall of an anti-racism: from political blackness to ethnic pluralism' in Geoff Andrews, Richard Cockett, Alan Hooper and Michael Williams (eds), *New Left, New Right and Beyond: Taking the Sixties seriously*, London: Palgrave Macmillan UK, pp. 168–81; Reshmi Dutt-Ballerstadt, 'Colonized loyalty: Asian American anti-Blackness and complicity', (2020); Anjana Mudambi, 'South Asian Americans and anti-Black racism: critically reflexive racialization as an anti-racist vernacular discourse', *Communication, Culture & Critique* 16 (1) (2023): 1–8.

25 Narayan, 'British Black Power'.

26 Pluriversality is a concept emerging from decolonial theory that provides a counternarrative to contemporary Northern assumptions of the universal. Pluriversality is not cultural relativism (a world of independent units) but an encounter of 'different cosmologies'. See Mia Perry, 2021, 'Pluriversal literacies: affect and relationality in vulnerable times', *Reading Research Quarterly* 56 (2) (2021): 293–309; and Walter D. Mignolo, 'Delinking', *Cultural Studies* 21 (2) (2007): 449–514.

27 Sivanandan, 'From resistance to rebellion', p. 130.

28 Sivanandan, 'From resistance to rebellion', p. 136; see also Jenny Bourne, 2016, 'When Black was a political colour: a guide to the literature', *Race & Class* 58 (1) (2016): 122–30.

29 Harriet Swain, 2020, 'Payback time: academic's plan to launch Free Black University in UK', *The Guardian*, 27 June, https://www.theguardian.com/education/2020/jun/27/payback-time-academics-plan-to-launch-free-black-university-in-uk, accessed 14.06.2024.

30 Melz Owusu, 2020, 'Young Black students need a decolonised education, and Melz Owusu wants to make it happen', 10 July, https://nakedpolitics.co.uk/2020/07/10/young-black-students-need-a-decolonised-education-and-melz-owusu-wants-to-make-it-happen/.

31 Naava Busenze Balagadde, 2023, 'Resilience' ', 5 October, *The Racial Justice Network*, https://racialjusticenetwork.co.uk/the-bounce-back-storytelling-as-a-form-of-resilience/, accessed 14.06.2024.

32 Sophia Siddiqui, 'Anti-racist organising today: a roundtable discussion', *Race & Class* 65 (1) (2023): 119–33.

33 Sivanandan, 'From resistance to rebellion'.

34 Sivanandan, *Communities of Resistance*.

35 Arun Kundnani, 'Introduction', *Communities of Resistance*, pp. 14–20.

36 A. M. Ranawana, 2022, *A Liberation for the Earth: Climate, race and cross*, London: SCM Press.

37 Per Frostin, 'The hermeneutics of the poor – the epistemological "break" in Third World theologies', *Studia Theologica – Nordic Journal of Theology* 39 (1) (1985): 127–50; Priya Guns, 'From memory to a re-imagining; learning from Sivanandan', *Race & Class* 65 (1) (2023): 34–8.

38 Sivanandan, *Communities of Resistance*; Julian Go and Jake Watson, 'Anticolonial nationalism from imagined communities to colonial conflict', *European*

Journal of Sociology / Archives Européennes de Sociologie 60.1 (2019), 31–68; Julian Go, 2023, 'Thinking against empire: anticolonial thought as social theory', *The British Journal of Sociology* 2023, https://doi.org/10.1111/1468-4446.12993; Sujata Patel, 'Anti-colonial thought and global social theory', *Frontiers in Sociology* 8 (2023), https://doi.org/10.3389/fsoc.2023.1143776; Odd Arne Westad, (ed.), 2005, 'The revolutionaries: anticolonial politics and transformations', in *The Global Cold War: Third World interventions and the making of our times*, Cambridge: Cambridge University Press, pp. 73–109; Bonny Ibhawoh (ed.), 2018, 'Nationalists and anti-colonists' in *Human Rights in Africa*, New Approaches to African History, Cambridge: Cambridge University Press, pp. 130–72.

39 Samreen Mushtaq and Amin Mudasir, '"We will memorise our home": exploring settler colonialism as an interpretive framework for Kashmir', *Third World Quarterly* 42.12 (2021), 3012–29; Priyamvada Gopal, 2019, *Insurgent Empire: Anticolonial resistance and British dissent*, London and New York: Verso; Anila Zainub and George J. Sefa Dei (eds), 2019, *Decolonization and Anti-Colonial Praxis: Shared lineages*; Anti-Colonial Educational Perspectives for Transformative Change, vol. 8, Leidenand Boston, MA: Brill Sense.

Conclusion

16

Where Do We Go From Here?

HARVEY KWIYANI AND PENIEL RAJKUMAR
WITH BENJAMIN ALDOUS

Ben: Good afternoon. Thanks both of you for joining me. As we've been working on this book and the variety of chapters from across a range of traditions and confessions, can you share a few highlights or reflections on what has been brought together.

Peniel: I think the book does well to cover the ideas of decolonizing mission and reimagining mission from the perspective of marginality. I think since we have ecumenical as an integral part of the title this closing chapter might also consider some focus on aspects of 'lived' ecumenism in Britain in the twenty-first century. The book and the chapters do well in bringing together perspectives from various denominations. How can we in the light of grassroots experiences think of lived ecumenism in a new way through the lenses of mission – churches coming together to a form of 'lived' ecumenism in missional action and missional thinking? In paying attention to the grassroots we might find an ecumenical perspective that is decolonizing in nature, which can help transcend the Eurocentrism of our thinking of ecumenism and can help unthink the way ecumenism has been traditionally carried out.

Harvey: I find it refreshing that this book is focused on the British context, and for this reason, it is difficult to faithfully reflect on global ecumenism. Having said that, the truth is that because of migration and cultural diversity, global ecumenism is already present here in the UK. For me, I appreciate the mix of the voices and the themes. We have a very good mix of voices in the book. I am excited about the contribution that the book will make.

Ben: As you read through was there anything that stood out for you, Harvey, or voices you haven't heard before?

Harvey: I don't know many of the people who have contributed to this book. Thus, a lot of the voices were new to me, which made the book even more interesting. I appreciated Bisi Adenekan-Koevoets's essay on second-generation British Nigerians. While her focus is on British Nigerians, the theme of second-generation migrants (and their religious lives) speaks to the concerns of the rest of the migrant communities in the UK. If we're talking about 'lived' mission in the UK today, the faith of younger-generation migrants is one of the key themes. We all ought to be thinking and doing something about it. In addition, Lisa Adjei and Shermara Fletcher's chapter, which focuses on racial justice, offers us a very helpful perspective on an issue we cannot avoid. It reflects on some of the issues that we need to wrestle with. These issues need to be heard in ways that they haven't thus far.

Peniel: I was particularly struck with James Woodward's chapter because there's a certain counter-intuitiveness about what he says. Perhaps, I don't know, he was influenced by your book on Kosuke Koyama, *The God Who Walks Slowly*, Ben? I think there is something in it that goes against the current trend of thinking about mission. There is such a focus on younger people, fresh blood within churches, fast-paced explosive growth, and other things, whereas he says there is something in putting the brakes on, to pause to reflect about the elderly people in our midst. To consider the people who have been steadfastly faithful and that is something we could reflect on more. When we think of mission in twenty-first-century Britain there are lots of anxieties around mission. One is about the numbers and when it is tied to the recent census reports there is almost panic with people saying that Christians now make up less than 50 per cent of the population. But in all honesty, we know that has been the case for many years in terms of faithful practice of Christianity – which is foundational for mission. But there are faithful small congregations which are resilient. Therefore, what do we learn from the small, the slow and the steadfast? How do we look at these categories of mission which can free us into other ways of thinking of mission. I particularly found James's to be an interesting piece.

Harvey: The chapter from Anupama that delves into environment justice in ways that I found really helpful. My response as a reader was, 'How do we translate this into practical lived experiences in our congregations?' Again, I think climate change is a big issue; it will become even more important in the next few decades. Generally speaking, migrant communities will be more aware of climate change because here, in the UK today, we don't feel a lot of pressure about it. Many people who have come from other parts of the world will be more aware of the effects of changing weather patterns. So, for us here, how do we translate this into a conversation that our British brothers and sisters can listen to and engage in at congregational level on a week-to-week basis?

Peniel: How migrants experience church here and how migrants think of mission is also something that will probably (re)shape the landscape of mission. Migrant experiences are already shaping new understandings of mission in the UK. It's not like it's out in the future. The colour of mission in the UK is definitely changing in the sense that there is a reliance from the historic churches on migrants. I'd even say the survival of mainstream churches is probably going to depend on migrants, and this is something that people are in some quarters taking serious note of.

Is the church willing to receive the generous gift of migrants? That is something you touch on and mentioned in your own chapter, Harvey. How can the church be transformed by the gifts that come to the UK? The gifts that come from the outside? So there are aspects of mission to the UK from within the UK from people in the UK. If we can think of them as being in some sort of a partnership working hand in hand as Christians, as global Christians here in the local context, this could shape a new form of thinking locally about mission. Working hand in hand as Christians, holding together different cultures in creative tension and embracing new ways of living with difference is key. Very often the implicit message that someone like me hears is something like, 'You are an Indian, you have now come to the Church of England so you need to become one of us.' Our ideas of hospitality need to change. The concept of hospitality at the heart of mission needs to be rethought both in terms of its theology and practice. The tables have to be turned upside down so that everybody has an equal space around the table. There's this hymn by Fred Kaan, 'The Church is like a table, a table that is round' and that is a good metaphor for 'lived' mission in twenty-first-century Britain in the light of what is happening with migration.

Ben: What do you think is stopping that kind of move into true hospitality towards migrants, because that's not the reality for many. What are the things that we need to overcome both in the local but also in the national? What blinkers need to be removed or postures do we need to inhabit?

Peniel: I think learning to hold tradition hand in hand with change may be important. Overcoming fear and openness to difference is key. I once met an Indian family in a local church who said that they have been attending the church for several years but not many people actually talk to them except the priest. I think there is a problem in the culture of welcome. As a church many haven't acquired the skills of engaging with the other. Many probably think it's offensive to just accost somebody after church and speak to them. They probably think that people are best left alone to themselves.

How do we do cross-cultural growing together so that church becomes a place where the so called 'other' is received rather than rejected. When we look at Christianity it's a religion that has been shaped around the ultimate 'other' – revealed to us as 'Jesus Christ' who came to his own but his own received him not (John 1.11). How do we form a missiology which recognizes divine 'otherness' and then translates it into some form of 'lived' hospitality in the context of the church? There is a mission within the church itself also in terms of receptivity, in terms of openness, in terms of welcome.

Harvey: There's a wider conversation than what's taking place here. It is the fact that we all tend to do faith in ways that reflect our cultures. There is no church without culture, just as much as there is no culture-free theology. The challenge comes in when the cultural expressions of our church – our culturally shaped ecclesiologies – work like ours is the only way things need to be done. So, when someone does something different that may make sense to them but seem weird to us, it becomes difficult to engage with it. This cross-cultural thing only works if we are actually crossing cultures both ways. As we cross cultures, we get to see expressions of what God is doing among all humanity. In places like the UK today our diversity itself is a gift that allows us to experience others. These encounters allow us to see things from different perspectives and hear things through different voices. That's the gift we can enjoy together. But it's a shift from believing that one cultural expression of Christianity is the only way and that everybody else doing it differently must learn 'our' way before we can have relationship.

Ben: Do you think one of the problems in this whole discussion is that what often happens is migrants who come to the UK are the ones crossing cultural barriers but indigenous British people very often do not? There is not an onus on British people stepping across the threshold culturally.

Harvey: When I lived in Minnesota, I had a Kenyan friend who went to a church for three years and, for the entire three years, she was always welcomed as a visitor or a stranger. One day, she got tired and picked up the microphone to ask the congregation, 'For how long should I be a stranger among you?' What really hurt her was that when she brought a Kenyan dish to church potluck, nobody would touch it – foreign exotic food can be suspicious sometimes. In Britain, we are used to others crossing cultures to engage British culture. As such, many British people do not feel the need to engage other cultures. Of course, other cultures from around the world are already here. It's just a matter of engaging your neighbours. Unfortunately, the legacy of the British empire often makes it difficult to engage the world at our doorsteps.

Peniel: I think what you said is really fascinating, Harvey. We also need to be mindful of the question of power when we think of crossing cultures. Sometimes people cross cultures but with their power intact. For example, missionaries crossed borders but had their political and economic and cultural power that they exercised in pejorative ways. What is demanded in cross-cultural border crossings is *kenosis* – self-emptying. It's giving your power away so that you can grow through the gift you receive from the 'other'.

You've probably both heard me say this on different occasions, that the original sin of triumphalist Christianity is what one of my Korean friends, Heup Young Kim, called hostility – HOST-ility – which is this perpetual need to play host. We sometimes speak so much about hospitality but then want to be the host always and never learn the humility of being the guest at other people's tables and receiving the gifts that others offer. This spirit of non-reciprocity keeps the power unequally in your favour – aiding the perpetuation of your culture, civilization, values, visions and agendas. Then you always have the power. It is similar to Koyama's idea of the contrast of the crusading mind with the crucified mind. He has another analogy: *No handle on the cross*. The metaphor of the cross without a handle is that of a mission without control or coercion. We cannot hold the cross in the same way that one holds a sword. In that sense we need to be thinking of this when it comes to hospitality. Are we cognisant of the unequal power dynamics that are present in every form of relating to others?

How do we actually take on that missiology of *kenosis*, where you give up a little bit of yourself to become a bit more of Christ through receiving the other? We probably also need to recognize that as people who are called to be part of the household of God, we are to become living stones only together, only through a connection with each other and with Christ, otherwise we are just random stones that can be used to be thrown at other people. It is only when we are built together that God breathes life into us and we become living stones that constitute the household of God.

Harvey: Trying to shift the conversation forward a little, I think one of the issues that we can wrestle with is exploring, in this context of 'lived' missiology, what the gifts of the world are to the British church.

What can this British context receive from other Christians in the UK or around the world? That's why I think climate change ought to be a big missiological issue today. Parts of the Body of Christ are wrestling with it out there while it is difficult to make that conversation connect with UK Christians at the moment. The Body of Christ is suffering in other parts of the world.

Ben: And as Paul says, 'If one part of the body suffers, we all suffer.'

Peniel: Carrying on with this idea of 'When one part of the body suffers, the other parts of the body suffer', I am reminded of how the Indian theologians Sathianathan Clarke and Arvind P. Nirmal bring the body metaphor into play while discussing Christian solidarity with suffering communities.

Nirmal identifies three different modes of knowing: pathetic, empathetic and the sympathetic knowing, all of which have a place in building solidarity and liberation in the face of human suffering. Pathetic knowledge is first-hand knowledge of the suffering ones, empathetic knowledge draws on one's own experiences of suffering to identify alongside the suffering ones, and sympathetic knowledge arises out of a commitment to identify with the suffering ones.

Expanding this idea further through the body metaphor, Sathianathan Clarke says if somebody punches you in the stomach the stomach receives the punch in a different way. This is *pathetic* knowing. But it is not only the stomach that receives the blow, it is also processed by the brain producing a different form of knowledge which is *empathetic* knowing. Theologians who reflect with people who have been directly affected by violence understand this form of knowing. Finally, there's also the mouth which cries out in pain and that is what he calls *sympathetic* knowing. The mouth may not have been the part which is hurt and bleeding but it has a role in processing suffering. This can be a good metaphor for the church. The church needs to become that body where if one part of the body receives a blow, all have a responsibility to articulate that pain and respond to that pain in different ways. How we do that is important for mission especially in the context of climate change. How we respond contributes to the pain or to the way in which we address the pain.

Ben: It feels like we are beginning to wrestle with these things now. How do we do that in more concrete ways missiologically? What areas do we need to press into for the future? This chapter is entitled 'Where do we go from here?' I think we've outlined a few; for example the idea about the gift of the other for the British churches and how the gift of migrants will profoundly shape missiological discourse for the future. You've mentioned the concepts around power and *kenosis*. You've mentioned British colonial history which continues as a residue of power that sits in many of our institutions. And you're now outlining the relationship between climate justice and mission. Are there other areas that we're going to need to pursue in the future that are going to be key missiological conundrums or areas that need our attention?

Harvey: I think the shift that's going on at the moment has to lead us to a new missiology that is not dependent on imperialism. The Apostle Paul shifts the story of Christianity and brings it to the West via Philippi in Acts 16. For him, it needs to be in cities – Antioch, Rome, Corinth, and many others. But what Jesus does in the Gospels is actually the opposite. His movement is centred in Nazareth and Capernaum in Galilee which is really the extreme opposite of Rome, at least in the context of that time. For me a good deal of our missiology is still very much dependent on Rome. If we pay attention to what world Christians bring to the table, we begin to realize that actually we need to go back to Nazareth or Capernaum or northern Galilee to keep mission away from the centres of power. It's actually the uneducated Galileans who can turn the world upside down, not the powerful Romans.

Ben: Can you expand on that a bit more? Can you give some concrete examples? Where is Nazareth, I guess?

Harvey: Nazareth symbolizes for us the vulnerable congregations in our cities with just a few people gathering together, with no power and no resources. Such congregations, powerless as they may be, find ways to embed themselves in their communities. While resource churches have their place, it is possible, or even likely, that a great deal of mission in the UK will be carried out by Christian communities at the margins of society, by vulnerable local communities that do not really seem very promising yet God is working and using those powerless people to change history.

Peniel: I'm speaking primarily from a Church of England perspective, but what does it mean to own up to the past? What does it mean, missiologically, to take responsibility for a sinful past but also to live God's just future now? The future of God's reign. What does it mean for the church to live that future now? There are different ways in which we can engage with this. One is the question of racial justice which is one that people are increasingly happy to pursue. How do we engage in meaningful conversation and dialogue with people from different contexts but also from different faiths? Because we can fall into political correctness sometimes, we want to be seen with the right religious leaders rather than working with religious actors today who are probably working on some of the marks of mission that Anglican Christians hold close. For example, the fourth mark of mission concerns the transformation of unjust structures. Who are going to be our mission partners in this? They may not be saying the name of Jesus but some of the work that they're doing means that we need to be shoulder to shoulder with people of other faiths. So what does it mean to understand mission as solidarity in the context of interreligious engagement? This is probably one perspective on 'lived' mission in twenty-first-century Britain that we need to carefully consider.

Racial justice is also something that can be pursued alongside those from other faiths. The big theological question when it comes to engaging with the 'othering' of people is not to make them objects that serve our own ends. What does it mean to live fully into the reality that 'The earth is the Lord's and its fullness thereof' (Psalm 24.1–2)?

How do we recognize that in the context of relationships with both our neighbours and with the earth there is something that we can learn from communities who have understood this challenge in a different way and seek to work hand in hand with them? Also, the question of dealing with contested historical legacies that we face are probably two things we can expand on.

Ben: Harvey, do you want to add anything to dealing with historic injustice and the legacy of the history of colonialism for future missiological engagement?

Harvey: The deconstruction that is going on in aspects of our lives will come to mission sooner rather than later. The challenge is that, on the one hand, once you begin to talk about the challenge of that deconstruction, especially in connection with the colonial legacy of mission, people feel like you are talking about their ancestors (and, to some extent, this is true). People's barriers go up and it becomes an impossible conversation. However, there is a history here that we need to wrestle with. Some claim that talking about colonialism and mission is guilt-tripping them, but this is not even a good way to defend themselves. That's not what we are trying to do. We need to have this conversation.

Ben: Are there other ways to navigate past this problem? We can't always deny each other these conversations if we're to move on and be united, to heal and to be the church that God has called us to be.

Peniel: From an Indian background, the idea of cultivating the importance of truth-telling is important. We have the missional mandate of telling the truth to our children, which will help us to move beyond fractured histories to shared futures. That is going to be crucial in terms of mission education. We think of theological colleges usually when we speak of missional education. But education for a just future is something that starts with our children and in our families. How do we do that as an investment in mission? How do we speak to our children about the past in a way that frees us to inhabit a just future is a question for us to consider, especially so if we are to be the change that we want to see in the future.

I think that despite the challenges we see missiologically there is a hopeful future, a future rooted in reciprocity, of deepening understanding across traditions and confessions. I think we all acknowledge that there are difficult conversations that need to be had but they are crucial to overcoming our past and moving into a shared future.

Thematic Bibliography

Decolonial theology and method

Ahmad, Aijaz, 2008, *In Theory: Nations, classes, literatures*, Radical Thinkers 25, London and New York: Verso.

Boesak, A. Allan, 1997, *Farewell to Innocence: A socio-ethical study on black theology and power*, Maryknoll, NY: Orbis Books.

Byung-Chul, Han, 2021, *The Palliative Society: Pain today*, trans. Daniel Steuer, Cambridge: Polity Press.

Clarke, Sathianathan, 2001, 'Viewing the Bible through the eyes and ears of subalterns in India', http://www.religion-online.org/article/viewing-the-bible-through-the-eyes-and-ears-of-subalterns-in-india/.

Davids, Nuraan, 'Love in the time of decoloniality', *Alternation* 24 (1) (2019): 102–21, https://doi.org/10.29086/2519-5476/2019/sp24.2a5, accessed 12/08/2024.

De Sousa Santos, Boaventura, 2016, *Epistemologies of the South: Justice against epistemicide*, Abingdon; Routledge.

Gee, Tim, 2012, *Open for Liberation*, Winchester: Christian Alternative Books.

Havea, Jione, 2020, 'Repatriation of native minds' in Jione Havea (ed.), *Mission and Context*, Maryland; Fortress Academic.

Hoppers, C.A.O. (ed.), 2002, *Indigenous Knowledge and the Integration of Knowledge Systems: Towards a philosophy of articulation*, Claremont: New Africa Books.

Keller, Catherine, 2002, 'Process and Chaosmos: the Whiteheadian fold in the discourse of difference' in Catherine Keller and Anne Daniell (eds), 2021, *Process and Difference: Between Cosmological and Poststructuralist Postmodernisms*, Albany: State University of New York.

Kohan, Walter Omar, 2021, *Paulo Freire: A philosophical biography*, London: Bloomsbury.

Koyama, Kosuke, 1975, *Theology in Contact*, Madras: The Christian Literature Society.

Mātenga, Jay, 'Editorial: The emancipation of indigenous theologies in light of the rise of World Christianity', *Anvil* 39 (1) (2023).

McKinless, Ashley. 'Cornel West and Robert P. George on Christian love in the public square', *America: The Jesuit Review* (2019).

Mignolo, Walter D., 1999, 'I am where i think: epistemology and the colonial difference', *Journal of Latin American Cultural Studies* 8 (2): 235–45, https://doi.org/10.1080/13569329909361962.

Mignolo, Walter D., 'Delinking', *Cultural Studies* 21 (2), (2007): 449–514.

Mignolo, Walter D., 'Epistemic disobedience, independent thought and decolonial freedom', *Culture & Society* 26 (7–8) (2009): 159–81, https://doi.org/10.1177/0263276409349275.

Mignolo, Walter D., Decolonizing western epistemologies/building decolonial epistemologies' in Ada María Isasi-Díaz and Eduardo Mendieta (eds), 2011, *Decolonizing Epistemologies: Latina/o theology and philosophy*, New York: Fordham Press.

Oliver, Gordon, 2006, *Holy Bible, Human Bible*, London: Darton, Longman and Todd.

Vellem, Vuyani, Patricia Sheerattan-Bisnauth and Philip Peacock (eds), 2019, *Bible and Theology from the Underside of Empire*, Johannesburg: SUN MeDIA MeTRO.

Vellem, Vuyani, 'Un-thinking the West: The spirit of doing Black Theology of Liberation in decolonial times', *HTS Teologiese Studies* 73 (3) (2017).

Vinayaraj, Y. T., 2015, *Intercessions: Theology, liturgy and politics*, New Delhi: ISPCK.

Wirzba, Norman, 2021, *This Sacred Life: Humanity's place in a wounded world*, Cambridge: Cambridge University Press.

Zainub, Anila, and Sefa Dei, George J. (eds), 2019, *Decolonization and Anti-Colonial Praxis: Shared lineages*, Leiden and Boston: Brill Sense.

World Christianity and missions

Adebayo, Racheal, 2018, 'The religion and spirituality of black churchgoing teenagers'. PhD dissertation, University of Warwick.

Adedibu, Babatunde Aderemi, 'Reverse mission or migrant sanctuaries? Migration, symbolic mapping, and missionary challenges of Britain's Black Majority Churches', *Pneuma* 35 (3) (2013): 405–23.

Adedibu, Babatunde Aderemi, 'Origin, migration, globalisation and the missionary encounter of Britain's Black Majority Churches', *Studies in World Christianity* 19 (1) (2013): 93–113, https://doi.org/10.3366/swc.2013.0040.

Adenekan-Koevoets, Adebisi A., 2022, 'Nigerian Pentecostals and "reverse mission" in London and Amsterdam', PhD dissertation, University of Roehampton.

Adenekan-Koevoets, Bisi, 'Nigerian Pentecostal diasporic missions and intergenerational conflicts: case studies from Amsterdam and London', *Mission Studies* 38 (3) (2021): 424–47.

Adogame, Afe, 'African Christians in a secularizing Europe', *Religion compass* 3 (4) (2009): 488–501.

Adogame, Afe, 2013, *The African Christian Diaspora: New currents and emerging trends in world Christianity*, London: Bloomsbury.

Ajayi, Jacob F. Ade, 1965, *Christian Missions in Nigeria 1841–1891: The making of a new elite*, Evanston: Northwestern University Press.

Aldous, Ben, 2022, *The God Who Walks Slowly: Reflections on mission with Kosuke Koyama*, London: SCM Press.

Ayegboyin, Deji and S. Ademola Ishola, 1997, *African Indigenous Churches: An historical perspective*, Greater Heights Publications.

Barrett, Al and Ruth Harley, 2020, *Being Interrupted: Reimagining the Church's mission from the outside, in*, London: SCM Press.

Boahen, A. Adu (ed.), 1985, *Africa Under Colonial Domination 1880–1935*, Vol. 7, London: Heinemann; Berkeley: University of California Press.

Bosch, David, 1991, *Transforming Mission: Paradigm shifts in theology of mission*, Maryknoll: Orbis Books.

Burgess, Richard, 'Bringing back the gospel: reverse mission among Nigerian Pentecostals in Britain', *Journal of Religion in Europe* 4 (3) (2011): 429–49.

Carey, William, 1961, *An Enquiry into the Obligations of Christians to Use Means for the Conversion of the Heathens*, London: Carey Kingsgate.

Cartledge, Mark J., Sarah Dunlop, Heather Buckingham and Sophie Bremner, 2019, *Megachurches and Social Engagement: Public theology in practice*, Vol. 33, Leiden: Brill.

Catto, Rebecca Alice, 2008, 'From the rest to the West: exploring reversal in Christian mission in twenty-first century Britain', PhD dissertation, University of Exeter.

Chakwera, Lazarus McCarthy, 2000, 'The development of the eleventh hour institute to be utilized as a means of mobilizing, training, and sending missions workers from malawi and nearby countries to unreached peoples', Doctor of Ministry, Trinity International University.

Conklin, Alice L., 2000, *A Mission to Civilize: The Republican idea of empire in France and West Africa, 1895–1930*, California: Stanford University Press.

Corrie, John, 'The promise of intercultural mission', *Transformation* 31 (4) (2014): 291–302.

Droogers, André, 'The power dimensions of the Christian community: an anthropological model', *Religion* 33 (3) (2003): 263–80.

Etherington, Norman (ed.), 2005, *Missions and Empire*, Oxford: Oxford University Press.

Fraser, Liam Jerrold, 2021, *Mission in Contemporary Scotland*, Edinburgh: Saint Andrew Press.

Fyfe, Christopher, and Andrew F. Walls, 1996, *Christianity in Africa in the 1990s*, Edinburgh: Centre of African Studies, University of Edinburgh.

Gerbner, Katharine, 2018, *Christian Slavery: Conversion and race in the Protestant Atlantic world*, Philadelphia: University of Pennsylvania Press.

Goodall, Norman, 1954, *Gathered for What? An Address from the Chair of the Congregational Union of England and Wales delivered in Westminster Chapel, London on 10th May 1954*, Independent Press.

Goodall, Norman, 1964, *Christian Missions and Social Ferment*, London: The Epworth Press.

Green, Laurie, 2009, *Let's Do Theology: Resources for contextual theology*, London: Mowbray.

Haar, G. T., 1998, *Halfway to Paradise: African Christians in Europe*, Cardiff Academic Press.

Hanciles, Jehu, 2008, *Beyond Christendom: Globalization, African migration, and the transformation of the West*, Maryknoll, NY: Orbis Books.

Hanciles, Jehu J., 2021, *Migration and the Making of Global Christianity*, Grand Rapids, MI: Eerdmans.

Haymes, Brian, 1985, 'Covenant and the Church's mission' in Paul Fiddes, Roger Hayden, Richard Kidd and Keith Clements (eds), *Bound to Love: The covenant basis of Baptist life and mission*, London: The Baptist Union, 63–75.

Irudaya, Raj, 2007, *Mission to the Marginalised*, Chennai: Sri Venkatesa Printing House.

Isichei, Elizabeth, 1995, *A history of Christianity in Africa: From antiquity to the present*, Grand Rapids, MI: Eerdmans.

Kalu, O. U., 'African Christianity: Its public role', Book review, *International Bulletin of Missionary Research* 24 (1) (2000): 36.

Kalu, O., and O. Nnaemeka, 2005, *Religion, History, and Politics in Nigeria: Essays in honour of Ogbu U. Kalu*, University Press of America.

Koyama, Kosuke, 2009, 'Commission one after a century of violence: the search for a larger Christ' in David Kerr and Cathy Ross (eds), *Edinburgh 2010: Mission now and then*, Oxford: Regnum.

Kwiyani, Harvey, 2022, *Multicultural Kingdom: Ethnic diversity, mission and the Church*, London: SCM Press.

Manji, Firoze, and Carl O'Coill, 'The missionary position: NGOs and development in Africa', *International Affairs* 78 (3) (2002): 567–84, https://doi.org/10.1111/1468-2346.00267.

Morier-Genoud, Eric, 2018, 'Reverse mission: a critical approach for a problematic subject' in Veronique Altglas and Matthew Wood (eds), *Bringing Back the Social into the Sociology of Religion*, Leiden: Brill, 169–88.

Newbigin, Lesslie, 1983, *The Other Side of 1984: Questions for the Churches*, Geneva: World Council of Churches.

Newbigin, Lesslie, 1985, *Unfinished Agenda: An autobiography*, Geneva: WCC Publications.

Newbigin, Lesslie, 1986, *Foolishness to the Greeks: The Gospel and Western culture*, Grand Rapids, MI: Eerdmans.

Newbigin, Lesslie, 1989, *The Gospel in a Pluralist Society*, Grand Rapids, MI: Eerdmans.

Niles, D. Preman, 1999, *Council for World Mission: World mission today*, Council for World Mission.

Olofinjana, Israel, 2015, *Partnership in Mission: A Black Majority Church perspective on mission and church unity*, Watford: Instant Apostle.

Olofinjana, Israel, 'Reverse mission: towards an African British theology', *Transformation: An International Journal of Holistic Mission Studies* 37 (1) (2019): 52–65, https://doi.org/10.1177/0265378819877902.

Pope Francis, 2013, *Evangelii Gaudium, The Joy of the Gospel*, London: Catholic Truth Society.

Ross, Cathy, and Andrew Walls, 2008, *Mission in the 21st Century: Exploring the Five Marks of Global Mission*, London: Darton, Longman and Todd.

Ryrie, A., 2021, 'The failure of the first Protestant missionaries', available at https://www.gresham.ac.uk/watch-now/protestant-failure, accessed 28.03.2023.

Ryrie, A., 2022, 'How Protestant missionaries encountered slavery', available at https://www.gresham.ac.uk/watch-now/protestant-slavery, accessed 28.03.2023.

Sanneh, Lamin, 'The horizontal and the vertical in mission: an African perspective', *International Bulletin of Missionary Research* 7 (4) (1983): 165–71.

Sanneh, Lamin O, 2008, *Disciples of All Nations: Pillars of world Christianity*, Oxford: Oxford University Press.

SARC and CWM, 2009, *Combating Human Trafficking*, Delhi, India.

Song, C. S., 1988, *Theology from the Womb of Asia*, London: SCM Press.

Stanley, Brian, 'The World Missionary Conference, Edinburgh 1910: sifting history from myth', *The Expository Times* 121 (7) (2010): 325–31.

Stults, Donald Leroy, 2009, *Grasping Truth and Reality: Lesslie Newbigin's theology of mission to the western world*, Cambridge, UK: James Clarke.

Turner, Victoria, 2023, 'A happy ecumenical legacy for the London Missionary Society? Exposing the coloniality between Churches engaged in mission' in Anthony Reddie and Carol Troupe (eds), *Deconstructing Whiteness, Empire and Mission*, London: SCM Press, 120–36.

Ukah, Asonzeh Franklin-Kennedy, 2009, 'Reverse mission or asylum Christianity? A Nigerian church in Europe' in Toyin Falola and Augustine Agwuel (eds), *Africans and the Politics of Popular Culture*, University of Rochester Press, 104–32.

WCC, 'Together towards life: mission and evangelism in changing landscapes', *International Bulletin of Missionary Research* 2 (38) (April 2014).

Empire, colonialism and racism

'History, Heritage and Identity Online Symposium, November 12, 2020: Caribbean Institute for Health Research', https://uwi.edu/caihr/engagement/pg-history heritage.php, accessed 06.09.2023.

'Quakers to make reparation for slave trade and colonialism', *Quaker*, 31 May 2022, https://www.quaker.org.uk/news-and-events/news/quakers-to-make-reparation-for-slave-trade-and-colonialism.

Adams, Graham, 2016, 'Doubting Empire: growing as faithful children', in Vuyani Vellem, Patricia Sheerattan-Bisnauth and Philip Peacock (eds), *Bible and Theology from the Underside of Empire*, Johannesburg: SUN MeDIA MeTRO.

Akala, 2019, *Natives: Race and class in the ruins of empire*, Two Roads.

Archbishops' Anti-Racism Taskforce, 22 April 2021, *From Lament to Action: Key recommendations*, https://www.churchofengland.org/sites/default/files/2021-04/FromLamentToAction-report.pdf.

Bourne, Jenny, 2016, 'When Black was a political colour: a guide to the literature', *Race & Class* 58 (1) (2016): 122–30, https://doi.org/10.1177/0306396816643229.

Busenze Balagadde, Naava, 2023, 'Until the lion tells the story, the hunter will always be the hero', 10, https://racialjusticenetwork.co.uk/the-bounce-back-storytelling-as-a-form-of-resilience/.

Carey, Hilary M., 2011, *God's Empire: Religion and colonialism in the British world, c. 1801–1908*, Cambridge: Cambridge University Press.

Césaire, Aimé, 2008, *Discours sur le colonialisme*, Nachdr. Paris: Présence Africaine.

Church of England, 2023, 'Church Commissioners publishes full report into historic links to transatlantic chattel slavery and announces new funding commitment of £100m in response to findings', The Church of England, 1 October 2023, https://www.churchofengland.org/media-and-news/press-releases/church-commissioners-publishes-full-report-historic-links.

Clarke, Sathianathan, 1999, *Dalit and Christianity: Subaltern religion and liberation theology in India*, New Delhi: Oxford University Press.

Collins, Patricia Hill, 'On violence, intersectionality and transversal politics', *Ethnic and Racial Studies* 40 (9) (2017): 1460–73, https://doi.org/10.1080/01419870.2017.1317827.

Commission on Race and Ethnic Disparities, *The Report of the Commission on Race and Ethnic Disparities*, 31 March 2021, https://assets.publishing.service.gov.uk/government/uploads/system/uploads/attachment_data/file/974507/20210331_-_CRED_Report_-_FINAL_-_Web_Accessible.pdf

Cruchley, Peter, 'Silent no longer: the roots of racism in mission', *The Ecumenical Review* 72 (1) (2020): 98–107, https://doi.org/10.1111/erev.12490.

Dasgupta, Rohit, 2018, 'Ambalavaner Sivanandan and Black politics in Britain', https://www.theoryculturesociety.org/blog/rohit-dasgupta-ambalavaner-sivanandan-black-politics-britain.

Dussel, Enrique, 1981, *A History of the Church in Latin America: Colonialism to liberation (1492–1979)*, Grand Rapids, MI: Eerdmans.

Ellis, Kevin, 2023, 'See, Judge, Act. Wrestling with the effects of colonialism as an English priest in Wales' in Anthony Reddie and Carol Troupe (eds), *Deconstructing Whiteness, Empire and Mission*, London: SCM Press, 208–21.

Equal Justice Initiative, 2018, *Slavery in America: The Montgomery Slave Trade*, Montgomery, AL: Equal Justice Initiative, https://eji.org/files/slavery-in-america-summary.pdf.

Finney, Nissa, James Nazroo, Laia Bécares, Dharmi Kapadia and Natalie Shlomo (eds), 2023, *Racism and Ethnic Inequality in a Time of Crisis: Findings from the Evidence for Equality National Survey*, Bristol: Policy Press.

Fotheringham, Ellen, and Caitlin Boswell, 2022, '"Unequal Impacts": How UK immigration law and policy affected migrants' experiences of the Covid-19 pandemic', Joint Council for the Welfare of Immigrants, May 2022.

France-Williams, A. D. A., 2020, *Ghost Ship: Institutional racism and the Church of England*, London: SCM Press.

Frostin, Per, 'The hermeneutics of the poor – the epistemological "break" in Third World theologies', *Studia Theologica – Nordic Journal of Theology* 39 (1) (1985): 127–50, https://doi.org/10.1080/00393388508600037.

Go, Julian and Jake Watson, 'Anticolonial nationalism from imagined communities to colonial conflict', *European Journal of Sociology/Archives Européennes de Sociologie* 60 (1) (2019): 31–68, https://doi.org/10.1017/S000397561900002X.

Goodfellow, Maya, 2020, *Hostile Environment: How immigrants became scapegoats*, London and New York: Verso Books.

Gopal, Priyamvada, 2019, *Insurgent Empire: Anticolonial resistance and British dissent*, London and New York: Verso Books.

Grimshaw, Patricia, and Elizabeth Nelson, 'Empire: the civilising mission and indigenous Christian women in colonial Victoria', *Australian Feminist Studies* 16 (36) (2001): 295–309.

Guns, Priya, 'From memory to a re-imagining; learning from Sivanandan', *Race & Class* 65 (1) (2023): 34–8, https://doi.org/10.1177/03063968231166909.

Howard, Phillip, Bryan Yan Chen Johnson, and Kevin Ah-Sen, 2022, 'Ukraine refugee crisis exposes racism and contradictions in the definition of human', *The Conversation* (blog), https://theconversation.com/ukraine-refugee-crisis-exposes-racism-and-contradictions-in-the-definition-of-human-179150.

Heimer, Rosa dos Ventos Lopes, 'Bodies as territories of exception: the coloniality and gendered necropolitics of state and intimate border violence against migrant women in England', *Ethnic and Racial Studies* 46 (7) (2023): 1378–1406, https://doi.org/10.1080/01419870.2022.2144750.

Ibhawoh, Bonny (ed.), 2018, 'Nationalists and anti-colonists' in *Human Rights in Africa*, New Approaches to African History, Cambridge: Cambridge University Press, 130–72, https://doi.org/10.1017/9781139060950.006

Modood, Tariq, 1999, 'The rise and fall of an anti-racism: from political blackness to ethnic pluralism' in Geoff Andrews, Richard Cockett, Alan Hooper and Michael Williams (eds), *New Left, New Right and Beyond: Taking the Sixties seriously*, 168–81, London: Palgrave Macmillan UK, https://doi.org/10.1057/9780333981726_11.

Mudambi, Anjana, 'South Asian Americans and anti-Black racism: critically reflexive racialization as an anti-racist vernacular discourse', *Communication, Culture & Critique* 16 (1) (2023): 1–8.

Mukaria, Andrew Ratanya, 2020, *A Synopsis of Racism in the African Christian Mission of 19th and 20th Centuries*, Independently published.

Mushtaq, Samreen, and Mudasir Amin, '"We will memorise our home": exploring settler colonialism as an interpretive framework for Kashmir', *Third World Quarterly* 42 (12) (2021): 3012–3029, https://doi.org/10.1080/01436597.2021. 1984877.

Narayan, John, 'British Black Power: the anti-imperialism of political blackness and the problem of nativist socialism', *The Sociological Review* 67 (5) (2019): 945–67, https://doi.org/10.1177/0038026119845550.

Office for National Statistics. 'Ethnicity facts and figures', 22 December 2022, https://www.ethnicity-facts-figures.service.gov.uk/uk-population-by-ethnicity/ national-and-regional-populations/population-of-england-and-wales/latest.

Padilla, Elaine, 2018, 'In the belly of the colony', Political Theology Network.

Patel, Sujata, 'Anti-colonial thought and global social theory', *Frontiers in Sociology* 8 (2023): 1143776, https://doi.org/10.3389/fsoc.2023.1143776.

Perry, Mia, 'Pluriversal', *Reading Research Quarterly* 56 (2) (2021): 293–309, https://doi.org/10.1002/rrq.312.

Prison Policy Initiative, 'Race and ethnicity', https://www.prisonpolicy.org/research/ race_and_ethnicity/, accessed 10.08.2023.

Sanghera, Sathnam, 2021, *Empireland: How imperialism has shaped modern Britain*, London: Viking.

Shanthakumar, B., 2018, 'At the interstices of race, class and imperialism: A. Sivanandan (1923–2018)', *Socialist Project*, February, https://socialistproject. ca/2018/02/interstices-race-class-imperialism-sivanandan/.

Shukra, Kalbir, 1997, 'From Black Power to Black perspectives: the reconstruction of a black political identity' in Ba-Nikongo Nikongo (ed.), *Leading Issues in African-American Studies*, Durham, NC: Carolina Academic, 587–602.

Siddiqui, Sophia, 'Anti-racist organising today: a roundtable discussion', *Race & Class* 65 (1) (2023): 119–33, https://doi.org/10.1177/03063968231168013.

Sivanandan, A., 'Black Power: the politics of existence', *Politics & Society* 1 (2) (1971): 225–33, https://doi.org/10.1177/003232927100100204.

Sivanandan, A., 'From resistance to rebellion: Asian and Afro-Caribbean struggles in Britain', *Race & Class* 23 (2–3) (1981): 111–52, https://doi.org/10.1177/030 639688102300202.

Sivanandan, A., 1981, 'What is institutional racism?' Institute of Race Relations.

Sivanandan, A., 1982, *A Different Hunger: Writings on Black resistance*, London: Pluto Press.

Snoussi, D., and Mompelat, L., 2019, *We Are Ghosts – Race, class and institutional prejudice*, London: Runnymede Trust.

Tharoor, Shashi, 2016, *An Era of Darkness: The British Empire in India*, Delhi: Aleph Book Company.

Tran, Jonathan, 2022, *Asian Americans and the Spirit of Racial Capitalism*, Oxford: Oxford University Press.

Virdee, Satnam, 2014, *Racism, Class and the Racialized Outsider*, Basingstoke: Palgrave Macmillan.

Walia, Harsha, 2021, *Border and Rule: Global Migration, Capitalism, and the Rise of Racist Nationalism*, Chicago: Haymarket Books.

Weller, Paul. 2023. 'Coming full circle: Christianity, empire, whiteness, the global majority and the struggles of migrants and refugees in the UK' in Anthony Reddie and Carol Troupe (eds), *Deconstructing Whiteness, Empire and Mission*, London: SCM Press, 173–92.

Westad, Odd Arne (ed.), 2005, 'The revolutionaries: anticolonial politics and transformations' in *The Global Cold War: Third World Interventions and the Making of Our times*, Cambridge: Cambridge University Press, 73–109, https://doi.org/10.1017/CBO9780511817991.004,

York, Sheona, 2022, 'The UK Immigration Control responses to asylum: Exclusion, disbelief, stigma and neglect' in *The Impact of UK Immigration Law: Declining standards of public administration, legal probity and democratic accountability*, Cham: Springer International Publishing, 57–100.

Ecology

Abel, Guy J., Michael Brottrager, Jesus Crespo Cuaresma and Raya Muttarak, 'Climate, conflict and forced migration', *Global environmental change* 54 (2019): 239–49.

Bhattacharyya, Gargi, 2023, *We, the Heartbroken*, London: Hajar Press.

Bilak, Alexandra, and Walter Kälin, 'Climate crisis and displacement – from commitment to action', *Forced Migration Review* 69 (2022).

Garlick, M., and I. Michal, 'Human mobility, rights and international protection: responding to the climate crisis', *Forced Migration Review* 69 (2022): 58–61.

Go, Julian, 'Thinking against empire: anticolonial thought as social theory', *The British Journal of Sociology* 74 (3) (2023): 279–93, https://doi.org/10.1111/1468-4446.12993.

Inge, John, 2003, *A Christian Theology of Place*, Aldershot: Ashgate.

Perry, Keston K., '(Un)just transitions and Black dispossession: the disposability of Caribbean "refugees" and the political economy of climate justice', *Politics* 43 (2) (2023): 169–85, https://doi.org/10.1177/02633957211041441.

Ranawana, A. M., 2022, *A Liberation for the Earth: Climate, race and cross*, London: SCM Press.

Sheldrake, Philip, 2001, *Spaces for the Sacred: Place, memory, and identity*, Baltimore: Johns Hopkins University Press.

Inter-generational

Adams, Graham, 2024, *God the Child: Small, weak and curious subversions*, London: SCM Press.

Bateson, M. C., 2010, *Composing a Further Life: The age of active wisdom*, New York: Vintage Books.

Bengston, V. L., with N. M. Putney and S. Harris, 2013, *Families and Faith: How religion is passed down across generations*, Oxford: Oxford University Press.

Bhakiaraj, Paul Joshua, 2014, 'The whole household of god: how children can deepen our theology and practice of missional ecclesiology' in Bill Prevette, Keith White, C. Rosalee Velloso Ewell and D. J. Konz (eds), *Theology, Mission and Child: Global perspectives*, Oxford: Regnum.

Bunge, Marcia J. (ed.), 2021, *Child Theology: Diverse methods and global perspectives*, Maryknoll, NY: Orbis Books.

Butler, R., 1995, 'Ageism' in G. Maddox (ed.), *The Encyclopedia of Aging*, New York: Springer.

Bytheway, B., 1995, *Ageism*, Buckingham: Open University Press.

Bytheway, B., 2011, *Age and Time in Unmasking Age*, Bristol: Policy Press.

Carstensen, L. L., and C. R. Hartel (eds), 2006, *When I'm 64*, Washington, DC: National Academies Press.

Coleman, P. G., 1984, 'The Netherlands: poverty and disability in old age' in R. Walker, R. Lawson and P. Townsend (eds), *Responses to Poverty: Lessons from Europe*, London: Heinemann, 266–82.

Coleman, P. G., 'Assessing self-esteem and its sources in elderly people', *Ageing and Society* 4 (1984): 117–35.

Coleman, P. G., 1986, *Ageing and Reminiscence Processes, Social and clinical implications*, Chichester: John Wiley & Sons.

Coleman, P. G., 2011, *Belief and Ageing: Spiritual pathways in later life*, Bristol: The Policy Press.

Coleman, P. G., and A. O'Hanlon, 2004, *Ageing and Development: Theories and research*, London: Hodder Arnold.

Coleman, P. G., and M. Mills, 2004, 'Memory and preservation of religious faith in an atheistic society: accounts of the practice of religion in the former Soviet Union', Proceedings of the International Oral History Association Conference (ed. A. Portelli), Rome.

Coleman, P. G., C. Ivani-Chalian and M. Robinson, 'Religious attitudes among British older people: stability and change in a 20 year longitudinal study', *Ageing and Society* 24 (2004): 167–88.

Constantineau, Corneliu, 2014, 'Welcome: biblical and theological perspectives on mission and hospitality with a child in the midst' in Bill Prevette, Keith White, C. Rosalee Velloso Ewell and D. J. Konz (eds), *Theology, Mission and Child: Global perspectives*, Oxford: Regnum.

De Lange, F., 2015, *Loving Later Life: The Ethics of Aging*, Grand Rapids, MI: Eerdmans.

Erikson, E. H., 1950, *Childhood and Society*, New York: Norton.

Fleming Drane, Olive M., Anne Richards et al., 2018, *Through the Eyes of a Child: New insights in theology from a child's perspective*, London: Church House Publishing.

Friedman, D. A., 2008, *Jewish Visions for Aging: A professional guide for fostering wholeness*, Woodstock, VT: Jewish Lights Publishing.

Gutmann, D., 1987, *Reclaimed Powers: Towards a new psychology of men and women in later life*, New York: Basic Books.

Hauerwas, S., C. B. Stoneking, K. G. Meador and D. Cloutier (eds), 2003, *Growing Old in Christ*, Grand Rapids, MI: Eerdmans.

Hay, David, and Rebecca Nye, 2006, *The Spirit of the Child*, rev. edn, London and Philadelphia: Jessica Kingsley Publishers.

Jewell, A. (ed.), 1999, *Spirituality and Ageing*, London: Jessica Kingsley Publishers.

Jewell, A. (ed.), 2001, *Older People and the Church*, Peterborough: Methodist Publishing House.

Jewell, A. (ed.), 2004, *Ageing, Spirituality and Well-being*, London: Jessica Kingsley Publishers.

Johnson, M. L. (ed.), 2005, *The Cambridge Handbook of Age and Ageing*, Cambridge: Cambridge University Press.

Johnson, M., and J. Walker (eds), 2016, *Spiritual Dimensions of Ageing*, Cambridge: Cambridge University Press.

Koyama, Kosuke, 'A holy mystery: welcoming a little child' in *The Living Pulpit* (October–December 2003).

Kwiyani, Harvey C., 2019, *Our Children Need Roots and Wings: Equipping and empowering young diaspora Africans for life and mission*, Missio Africanus.

Lancaster, L. C., and D. Stillman, 2002, *When Generations Collide: Traditionalists, BabyBoomers, Generation Xers, Millennials: who are they, why they clash, how to solve the generational puzzle at work*, New York: HarperBusiness.

Laslett, P., 1996, *Fresh Map of Life: The emergence of the Third Age*, London: Macmillan.

MacKinlay, E., 2001, *The Spiritual Dimension of Ageing*, London: Jessica Kingsley Publishers.

MacKinlay, E., 2006, *Spiritual Growth and Care in the Fourth Age*, London: Jessica Kingsley Publishers.

MacKinlay, E. (ed.), 2008, *Ageing, Disability and Spirituality: Addressing the Challenge of Disability in Later Life*, London: Jessica Kingsley Publishers.

McAdams, D. P., 2006, *The Redemptive Self: Stories Americans Live By*, New York: Oxford University Press.

Meilaender, G., 2013, *Should We Live Forever? The Ethical Ambiguities of aging*, Grand Rapids, MI: Eerdmans.

Mercer, Joyce Ann, 2005, *Welcoming Children: A practical theology of childhood*, St Louis, MO: Chalice Press.

Moody, H. R., 1994, *Aging, Concepts and Controversies*, California: Pine Forge Press.

Moody, H. R., 1996, *Ethics in an Aging Society*, Baltimore: The John Hopkins University Press.

Morisy, A., 2011, *Borrowing from the Future: A Faith-Based Approach to Intergenerational Equity*, London: Continuum International Publishing Group.

Myerhoff, B., 1992, *Remembered Lives: The Work of Ritual, Storytelling, and Growing Older*, Michigan: The University of Michigan Press.

Palmore, E., 1999, *Ageism: Negative and Positive*, 2nd edn, New York: Springer.

Palmore, E. B., L. G. Branch and D. K. Harris (eds), 2005, *Encyclopedia of Ageism*, Binghamton, NY: Haworth Pastoral Press.

Reddie, A. G., 2001, *Faith, Stories and the Experience of Black Elders: Singing the Lord's Song in a Strange Land*, London: Jessica Kingsley Publishers.

Reynolds, Tracey, and Elisabetta Zontini, 'Transnational and diasporic youth identities: exploring conceptual themes and future research agendas', *Identities* 23 (4) (2016): 379–91.

Sarton, M., 1995, *Endgame: A journal of the Seventy-Ninth Year*, New York: Norton.

Scanlan, Mark, 2021, *An Interweaving Ecclesiology: The Church, mission and young people*, London: SCM Press.

Small, H., 2007, *The Long Life*, Oxford: Oxford University Press.

Smith, James K. A., 2009, *Desiring the Kingdom: Worship, Worldview and Cultural Formation*, Grand Rapids, MI: Baker Academic.

Stollar, R. L., 2023, *The Kingdom of Children: A liberation theology*, Grand Rapids, MI: Eerdmans.

Tan, Rosalind, Nativity A. Petallar and Lucy A. Hefford (eds), 2022, *God's Heart for Children: Practical theology from global perspectives*, Carlisle: Langham Global Library.

Thane, P., 2000, *Old Age in English History, Past Experiences, Present Issues*, Oxford: Oxford University Press.

Tinker, A., 1997, *Older People in Modern Society*, 4th edn, London: Longman.

Tornstam, L., 2005, *Gerotranscendence: A Developmental Theory of Positive Aging*, New York: Springer Publishing Company.

Van Dijk, Rijk, 1999, 'Pentecostalism, gerontocratic rule and democratization in Malawi: The changing position of the young in political culture' in *Religion, globalization and political culture in the Third World*, London: Palgrave Macmillan UK, 164–88.

Vincent, J., 2003, *Old Age*, London: Routledge.

Poverty and class

Brower Latz, D., C. Murphy Elliott and S. Purcell, 2023, *Church on the Margins. What does it mean to be a church on the margins?*, Manchester: Church Action on Poverty.

Charlesworth, M., and N. Williams, 2017, *A Church for the Poor*, Eastbourne: David Cook.

Cooper, N., C. Howson and L. Purcell, 2022, *Dignity, Agency, Power*, Glasgow: Wild Goose Publications.

Donaldson, A., 2010, *Encountering God in the Margins*, Dublin: Veritas Publications.

Duncan-Smith, I., 2007, *Breakthrough Britain: Ending the costs of social breakdown*, London Centre for Social Justice.

Forrester, D., 2001, *On Human Worth*, London: SCM Press.

Green, L., 1987, *Power to the Powerless: Theology Brought to Life*, Basingstoke: Marshall Pickering.

Hirst, Michael, 'Poverty, place and presence: positioning Methodism in England, 2001 to 2011', *Theology and Ministry* 4 (2016): 4.1–25.

King, M. L. Jr, 1967, *Where do we go from here? Annual Report Delivered at the 11th Convention of the Southern Christian Leadership Conference*, 16 August, Atlanta, GA, http://www-personal.umich.edu/~gmarkus/MLK_WhereDoWeGo.pdf, accessed 29.06.2023.

Larner, Luke (ed.), 2023, *Confounding the Mighty: Stories of Church, social class and solidarity*, London: SCM Press.

Lister, R., 2004, *Poverty*, Cambridge: Polity Press.

Lithicum, R., 2003, *Transforming Power*, Downers Grove: InterVarsity Press.

McGarvey, D., 2018, *Poverty Safari*, London: Picador.

Power M., 2020, 'Fratelli Tutti: Pope Francis delivers new teaching aimed at healing divisions in the face of coronavirus', The Conversation, 5 October 2020, https://theconversation.com/fratelli-tutti-pope-francis-delivers-new-teaching-aimed-at-healing-divisions-in-the-face-of-coronavirus-147487, accessed 29.06.2023.

Roddick, A., 2020, 'A marginal God' in United Reformed Church, *In the Thick of It: Stories, experiences and reflections on God's kingdom in the margins*, London: United Reformed Church.

Walsh, T., 2022, 'Poverty is many things' in N. Cooper, C. Howson and L. Purcell, *Dignity, Agency, Power*, Glasgow: Wild Goose Publications.

Political theology

Adams, Graham, 2022, *Holy Anarchy: Dismantling domination, embodying community, loving strangeness*, London: SCM Press.

Atherton, J., 2000, *Public Theology for Changing Times*, London: SPCK.

Brown, Sally A., and Patrick D. Miller (eds), 2005, *Lament: Reclaiming practices in pulpit, pew, and public square*, Louisville, KY: Westminster John Knox Press.

Brueggemann, Walter, 'The costly loss of lament', *Journal for the Study of the Old Testament* 11 (36) (October 1986): 57–71.

Buchanan, Colin, 1994, *Cut the Connection: Disestablishment and the Church of England*, London: Darton, Longman and Todd.

Chaplin, Jonathan, 2022, *Beyond Establishment: Resetting Church-State relations in England*, London: SCM Press.

Clements, Keith, 2017, *Dietrich Bonhoeffer's Ecumenical Quest*, Geneva: World Council of Churches.

Cornwall, Pete, 1983, *Church and Nation*, Oxford: Basil Blackwell.

Groves, Richard (ed.), 1998, *Thomas Helwys: A short declaration of the mystery of iniquity*, Macon, GA: Mercer University Press.

Kee, Alistair, 1982, *Constantine Versus Christ: The triumph of ideology*, London: SCM Press.

Leech, Kenneth (ed.), 2001, *Setting the Church of England Free: The case for disestablishment*, Croydon; The Jubilee Group.

MacLeod, George, 1936, *Speaking the Truth in Love: The modern preacher's task*, London: SCM Press.

Madges, William, 2015, *Pope Francis's revolution of Tenderness and Love*, trans. W. Kasper, New York: Paulist Press.

Murray, Stuart, 2004, *Post-Christendom: Church and mission in a strange new world*, Carlisle: Paternoster.

Patta, Raj Bharat, 2022, 'The newness of the new commandment', Political Theology Network.

Robinson, John, 1963, *Honest to God*, London: SCM Press.

Robinson, John, 1972, *The Human Face of God*, London: SCM Press.

The Kairos Document, 1985, 'Challenge to the Church; a theological comment on the political crisis in South Africa', British Council of Churches.

United Church of Christ, 'Barmen Declaration', https://www.ucc.org/beliefs_barmen-declaration/, accessed 15.12.2021.

Watts, Alan, 1976, '"Wash Out Your Mouth"', in Robert Sohl and Audrey Carr (eds), *The Gospel According to Zen: Beyond the death of God*, London: Mentor New American Library, 16–17.

Wright, Nigel, 2000, *Disavowing Constantine: Mission, Church and the social order in the theologies of John Howard Yoder and Jürgen Moltmann*, Carlisle: Paternoster.

Religious diversity and dialogue

McDonald. K. (ed.), 2014, *The Gift of Dialogue, the Encyclical Ecclesiam Suam and the key documents of Vatican II on Interreligious Dialogue and Ecumenism*, London: Catholic Truth Society.

ONS (Office for National Statistics), 2003, *Ethnic Group Statistics: A Guide for the Collection and Classification of Data*, London: HMSO.

ONS (Office for National Statistics), 2022, *Religion England and Wales Statistical Bulletin*, https://www.ons.gov.uk/peoplepopulationandcommunity/culturalidentity religion/bulletins/religionenglandandwales/census2021, accessed 06.08.2023.

Weller, Paul, 1986, 'The theology and practice of inter religious dialogue: a Baptist contribution to ecumenical debate in England', unpublished dissertation, MPhil in Social and Pastoral Theology, University of Manchester.

Weller, Paul, 2004, 'Identity, politics and the future(s) of religion in the UK: the case of religion question in the 2001 Decennial Census', *Journal of Contemporary Religion* 19 (2004): 3–21.

Weller, Paul, 2005, *Time for a Change: Reconfiguring religion, state and society*, London: T. & T. Clark.

Weller, Paul, 2006, *God, Jesus and Dialogue: The Beach Lectures for 2005*, Bracknell: Centre for the Study of Religious and Cultural Diversity, Occasional Papers, No. 3, Newbold College.

Weller, Paul, 'Theological ethics and interreligious relations: a Baptist Christian perspective', *Internationale Kirchliche Zeitschrift/Bern Interreligious Oecumenical Studies* 1 (2014): 119–40.

Weller, Paul, 'Balancing within three dimensions: Christianity, secularity and religious plurality in social policy and theology', *Internationale Kirchliche Zeitschrift/Bern Interreligious Oecumenical Studies* 3, published as a themed edition on 'Religious minorities and interreligious relations: social and theological challenges' of *Studies in Interreligious Dialogue* 26 (2) (2016): 131–46.

Weller, Paul, 'Changing socio-religious realities, practical negotiation of transitions in the governance of religion or belief, state and society', *Internationale Kirchliche Zeitschrift/Bern Oecumenical Studies*, published as themed edition on 'Secular society and religious presence: religion-state relations' of *Interreligious Dialogue* 30 (2) (2020): 145–62.

Weller, Paul, 'Historical sources and contemporary resources of minority Christian Churches: a Baptist contribution', *Internationale Kirchliche Zeitschrift* 111 (3–4) (2021): 140–57.

Weller, Paul, and Ahmed Andrews, 'Counting religion: religion, statistics and the 2001 Census', *World Faiths Encounter* 21 (1988): 23–34.

Weller, Paul, Kingsley Purdam, Nazila Ghanea and Sariya Cheruvallil-Contractor, 2013, *Religion or Belief, Discrimination and Equality: Britain in global contexts*, London: Bloomsbury.

Congregational/denominational studies

Baglyos, Paul A., 'Lament in the liturgy of the rural church: an appeal for recovery', *Currents in Theology and Mission* 36 (4) (August 2009): 253–63.

Hopewell, James F., 1988, *Congregation: Stories and structures*, ed. Barbara G. Wheeler, London: SCM Press.

Major, Heather J., 2022, 'Living with churches in the Borders: mission and ministry in rural Scottish parish churches', PhD Thesis, University of Glasgow.

McClendon Jr, James, 'What is a Baptist theology?', *American Baptist Quarterly* 1 (1) (1982): 16–39.

Methodist Church, 2020, *God For All: The connexional strategy for evangelism and growth*, London: Methodist Church.

Moschella, Mary Clark, 2008, *Ethnography as a Pastoral Practice: An introduction*, Cleveland, OH: Pilgrim Press.

Pemberton, Glenn, 2012, *Hurting with God: Learning to lament with the Psalms*, Abilene, TX: Abilene Christian University Press.

Pemberton, Glenn, 2014, *After Lament: Psalms for learning to trust again*, Abilene, TX: Abilene Christian University Press.

Roberts, Vaughan, and David Sims, 2017, *Leading by Story: Rethinking church leadership*, London: SCM Press.

(Re)engaging spirituality

Adogame, A. 'Engaging the rhetoric of spiritual warfare: The public face of *Aladura* in diaspora', *Journal of Religion in Africa* 34 (4) 2004: 493–522.

Albrecht, Daniel E., 'Pentecostal spirituality: ecumenical potential and challenge', *Cyberjournal for Pentecostal-Charismatic Research* 2 (1) (1997): 1–52.

Anderson, Allan Heaton, 2018, *Spirit-filled world: Religious dis/continuity in African Pentecostalism*, London: Palgrave Macmillan, p. 8.

Anderson, Allan H., and Walter J. Hollenweger, 1997, 'African Pentecostal churches and concepts of power' in *Africa Forum, Council of Churches for Britain and Ireland*, 1–4.

Barlow, Frank (ed.), 1992, *The Life of King Edward who Rests at Westminster Attributed to a Monk of Saint-Bertin*, 2nd edn, Oxford: Clarendon Press.

Birchall, Christopher, 2014, *Embassy, Emigrants and Englishmen: The three hundred year history of a Russian Orthodox Church in London*, Jordanville, NY: Printshop of St Job of Pochaev.

Carroll, Timothy, 2015, 'An ancient modernity: ikons and the re-emergence of Orthodox Britain' in Timothy Willem Jones and Lucinda Matthews-Jones (eds), *Material Religion in Modern Britain: The spirit of things*, London: Palgrave MacMillan.

Catsiyannis, Timotheos, 1993, *The Greek Community of London (1500–1945)*, London: privately printed.

Gillquist, Peter, 1989, *Becoming Orthodox: A journey to the ancient Christian faith*, Chesterton, IN: Conciliar Press.

Harris, Jonathan, 2009, 'Silent minority: the Greek community of eighteenth-century London' in Dēmētrēs Tziovas (ed.), *Greek Diaspora and Migration Since 1700: Society, politics and culture*, London: Ashgate Publishing.

Husserl, Edmund, 1991, *On the Phenomenology of the Consciousness of Internal Time 1893–1917*, trans. John Barnett Brought, London: Kluwer Academic Publishers.

Istavridis, Vasil, 'The work of Germanos Strenopoulos in the field of inter-Orthodox and inter-Christian relations', *The Ecumenical Review* 11 (3) (1959): 291–9.

Kalu, O., 2008, *African Pentecostalism: an introduction*, Oxford: Oxford University Press.

Lackenby, Nicholas, 2024, 'Peoplehood and the Orthodox person: a view from central Serbia', *Journal of the Royal Anthropological Institute*.

Meyer, Birgit, '"Make a complete break with the past." Memory and post-colonial modernity in Ghanaian Pentecostalist discourse', *Journal of Religion in Africa* 28 (3) (1998): 316–49.

Moltmann, Jürgen, 1978, *The Open Church: Invitation to a messianic lifestyle*, London: SCM Press.

Nyanni, Caleb Opoku, 2021, *Second-Generation African Pentecostals in the West: An emerging paradigm*, Eugene, OR: Wipf and Stock Publishers.

Ojo, Matthews A., 'Pentecostalism and charismatic movements in Nigeria: factors of growth and inherent challenges', *The WATS Journal: An Online Journal from West Africa Theological Seminary* 3 (1) (2018): 5.

Schaff, Philip (ed.), 1899, 'The Canons of the Holy and Altogether August Apostles' in *Nicene and Post-Nicene Fathers Series II, Volume 14, The Seven Ecumenical Councils*.

Williamson, Marianne, 1992, *A Return to Love: Reflections on the principles of a course in miracles*, New York: HarperCollins.

Index of Names and Subjects